Police Encounters

Stanford Studies in Middle Eastern and Islamic Societies and Cultures

Police Encounters

Security and Surveillance in Gaza under Egyptian Rule

Ilana Feldman

Stanford University Press
Stanford, California

Stanford University Press
Stanford, California

This Book is printed on acid-free paper

Library of Congress Cataloging-in-Publication Data

Feldman, Ilana, 1969– author.
  Police encounters : security and surveillance in Gaza under Egyptian rule / Ilana Feldman.
     pages cm
  Includes bibliographical references and index.
  ISBN 978-0-8047-9395-7 (cloth) — ISBN 978-0-8047-9534-0 (pbk.)
  1. Police—Gaza Strip—History—20th century.   2. Internal security—Gaza Strip—History—20th century.   3. Police patrol—Gaza Strip—Surveillance operations—History—20th century.   4. Gaza Strip—Politics and government—20th century.   5. Egypt—Politics and government—1952-1970.   I. Title.
  HV8242.24.A2F45 2015
  363.2'3209531—dc23

                                                                              2014038874

ISBN 978-0-8047-9537-1 (electronic)

Typeset by Newgen in 11/13.5 Adobe Garamond

Printed and bound in Great Britain by
Marston Book Services Ltd, Oxfordshire

Contents

Illustrations

Map

Figures

Note on Transliteration

FOR EASE OF READING I have used a modified version of the *International Journal of Middle East Studies* transliteration system, excluding diacritical marks except for the 'ayn (') and the hamza ('). When quoting from spoken Arabic, or referring to terms used in spoken Arabic, I have transliterated them according to local pronunciation. For names and terms that have a common transliteration in English (e.g., Gamal Abdel Nasser, fedayeen) I have used that spelling.

Acknowledgments

THIS BOOK HAS BEEN LONG IN GESTATION. Its roots lie in fieldwork and archival research I conducted, many years ago now, for my first book, *Governing Gaza*. I thank the people, institutions, and funding agencies who made the initial research possible and those who permitted me to undertake the additional research that followed. Financial support was provided by the Near and Middle East Program of the Social Science Research Council, the Council of American Overseas Research Centers, the Wenner-Gren Foundation, and New York University. I appreciate the ongoing research support provided by George Washington University, especially from the Elliott School of International Affairs and the Institute for Middle East Studies. I am grateful to the archivists and librarians at the Israel State Archives, the Egyptian National Archives, the United Nations Archives in New York, the UN Relief and Works Agency for Palestine Refugees in the Near East Archives in Amman, the New York Public Library, the National Archives in London, and the American Friends Service Committee Archives in Philadelphia. I am particularly thankful to the people in Gaza who taught me about its history, shared their life experiences with me, and helped me in innumerable ways during my time there.

As I have worked on this project over the years I have benefited from many excellent research assistants, including Ashley Makar, Elizabeth Williams, and Daniel Blatter. As an assistant, in this and other projects, Doaa' el Nakhala has been indispensable. Her efficiency, precision, and insight provided crucial support. I often learn from my students, and I am especially appreciative of the excellent graduate students in my fall 2013 seminar, Anthropology of Security, who provided helpful feedback on the manuscript.

My capacity to write and think is enhanced by a vibrant community of colleagues and friends, in Washington DC and beyond. At George Washington University, I particularly thank my colleagues in the Anthropology Department, the History Department, and the Institute for Middle East Studies for creating such collegial and congenial intellectual environments. I am always made smarter by my shared reading and thinking with Mona Atia, Johanna Bockman, Elliott Colla, Dina Khoury, Melani McAlister, and Andrew Zimmerman. And I am further supported, intellectually and personally, by Pamila Gupta, Rachel Heiman, Kevin Martin, Shira Robinson, Rashmi Sadana, Sara Scalenghe, and Miriam Ticktin. Kate Wahl at Stanford University Press has been an enthusiastic supporter and helpful reader of this book. I also thank two anonymous reviewers for supportive and incisive feedback.

Police Encounters

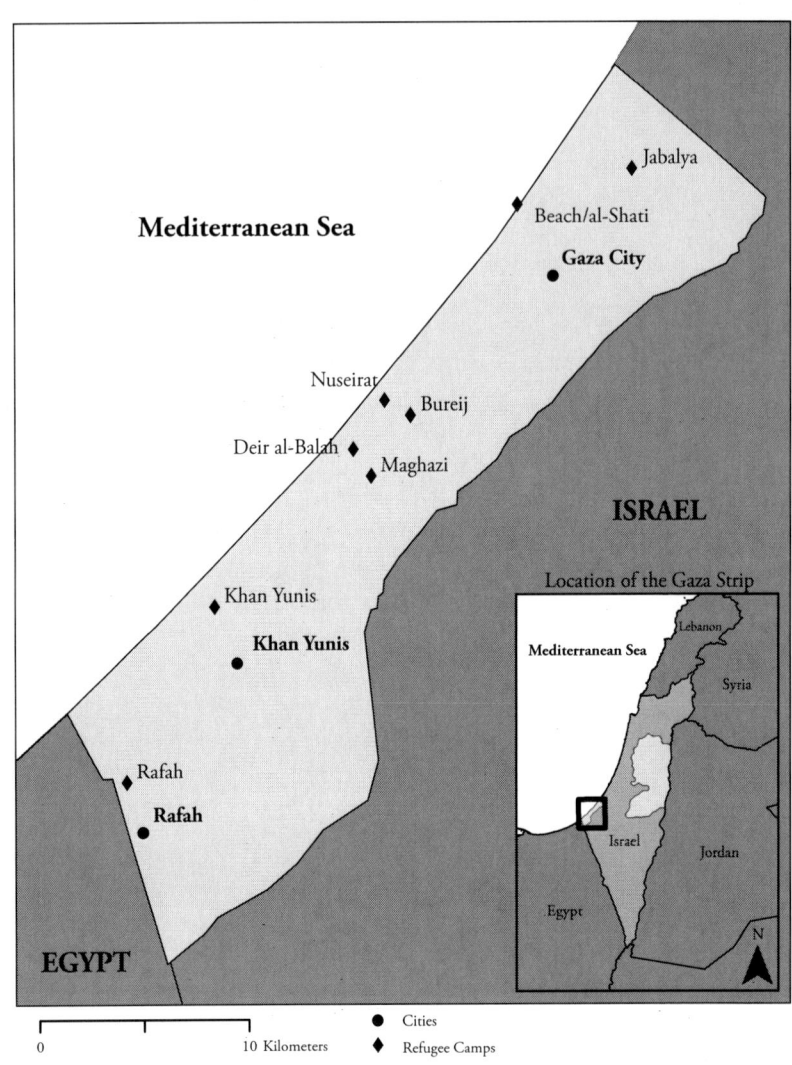

MAP *The Gaza Strip. Sources: UNRWA, GADM, OSM.*

NOTES: The refugee camps, cities, and territorial borders displayed on this map represent approximations of their on-the-ground locations. Cartographer: Jillian Sherman, 2014. Israel TM Projection.

Introduction

Security Society in Gaza

IN MARCH 1961 a Palestinian doctor got drunk at a dinner party in Gaza City. Shortly thereafter, a report on the matter was submitted to the police.[1] The occasion for the party was the visit to Gaza of a UN Relief and Works Agency for Palestine Refugees in the Near East (UNRWA) doctor from Beirut, and its attendees included local doctors and an officer in the UN peacekeeping force then stationed in the Gaza Strip. The report was unsigned, but it appears to be the work of an informer. It was followed a few days later by a police officer's report confirming the first account. Noting the time the party began and ended, including the license plate number of the peacekeeper's car, and listing the names of all attendees, these reports provide a detailed account of the evening, thereby revealing something of the breadth of security concerns and practice during the Egyptian Administration of the Gaza Strip.

Although everyone at the party drank alcohol, Dr. Abu Ramadan was the only one who misbehaved. He began to complain about "dogs" on the radio and to "say things that he had no business talking about." He then threw up in the bathroom and afterward drank three cups of coffee. At this point the party ended. The first report concluded by stating, "This kind of behavior is not becoming of the head of the doctors [syndicate]." These detailed reports about a seemingly minor social indiscretion were part of the work of the Egyptian Administration's Mabahith al-'Amma (literally General Investigation Department, rendered in English as the Criminal Investigation Department, or CID), a unit of the Interior Security Directorate.

The reports describe some lapses in judgment (Dr. Abu Ramadan seems not have shown himself in his best light on this occasion) but do not allege the commission of a crime. Nonetheless, this otherwise unremarkable social event was clearly of interest to the police. The details provided suggest an informer's presence at the party, and they indicate matters that preoccupied security personnel: the presence of foreigners, the possibility of uncontrolled talk, and—indeed—impropriety. Although the reports make clear judgments about the doctor's behavior, they imply, rather than explicitly state, the potential political implications of the "things he had no business talking about." Uncovering and documenting political talk and action was central to the mission of police serving under Egyptian rule in Gaza.

This account of the party was one of many investigations preserved in a single CID file. Other reports describe additional police concerns, including unauthorized border crossings and ordinary crime. One report describes the activities of another physician, who practiced at the Bureij hospital in the middle area of the Strip and who had opened a private clinic in his home. The clinic was serving a large number of people who were "not residents of Palestine . . . but citizens of the UAR [United Arab Republic]," and who were coming illegally from the Sinai for treatment. Because the doctor sent many of these patients to the Bureij hospital for X-rays, the facility was becoming overcrowded with "too many Sinai residents," sometimes resulting in the denial of "treatment to locals."[2]

Still other reports in the file describe the apparent theft of medicine from the Shifa hospital pharmacy in Gaza City, the investigation that followed, and the discovery that the medicine had been misplaced within the hospital.[3] This attention to a potential theft confirms the relevance of regular criminal activity to a security field that was replete with other concerns. This single file, produced in the course of the nearly twenty years of Egyptian rule in Gaza (1948–67), reveals a policing apparatus that concerned itself with the control of social and moral order as well as crime and politics, that engaged in the surveillance of seemingly ordinary activity, and that relied on informers as much as professional police.

This study of policing and security practices in Gaza during the period of Egyptian rule explores the range of matters that occupied police personnel, the mechanisms through which Gazans came to participate in the police project, and the avenues for influence and effect that were sometimes produced in a system designed for control and containment. It is an apparent paradox of Egyptian rule that security practices such as surveillance, control, and even police violence are among the most and the least positively remembered aspects of this period by Gazans.[4] When I talked with Gazans about this time, I repeatedly heard from people that they had no worries about crime then, that you could sleep with your door open, that your personal safety was never at risk. At the same time, and sometimes by the same people, I was told that the Egyptians were harsh in their repression of independent political activity and that there was very limited freedom of expression. Policing was a space of both constraint and possibility, of control and action. Security practices produced uncertainty, suspicion, and comfort—all at the same time. These different security effects and the range of practices that produced them were part of the same security field. They were all part of Gaza's "security society."

This security society was a field of both governance and action. The broad scope of police concern, the number of people engaged in the policing project, and the range of techniques police deployed were part of a wide network of deeply unequal relations through which Gaza's population was controlled and within which people tried to influence government policy, their neighbors' behavior, and their families' futures. Gaza is a distinctive site for considering the dynamics and effects of expansive policing practices, but it is by no means exceptional. Police practices and procedures were directly connected, through personnel and planning, to the colonial policing that existed in Palestine before 1948 and the increasingly authoritarian policing that developed in Egypt during the 1950s. These practices also resonate with forms of surveillance, investigation, and interdiction that are found across the globe, under authoritarian regimes as well as democratic ones, as governments respond to apparent threats by expanding, and extending the reach of, their security apparatuses.

Policing and security need to be understood within the wider context of Egyptian rule in Gaza, itself subject to a range of evaluations by

Gazans. Egypt came to govern Gaza as a result of war in 1948, a failed effort to maintain Arab Palestine. Throughout the twenty years of this administration, the majority of it during Gamal Abdel Nasser's presidency, Egypt's rhetorical stance was as a defender of Palestinian rights, even if it did not always advance Palestinian objectives in practice. Gazans remember much about this time very positively, to the extent that they often describe it as the "golden age" for Gaza. Egyptian administrators, following similar policies being pursued in Egypt proper at the same time, made universal primary and secondary education a reality for the first time, provided scholarships for Palestinians to study in Egyptian universities, and promised government jobs to university graduates. Many in the increasingly highly educated Palestinian population were able to get well-paying jobs in Gulf countries. Egyptian policy was also directed at the economy within Gaza. The administration sold plots of land at very low prices to civil servants and made Gaza a duty-free zone, encouraging the development of hotels and restaurants to cater to bargain shoppers. Even as Egypt exercised strong control over independent political expression, Gaza was a crucial space for the reemergence of organized Palestinian politics in the post-1948 period: Fatah, long the most important Palestinian political organization, was founded by refugees to Gaza.

After 1948, the borders, political status, and population of the territory were all new, and each was cause for concern among Egyptian administrators and their security apparatus. The circumstances that created the Egyptian Administration, and that also created the Gaza Strip, highlight how unsettled and insecure this space was. Before 1948 Gaza was an administrative district within the larger territory of Palestine, governed by Great Britain under mandate from the League of Nations. Much of the period of the British Mandate was marked by conflict, between Palestine's native population and incoming Jewish settlers, and between Palestinians (both Jewish and Arab) and British rulers. In 1947 the British government gave up trying to quell these conflicts and turned the matter over to the United Nations (the successor to the League of Nations). The United Nations' proposal to divide the territory into two states—one Jewish, one Arab—seemed profoundly unfair to the Arab community, which represented around 70 percent of the country's population and owned around 90 percent of the land, and they rejected the plan.[5]

Fighting began inside Palestine before the end of the Mandate on May 15, 1948. With the end of the Mandate and the formal establishment of the State of Israel, neighboring Arab countries, including Egypt, joined the battle. The Egyptian army entered Palestine through Rafah, along the Gaza-Sinai border, and its forces moved northward through the territory that would become the Gaza Strip.[6] The war did not go well for the Egyptian army; a large contingent of its forces (including a young Gamal Abdel Nasser) was trapped by the Israeli army in Faluja. Basically defeated, the Egyptians signed an armistice agreement with Israel that gave them control over what came to be called the Gaza Strip. This agreement delineated the "provisional borders" of this new territory, twenty-seven miles long and seven miles across at its widest point. The armistice agreement concluded the fighting between Egypt and Israel, but it did not create peace. The length of the Gaza Strip was, therefore, a border with a hostile country (one with a significant military advantage). This fact alone created tremendous security concerns for Egyptian administrators in Gaza and made border control a key focus of attention throughout the administration. The nature of that attention changed over time: at first any crossings by Palestinians were met with strong punishment, but later Egypt supported Palestinian guerrilla attacks across the line. At no point was truly independent Palestinian movement permitted (even if it could not always be stopped).

Egypt governed the Strip until its 1967 occupation by Israel, with a four-month interlude from November 1956 to March 1957 when Israel occupied it as a result of the Suez Crisis. The status of the territory—previously a part of the larger Palestine Mandate, supposedly (though never actually) on the road to independence—became even more undefined. Unlike Jordan, which both governed and annexed the West Bank, Egypt, rhetorically at least, administered Gaza as a Palestinian territory. From the beginning, and partly in an effort to distinguish itself from regimes like that of Jordan, Egypt claimed only caretaker status, preserving Gaza to be part of a future independent Palestine. The first formal (though never substantive) indication of this stance was the establishment of the All-Palestine Government in Gaza in 1948.[7] Other institutional arrangements followed in later years of the administration, but none of them ceded actual Egyptian authority over Gaza. Even as the administration was internationally recognized, the territory itself was deemed *res nullius*—not under any existing sovereignty.[8] It was governed as a separate territory, but it was not part of any independent state.[9]

The creation of the Gaza Strip also transformed the area's population, in several respects. Before 1948 around eighty thousand people lived in the area that became the Strip. They were joined by 200,000–250,000 refugees, largely from villages in southern Palestine. The vulnerability of the new population—displaced refugees and largely dispossessed natives—made them a source of considerable concern. A population under duress could easily become a threat. As might be expected, this enormous social transformation created both solidarity and resentment. Even if Egypt claimed to govern on behalf of Palestine, this stance did not mean that its officials necessarily trusted Palestinians. It is clear that by and large they did not. And Palestinians were often equally wary of Egyptians, sometimes doubting their commitment to the liberation of Palestine (reports that the army had fought in 1948 with defective weapons were seen by many as evidence of perfidy). In addition to changes in demography and solidarity, the political status of Gaza's residents was reconfigured by the loss of Palestine. Before 1948 everyone was a citizen of not-yet-independent Palestine. After 1948 no one was a legal citizen at all, a fact that was of crucial importance for governance, for policing, and for politics. Despite its legal absence, the concept and practice of citizenship remained important for both how Egyptians governed Gazans and how Gazans made claims on Egyptians.[10]

Where citizenship was a real, if not fully realized, social and administrative category, the demographic makeup of post-1948 Gaza meant that refugeedom and the refugee were fundamental, and foundational, categories. The presence of large numbers of refugees also changed the physical landscape of Gaza's interior. Eight refugee camps were established throughout the Strip to shelter the large number of displaced persons. These camps housed about half the refugee population, with the remainder living in Gaza's cities and towns, transforming the character of these places as well. The Israeli takeover of Palestinian territory meant that most of Gaza's native population was dispossessed of its land, which lay on the other side of the armistice line. The economic and social connections that had sustained the area were destroyed by the war and the new borders it had produced. Egyptian administrators—and international aid workers—had to provide assistance to this destabilized and impoverished population. Because of the large number of refugees in Gaza, and the fact that they accounted for a high percentage of the population, UNRWA was as significant a service actor as the administration. Health care, education, and rations were all provided to refugees by UNRWA, which sometimes also embarked on infrastructure projects. Policing and security remained the provenance of the administration alone.

Gaza-specific security concerns were joined by more general Egyptian concerns about controlling politics and public life.[11] In July 1952 a coup by Egyptian military officers, known as the Free Officers, brought an end to monarchical rule in Egypt. In 1954 Gamal Abdel Nasser took over the presidency of Egypt. Among the consequences of the new regime were the abolishment of political parties, the strict control of any opposition, and the creation of what would become an infamous security regime.[12] Police in Egypt tapped telephones and surveilled activity; they arrested, imprisoned, and sometimes tortured political activists.[13] These practices continued, and even intensified, under the regimes that followed Nasser.[14] For example, anger at the seemingly unchecked power of security personnel was one factor that contributed to the uprising that led to Hosni Mubarak's removal from office in February 2011.[15] Gaza under Egyptian rule witnessed the same interest in containing political activity and experienced the same sorts of policing techniques as deployed in Egypt.

To address the range of threats they identified in Gaza, Egyptian administrators established an extensive police force with expansive authority and jurisdiction. Few moments in life were beyond the scrutiny of the security establishment—to wit, the report on the drunk doctor—and few techniques of control were off-limits to police. One obvious effect of these multiple techniques deployed in a wide array of sites was that security personnel exercised a high degree of control over people's lives, their actions, and their relationships. A less self-evident effect, but a significant one nonetheless, was that the security apparatus—its practices and its concerns—also became a venue through which people pressed claims and exerted influence. These actions took a variety of forms, including gossip and informing, petitions and protest. Influence was also sometimes a by-product of policing itself, even if people were not entirely aware that they were taking action. A key example of this dynamic is the way the surveillance of public opinion (street talk) sometimes led to a change in government policy. Security was at once a mechanism of governance and a means of acting politically. This book explores the range of techniques of policing, including public participation, widespread surveillance, reliance on informants, and police violence. It also considers the diverse spaces and objects of police intervention and investigation: political activity, petty crime, border control, and the management of public and moral life. In developing and implementing these practices, the history of colonial police in Palestine provided both personnel and procedural guidance.

Palestine Police in the British Mandate

Before there was the Gaza Strip there was Palestine. And before there was the Egyptian Administration there was the British Mandate. The Mandate itself, and its policing, was embedded in a broader system of colonial policing and counterinsurgency operations.[16] Palestine was a crucial node in a network of moving personnel and procedure. British members of the Palestine Police were part of a circulating security force of empire. When the Palestine Police was first established, many of its British personnel came from the Royal Irish Constabulary and its Auxiliary Division (the Black and Tans).[17] When the Palestine Mandate concluded, many police officers went on to serve in Malaya.[18] Georgina Sinclair argues that the repeated emergencies in Palestine made its policing practices exemplary for the broader empire and that it became a key site for training people for leadership in the colonial police forces.[19] The centrality of policing Palestine to the broader British Empire made service in its police an act of British civic responsibility, tied as much to a British national community as to the Palestinian public and Palestinian police.

The story of empire is in significant part a story of efforts—often brutal, sometimes sophisticated—to maintain control over spaces whose populations object to the colonial presence. As such, police forces and policing practices are at the heart of the imperial experience. Whether in settler-colonies with European populations to protect or in neocolonial orders in which it is the capacity for resource extraction that must be safeguarded, controlling resistance, insurgency, and crime is vital to imperial stability.[20] Colonial police forces were uncomfortably located somewhere between military and civilian forces. As circumstances on the ground changed—an uprising begun or quelled—this location changed as well. In Mandate Palestine, and not only in Palestine, the attempt to make the force more civilian, and therefore more "professional," occupied considerable energy of the commanders of the force.[21] At the same time, the regular insurgencies that characterized the Mandate meant that these efforts were at best only partly successful.

Administrative concern about police professionalism was connected to the endemic condition of colonial violence. Violence was central to efforts to subdue native populations and in many struggles for decolonization.[22] Although the most famous violence of the colonial era was that of the Belgians in the Congo and the French in Algeria, recent scholarship has illuminated the brutality that often accompanied British colonial experiences.[23] In this context of inevitable violence, it was particularly important to colonial administrators that police forces be well ordered: ready to engage in state-directed violence when deemed necessary and able to control the impulses to disordered violence that encounters with natives could engender. If police exercised self-control, it was easier for colonial authorities to cast criminality as a "native problem."[24] To develop this control, it was necessary to instill in police officers a sense of themselves as not only professional actors but also imperial citizens.

In Palestine the police force was composed of both British and Palestinian officers, who worked together with varying degrees of comfort. As opposition to the Mandate and Zionist settlement in Palestine heated up, Arab Palestinian personnel found themselves in the difficult position of being called upon to act against their own community. As part of an effort (only occasionally successful) to manage these tensions, police work in Palestine was pursued through a model of professionalization that emphasized ethical comportment, disciplined distinction, and centralized control. A persistent challenge in developing a professional force was establishing and maintaining both appropriate distance between police and public and adequate camaraderie and esprit de corps within the force. To accomplish the first goal, policies recommended against posting Palestinian personnel to their hometown or district.[25] Marriage between British police personnel and local women was strongly discouraged.[26] To accomplish the second, there were proposals to train Jews and Arabs together and to make British police work closely with, and sometimes under the command of, Palestinian personnel.[27] Although these efforts were substantial, in their memoirs British members of the force suggest that their effects were limited.[28] As one former policeman put it: "Looking back, however, I think we could have done better by way of fostering a truly international spirit."[29]

Both the degree of cooperation among national groups and the professionalism of the force were put to the test by the 1936–39 rebellion in Palestine. British personnel felt that their Palestinian counterparts were more loyal to their nation than to the force. As the 1938 annual report of the Police Department stated, "The Arab personnel of the Force could no longer be regarded as reliable."[30] As frustrated as they were with the refusal, or inability, of Palestinian officers to police rebellion, British officers expressed understanding for the conditions that fostered this refusal. In his history of the force, one former officer described conditions during the 1936–39 rebellion: "It was clearly now asking too much of a Moslem policeman whose wife and family were resident in the town to stand out fearlessly and belabour into the mob. . . . [This] was to invite one's own destruction and a revenge attack upon one's own children who attended the school and one's own wife who used the local market place."[31] For Palestinian policemen the political situation in Palestine meant that they were frequently put in the position of having to balance their national identity, their personal safety, and their professional requirements.[32]

Like much about Mandate rule this conflict could never be wholly resolved. And in the last years of British rule in Palestine, policing followed an increasingly militarized model. Following recommendations by "imperial expert" Charles Tegart, police fortresses were built around the country, a mobile force was established with recruits from the British military, and the overall force had an increasing "security orientation."[33] It was this experience in counterinsurgency that made the British personnel in the Palestine police so well suited for other colonial conditions. As for the Palestinians in the force, some who lived in Gaza, or who came to Gaza in 1948, went on to serve as police during the Egyptian Administration.

How to Think About Policing

In contexts of colonialism, of security states, and of many urban environments, policing is very easily located as part of what Althusser calls the "repressive state apparatuses."[34] It is an arm of government that seems to operate more through coercion than consent, and it appears to be one of the key means through which states monopolize the "legitimate use of force."[35] There is no doubt that the policing system in Gaza under Egyptian rule was an expression of state force and often operated to constrain and contain popular desires and demands. And yet this coercive framework does not provide a wholly adequate account of the effects of this policing. Making sense of the complicated ways that multiple ideas about security and multiple tactics of policing insecurity intersect requires an analytic that does not only focus on its repressive or coercive capacities. For this sort of approach, many scholars turn to Michel Foucault's *Discipline and Punish*.[36] As is well known, Foucault looks at apparently repressive governing forms and considers precisely what is produced through them. Through consideration of the military, education, and prisons in Europe, he argues that a key product is subjectivities: both the disciplined, obedient subject and the incorrigible, ungovernable delinquent.

Building on this work, a great deal of the scholarship on policing explores ways that it works as a form of disciplining, as a means through which people are evermore precisely defined and categorized. Very often this disciplining works in the service of particular political projects of social control.[37] Surveillance is a crucial technique in this project. Advances in surveillance technologies allow for increasing specificity of the observed subject, and thereby permit a population to be searched for its criminal elements.[38] The dynamics of policing in Gaza during the Egyptian Administration certainly support the general diagnosis of its disciplinary operations, interest in expansive knowledge, and use of intrusive security practices, but they also highlight a practice that frequently relied more on indistinction than on precision. Just as it is broadly correct but insufficient to note that policing in Gaza was coercive, so too was discipline part of the policing dynamic but not all that needs to be understood about it.

Yet another approach to police work tacks from a different angle: asking about the place of policing in democratic life and in democracy promotion. This line of inquiry considers the ways in which police practice both follows the requirements of democratic governance (e.g., following the rule of law, respecting citizens' freedom and dignity) and allows for appropriate forms of protest and complaint. Often prescriptive as much as descriptive, the investigation of the democratic potential and limits of policing is often in conversation with ideas about cosmopolitanism, especially in relation to the policing of immigrants and asylum seekers in democratic countries.[39]

One problem with this approach, at least for considering policing in Gaza, is that it often proceeds with an assumption that a sharp line can be drawn between democratic and totalitarian policing, with the political goal being to make policing more democratic. I would not dispute that there are important (ethical, political, practical) distinctions between these different governing systems and their related policing practices, but focusing too much on category differences can sometimes impede an understanding of the effects of police practice. That is, it may obscure both how repressive policing can sometimes enable forms of political action and the potential of seemingly democratic practices like community policing to constrain popular politics. Whatever the governing form, policing is important in shaping relations between governor and governed, among the population, within the locale, and with the wider world.[40]

The different character of policing practices in different places and times does matter for how those relationships develop. Making an argument for better, democratic policing, the criminologist Ian Loader argues that too often policing is shallow and wide when it should instead be deep and narrow.[41] By "shallow" he means that recognition of police effect is limited to protecting people from "crime and disorder,"[42] whereas "deep" policing would acknowledge the importance of policing to shaping subjectivities and political belonging.[43] By "wide" he means the extensive visible display of police presence and entrance of police into a broad range of situations. "Narrow" policing, in contrast, would be accomplished by ~ained, reactive, rights-regarding agencies of minimal interference and last resort."[44] Loader's project is a prescriptive one, to make a case for how to do better policing. Mine is a diagnostic one, to better understand the dynamics and effects of policing in Gaza. Using Loader's terms, but twisting them a bit, I would argue that policing in Gaza was deep and wide. This policing practice was self-consciously ambitious in its aims to shape "membership in a political [and social] community,"[45] and it did so in part through its expansive presence in that community.[46]

In thinking about how policing works to shape political and social community, another part of Foucault's work can be helpful. I refer here to his investigation of security, a practice that he distinguishes from both sovereignty and discipline. Foucault describes security as involving a particular relationship of space, event, and population. He highlights the importance of "the temporal and the uncertain," suggesting that "the specific space of security refers then to a series of possible events."[47] He distinguishes discipline and security, suggesting that where the former "regulates everything," the latter "lets things happen."[48] Letting things happen is not a matter of unconcern but rather a technique to prevent the emergence of other things that are deemed to pose a more general threat (e.g., allowing some people to go hungry to avoid a general problem of scarcity). The capacity to know which things to let happen requires a detailed knowledge of people and place and an analysis of the relations among these details. Foucault further contrasts the way that security relates to people as population—observing people as a "multiplicity of individuals . . . bound to the materiality within which they live"—with sovereignty's interest in "a set of legal subjects" and discipline's interest in "bodies capable of performance."[49]

Although Foucault's arguments about different techniques of power sometimes appear to suggest a replacement of one form by another—that is, a historical movement from sovereignty, to discipline, to security and governmentality—he insists that they coexist. What he aims to identify is a shift in emphasis, where different epochs display greater reliance on certain of these technologies. So what he suggests might be called a "society of security"[50] is one that is dominated by the security form. Thinking about Gaza under the Egyptian Administration as a security society is helpful, but this cannot involve a direct application of Foucault's descriptions. Policing in Gaza, and governance more broadly, does seem to have deployed many of the relations among space, event, and population that Foucault identifies with security, but with a difference. His exploration of the emergence of security as the dominant governing framework is a story of liberalism. This is in part why the concept of letting things happens—laissez-faire—plays such a key role in this form of security. Egyptian rule in Gaza was not liberal, and laissez-faire was not a dominant part of its practice, although it too was concerned with both the limits of government and the welfare of the population.

What does a security relation to population look like if it does not proceed within the frame of "letting things happen"? In Gaza, at least, the framework appears to have been uncertainty. Uncertainty is not quite the same as risk, in part because risk can be calculated. Indeed, risk is a way of managing uncertainty. In Gaza uncertainty was not contained by statistics but circulated via rumors and surveillance, through informants and police personnel. It defined police encounters in the interrogation room and in the street. Suspicion (a key expression of uncertainty) shaped relations among all the actors in Gaza and helped define both political and social possibility. The administration worked to manage and control the Gazan population by significantly expanding police presence and by maintaining a degree of uncertainty about when and where that expansion would be found. It should be further noted that uncertainty was not just a policing technique; it was also an existential condition. Policing did not just produce fear; it responded to and made use of existing fears. But in contrast to how the effects of totalitarian and authoritarian policing through fear are often described, people in Gaza's security society did not live in isolation and loneliness.[51] They did live in and with chronic apprehension, and that state of affairs shaped both how they were governed and how they acted in the world.

Policing and Security Society

In thinking about security society in Gaza, I draw also from Partha Chatterjee's consideration of the "politics of the governed." I develop "security society" as a third category to employ alongside his two key concepts of civil society and political society.[52] Chatterjee argues that in postcolonial India it is useful to think of people as being largely governed in one of two ways: as citizens (in the classic sense) or as population (in the Foucauldian sense). In turn, people act politically, make claims of government, in two different contexts and with two different kinds of tactics: as members of civil society using the language of rights or as part of political society engaging in practices on the ground that change their circumstances. Chatterjee's descriptions of India do not map perfectly onto conditions in Gaza—the absence of a national state being only one notable difference—but the conceptual framework he offers is helpful to think with. And it is especially so with the addition of "security society." Security matters are not a central focus of Chatterjee's discussion, but he indicates that they could be considered within the context of political society.[53] This incorporation is not adequate to account for dynamics in Gaza. The "security society" category, with distinct modes of governing and of acting politically, is necessary for understanding the character of policing here. Furthermore, distinct from Chatterjee's proposal about India, everyone in Gaza was governed through all three forms and also acted politically through all three mechanisms. Different contexts and times brought different features to the fore.

When Gazans were governed via security, they were approached as security threats. And they could act politically through security society by mobilizing policing techniques to other ends, in part by changing the threat calculations of security services (to make not responding to a popular demand riskier than doing so). The identification of security threats relied on two processes that appear to move in opposite directions but were in fact often simultaneous and mutually reinforcing: the identification of "the people" as a collective unity (that required protection and could be a source of threat) and the separation of this category into constitutive parts (that could pose threats to each other and could also come together in different configurations).[54] Citizens, population, and the people as security threat were all part of the governing landscape in Gaza.

Policing as Governance
Citizens are governed as legal and political subjects. Populations are governed as targets of welfare and other forms of intervention. Security threats are governed as potential problems and sources of suspicion.

Policing practice in Gaza during the Egyptian Administration indicates that everyone fell into the category of "security threat." At times this everyone was identified as "the people": a collectivity that both required protection and was seen as a possible threat. At times this category was disaggregated, and to this end some policing techniques worked precisely by distinguishing persons. This attention to persons and people as security threats did not mean that suspects were transformed into "objective enemies" or "objective opponents,"[55] as Hannah Arendt argues was the case for totalitarian policing. They remained in the realm of the uncertain—carrying the permanent potential for threat—that Foucault defined as central to security. Gazans who might stand in political opposition to the regime (and therefore be "enemies" in that context) were also Palestinian subjects (and therefore "friends," or at least objects of compassion and putative solidarity). People whose behavior identified them as threats to moral order could also act in service of the police. And in fact their social vulnerability could make them more likely to do so.

What were the terms by which people were identified as possible security threats? The evidence from policing practices indicates that there were two key fields of security concern: national interest and social propriety. Given the tense location and conditions of Gaza during (and before and after) the Egyptian Administration, it is not surprising that many of the security concerns that drove policing practice during the Egyptian Administration were about the security and stability of the governing order. And much of this book describes policing objects and tactics that were clearly directed toward that security—including the direct control of political activity; efforts to produce a compliant, unthreatening population; and the patrolling of borders to stave off political conflict. The surveillance of everyday activity sought to track and therefore to head off any threat to this stability from Gaza's population. The control of political and military activity was additionally about protecting Egyptian forces from Israeli attack.

Although regime stability and the national interest may seem more evidently relevant to security discourse—and Egyptian administrators clearly defined any independent political activity as a possible threat to national security and therefore to be controlled—police practice makes clear that propriety was also a central concern.[56] For one thing, public order, and therefore seemingly private behavior, was viewed as relevant to the national interest. In these circumstances, the policing of morality and comportment that is part of any social order took on a heightened security valence. Additionally, propriety was a police matter because relationships between people were viewed as police matters, and the moral life of the community was a key terrain where these relations were worked out. Reputation also played an important role in this process. Identifying propriety as a matter relevant to the police also was a technique for promoting expansive entry into people's lives, and therefore for assisting in the policing of politics as expressed in personal, familial, and social contexts. Recognizing the importance of this range of concerns to the security field helps explain the variety of spaces and behaviors that police concerned themselves with, the terms by which they addressed the population, and the ways that people responded to them.

Policing as a Means of Action

That security society was also a space within which people acted, and that the policing techniques through which they were governed also provided mechanisms for such action, is an important part of the picture. As a space of action, civil society is defined by associational life and rights claims. Political society is defined by communities in action, what Chatterjee calls "popular politics" and what Asef Bayat calls the "quiet encroachment of the ordinary."[57] Security society is a space defined by practices of surveillance and informing, by the forwarding of claims through expressions of suspicion, and by networks of relations that are defined by hesitancy as much as comfortable connection. When people in Gaza acted politically through security society, they did so in part by mobilizing these policing techniques to other ends.

People engaged in various sorts of actions. Some were framed in explicitly political terms and took the form of petitions and protests. In these actions, which were the minority, security concerns provided a basis for pressing claims for representation, protection, and militarization. Because of the significant constraints imposed on such explicit politics, political life pursued through security society often took the form of the apparently incidental, of small-scale pushback at particular arrangements.

Suspicion, rumor, and apprehension are all well suited for such, often extremely localized, redirections. People used the same practices that police deployed in controlling their actions as mechanisms for pressing interests and claims, though never to equal effect. These claims were sometimes directed at the government and sometimes at other members of their community.

This last point is crucial for understanding the dynamics of security society in Gaza. It is easy to slip into speaking in dyadic terms of government control and popular resistance, of state-imposed constraints and people's demands for freedom (and I sometimes speak in these terms here). But this dyadic relationship is only one part of the dynamic at play in Gaza, only one node in a larger network of relations. Acting politically was not just about acting against or in relation to governing authorities. It is important to consider the multiple relations within the population and the very significant efforts by people to exercise control over others in their community. It was easier for people to impose themselves on other Gazans, to control their behavior, than it ever was to exert influence on government. In these efforts people identified the same security threats as the police did. In so doing, they sometimes deployed an explicitly political language, particularly the discourse of nationalism, to suggest that others were involved in corruption or betrayal. Even more frequently, though, or at least so it seems from the available sources, they used the notion of propriety, and especially gendered propriety, to assert control over public space, private behavior, and social practices. Claims about improper behavior provided a means for bringing police authority to bear on what might otherwise be personal conflicts. They also motivated direct action that people sometimes took against each other. Such efforts were sometimes directly linked to charges of national betrayal.

The concepts of security and security society provide an analytic that shows how political mobilization for the nation and social mobilization for proper behavior in the community were linked. They help in exploring the multiple avenues through which control was exercised and rebuffed. They clarify the multiple relations that shaped the policing dynamic. Security society was a tremendously unequal space. The police had an array of coercive powers at their disposal that other people could never mobilize. Yet this inequality did not mean that police held all the cards. Not only were people occasionally able to push back at government policies they opposed, to insist on changes in procedures they found problematic; they were also able to mobilize security techniques—suspicion, informing, moral suasion, and coercion—to shape the behavior of others in their community. Gazans' widespread participation in security work was to a considerable degree a product of fear and coercion, but it was never just that. It was also a product of the sometimes-positive evaluation of these techniques and of their usefulness to Gazans in getting things done for themselves.

Relationships, Categories, and Police Practice

In Gaza policing was a space and a vector of interaction and relation between the population and government. Working out this relationship also meant working out who that population was: as a totality, as an array of social groupings, and as a collection of individuals. So one task of policing, and it did not fall only to the police, was the work of naming: both addressing "the people" as a whole and disaggregating that category into a range of social and political categories with diverse allegiances and conflicts. Policing was thus as much about identifying subject positions as it was about controlling specific behavior. Policing also provided a mechanism through which people—within and sometimes in opposition to the categories with which they were identified—interacted with one another. In the early years of the administration these subject categories included spies and traitors, victims and neighbors. In later years some of these subject positions transformed into dissidents or activists, criminals, guerrillas (fedayeen), and nationals or citizens. These local subject categories also intersected with the global category of humanity. Police did not produce these subject positions either alone or out of nothing—and in fact sometimes they clearly emanated from within the population—but policing as a practice helped shore up these categories as meaningful and also used them as an instrument of control.

Police practice involved questions about both social and political relations. Political questions included, What can be demanded of government? What degree of free political expression is possible? What independent political activity is allowed? What venues for claim making exist?

Questions about social relations included, What obligations do Gazans have to one another? What obligations do Egyptians have to Palestinians? What kinds of sociability are possible between Egyptians and Palestinians and between internationals and Palestinians? What sorts of behavior are deemed proper? Answering these questions, even provisionally, required continuing work around the question of who, and what, were the subjects in Gaza and what were the relationships among them.

The categories through which people worked out political relations included "citizen," "subject," "native," "refugee," "Palestinian," and "human." As citizens, Gazans interacted with government authorities to make a set of claims. As subjects of rule (population), they received services and dispensations. As native Gazans or refugees—significant and distinct social categories within the local community—they were differently connected to the place of Gaza and to Palestine more generally. These territorial relationships formed a basis of political claims (to return, to defense, to representation), of social dynamics (as people worked out the boundaries of community), and of security concerns (as people's connections to here and there were identified as potential motivators for unauthorized actions). As Palestinians particularly and part of humanity generally, Gazans claimed a connection to the "international community." As Palestinians, they argued that the international community bore responsibility for their plight, having supported the partition of Palestine, and therefore also had responsibility to both aid them and help resolve the situation. As part of humanity, Gazans located themselves inside this international community and pressed an explicitly relational set of claims about equity, justice, and mutual obligation among its members.

Social relations were worked out in significant part through the additional categories of neighbors and kin. One of the striking features of conditions in Gaza in the aftermath of the *nakba* (catastrophe), which brought masses of refugees into Gaza and dispossessed much of the native population of its land, was the disruption of preexisting neighborly relationships. These relationships were disrupted because the demography had changed: there were new people nearby, living as neighbors and making claims on one another. They were also disrupted because circumstances had changed so dramatically for the worse. People who used to be in a position to give found themselves in need. People whose homes had been centers of hospitality found themselves living in tents. People whose lands provided sustenance for their families and their neighbors found themselves dependent on rations. And people who were still in a position to be "neighborly" found the demands on their care to be substantially increased.[58] All these conditions introduced new tensions into the dynamics of social proximity, but they did not utterly upend them.

Kinship relations were likewise strained by the 1948 experience. Families existed on both sides of the new categorical distinction between natives and refugees. And all of the difficulties associated with these new conditions affected family dynamics. Still, family ties remained economically, socially, and politically important, and they played a significant role in security dynamics. Not only did powerful families create a challenge for police operations, as taking them on had the potential to create more security problems than it might solve, but also family relations were one means through which people sought to promote and enhance their own security. As I have already suggested in invoking the centrality of propriety in policing, neighbor and kin relations were as much about the exercise of control as about the provision of care. The behavior and morality of those nearby was understood to be directly connected to a person's well-being and that of his or her family. To be a neighbor, therefore, was not just to be a potential source of assistance and conviviality, but also to be, possibly, a threat. This potential was not a creation of the conditions produced by the 1948 *nakba*, but it loomed significantly larger because of them.

Police Encounters in the Archives

To pursue this investigation of policing in Gaza under Egyptian rule I use a range of sources: interviews with retired police officers and other Gazans, memoirs, press accounts, and archival sources. I rely most heavily on the last, which include records of the police forces of the Egyptian Administration and of the United Nations peacekeeping force deployed to Gaza in 1957. The latter records are housed in the UN Archives in New York and are readily available to researchers. The former, as I described in some detail in *Governing Gaza*, have a more complicated story. They are part of a broad set of government documents seized by Israeli forces when they occupied Gaza, first in 1956 and then in 1967. They are housed in the Israel State Archives in Jerusalem. When I encountered them in the 1990s they were "openish." They had never been indexed or formally declassified, and archive employees made an ad hoc decision about which of the many boxes of Egyptian records were not about sensitive security matters and therefore available to me. In the midst of my research a decision was made (for reasons unrelated to my work) to close the files pending a formal review of their classification status. Given fair warning of the impending closure, I was able to photocopy large portions of these materials. To the best of my knowledge, they remain closed, and I have no expectation that they will be reopened.

The police records in these files include surveillance reports, interrogation transcripts, investigation files, reports on public opinion, informant statements, internal correspondence, and committee records (see Figure 1). The bulk of the records are from the on-the-ground work of policing, including both the surveillance operations of the security apparatus and the crime interdiction responsibilities of cops on the beat. They also include materials that went up the chain of command to the level of the governor-general (the highest authority in the Strip). There are some statements of policy and procedure, but the records are largely of police work in practice. They provide a rare window into the details of police procedure in the security states of the Arab world. As such, the significance of this material extends well beyond the particular history of Gaza.

In my reading of these sources I consider the police encounter, whether mundane or dramatic, as a kind of event. In the chapters that follow I recount many of these events: in the interrogation room, on the street, in the report. Policing events in Gaza can sometimes be identified as "critical" or "exemplary"[59]—in the sense of being both reflective and generative of social transformation[60]—but more frequently the archives are populated by a more quotidian sort of event, one whose effects were accumulative rather than immediately transformative. These events were no less important in shaping a social and political order, but it was a compilation of encounters that cemented, but did not necessarily dramatically redirect, the order of things. It was largely in such quotidian events—ones that, except for the peculiar history of these documents, might have left no historical record—that police and civilians had to

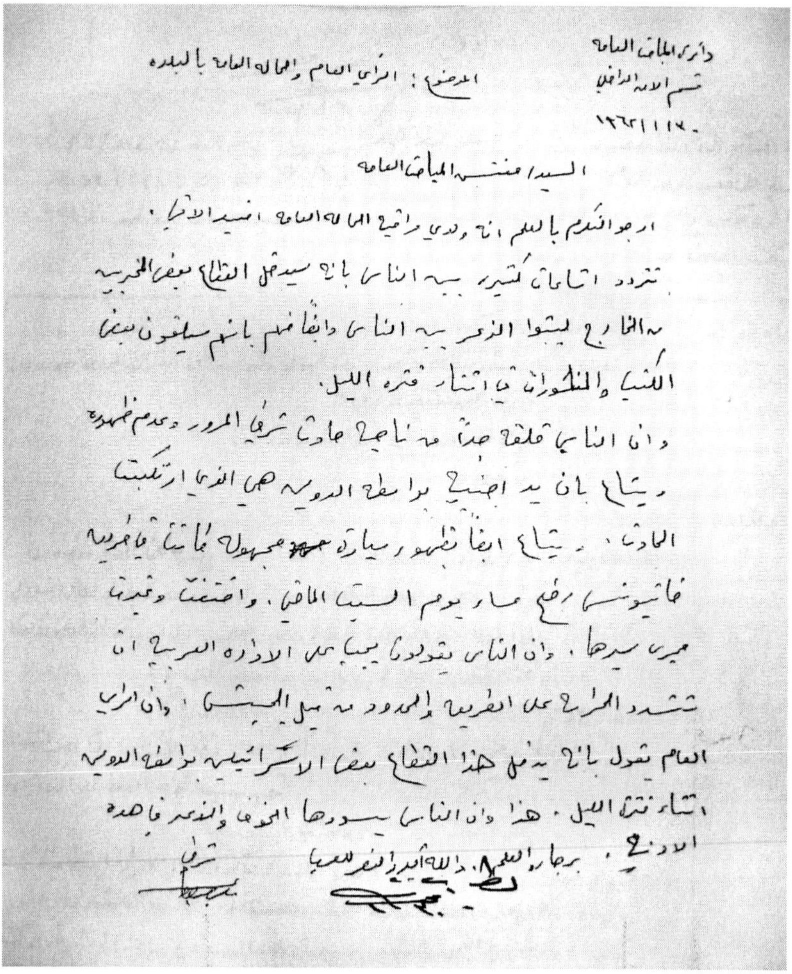

FIGURE 1 *Police report on public opinion describing people's worries about infiltrators, border control, and possible Israeli incursions, 1962. Source: Israel State Archives.*

repeatedly work out their roles (professional, political, and personal) and their relations with each other. It was also through these events that the security landscape was understood and produced.

As rich as these sources are, I should also note what they do not provide. By and large, they do not follow a case or an incident from beginning to end. Rather, they are snapshots of moments in the policing process. They do not offer an account of how police felt about their work and their relationships with the rest of the population. For some evidence about these matters, I make use of interviews I conducted with retired policemen in Gaza as well as conversations with other Gazans about their views of the police. The arguments I make in this book about these relationships are, though, based primarily on what they looked like in the details, on what was happening on the ground. At the same time, each of the documents I consider is engaged in its own interpretative work: making sense of what police saw on the street, determining which comments count as "public opinion," evaluating witness statements, analyzing threat. Together, these interpretations paint a vivid picture of the landscape of concern and the network of relations in Gaza. In exploring this police practice, the first and second chapters of the book further delineate the contours of the security field: both the identification of subjects and persons of concern and the structure and techniques that developed to respond those concerns. Chapters 3–5 explore the broad range of activities that police sought to control, from the mundane work of investigating petty crime to efforts to curb political upheaval.

The expansive policing practice in Gaza was, I have suggested, wide and deep. To return to Ian Loader's argument, he suggests that "wide" policing has the effect—in the name of security—of producing widespread insecurity. To a certain extent, this seems clearly to have been the case in Gaza. Even more, though, wide policing shows how insecurity and security could be produced together: security about daily life (little crime or violence) and insecurity about other members of the population, about political machinations inside and outside Gaza, and about the future. The "deep" effects (shaping subjectivities and political belonging) of Gaza's form of participatory policing included the production of uncertainty as a central feature of community identification and population-government relations; the formation of new relationships and intimacies in an altered community and governing structure; the recalibration of political and public demands; and the reconfiguration of borders and boundaries, both spatial and social, as key features of governing and community relations. I explore each of these effects in the chapters that follow.

The characteristics of policing and security in Gaza during the Egyptian Administration were by no means unique to either this place or this time. The contours of what I am calling security society certainly vary across locales, but the centrality of security threats and security concerns to governing dynamics in a range of places is evident. The array of issues that can be named as security concerns and persons who can be identified as security threats is considerable and varied. In Gaza these threats and concerns were generally articulated through the rubrics of national interest and social propriety. Responding to these concerns, and seeking protection from violations by others, was a significant factor in structuring a range of relationships in Gaza. The ways that these two seemingly separate areas of concern, which might appear to matter to quite different parties, were in fact seen not only as part of the same terrain but also as intrinsically connected, is noteworthy. Consideration of this shared field can broaden the understanding of which issues matter to security states and to the populations who live in those states. It can help explain how people can both fear and desire expansive policing.

1

Cultivating Suspicion and Participation

NOT LONG AFTER EGYPTIAN AUTHORITIES acquired formal control of Gaza, Egyptian military and administrative officers met in Khan Yunis with a group of mukhtars (village leaders). The purpose of this meeting, held in October 1949, was to enlist the cooperation of the mukhtars in controlling the population, particularly in keeping people from crossing the armistice line that marked the boundary between the new Gaza Strip and the new State of Israel. In his opening statement, Egyptian army officer Abdullah Sharqawi laid out the situation as a simple quid pro quo: "The Egyptian army," he said,

> came to Palestine specifically to help the people of Palestine and to defend against their enemies. In this effort it sacrificed money and men, and it is still ready to sacrifice whatever is asked of it. This is from our side, but from your side we ask that you help us to fulfill our mission with honor and security. The Egyptian army intends to respect that to which it has agreed, in regards armistice conditions.[1]

The armistice agreement between Egypt and Israel was signed on February 24, 1949. It brought an end to active hostilities, defined the provisional boundaries of the Gaza Strip, and identified Egypt as the responsible authority in that territory. According to the agreement, Palestinians were supposed to remain at a distance from the armistice line: the territory abutting the border was defined as a no-man's-land. But, suggesting that the Egyptian army was willing to be flexible and to take risks on behalf of the Palestinian people, if it received their full cooperation, Sharqawi indicated the following: "If we violate the letter of this condition and allow people to cross [into the no-man's-land] to the armistice line itself, in order to help them earn a livelihood, then we expect from the people that they will appreciate this sympathy from us and will not cross the armistice line under any circumstances. And the line is known to you also."

This meeting was an early instance in the process of establishing the expansive and wide police presence that the Egyptian Administration deemed necessary in Gaza. This broad presence required the cultivation of significant public participation in policing. It also required, and equally was required by, a condition of suspicion. That is, police needed to be everywhere because they viewed everybody with suspicion, and their ability to engage the public sufficiently in order to make it possible for them to be everywhere depended on ensuring that this suspicion was widely shared. The work of cultivating both participation and suspicion involved coercion and consent, the threat of force and the promise of support. These efforts to establish the conditions for policing not only show the complexity of police power and the population's response to it; they illuminate the multiplicity of attributes ascribed to both police and public. The people were identified as at once a source of threat and an object of protection. The police appeared as both part of the local community and apart from it. Trust among all these parties was tenuous, but mutual reliance was nonetheless necessary.

The demand for significant public participation in policing work was one prong of the Egyptian security strategy. The consolidation of a professional police force was another. Building up the force and its structure took time, and the first personnel were often people who had served in the Palestine Police during the British Mandate. They brought their training and prior experience to the job. Like police everywhere, they regularly confronted questions about their proper relationship with the public. Learning to create a degree of professional distance, even as one works to cultivate trust, is a central part of most police training.[2] The experience of the Mandate had confirmed that these questions were particularly acute, and sometimes unsolvable, in circumstances of conflict where the police were also party to the struggle.[3] During the Egyptian Administration "conflict" lay across the new border, but there were numerous tensions within Gaza that sometimes presented themselves as clashes of loyalty for police personnel.

The Gaza Strip was a brand-new space, in a difficult condition and with an unknown future. Its boundaries were a product of war. Its population was the result of the massive displacement of Palestinians. The approximately 250,000 refugees nearly overwhelmed the 80,000 natives of the area. Refugees lived everywhere: about half of the displaced in the eight refugee camps established throughout the Strip and the remainder in its towns and villages. Whether the refugees would ever be able to return home or whether the dispossessed natives would ever gain access to their property was unknown (and seemed increasingly unlikely as time went on). Quaker aid workers who arrived in Gaza in the midst of the emerging refugee crisis recorded the suffering and the demands of the displaced. In a typical statement, a refugee from Lydda insisted: "I want to return to my lands, my house and my friends. . . . This is a very bad life. All we ask is to be home and safe."[4] The Quakers also described the ways refugee needs could create security challenges in the camps. Refugees were sometimes injured in the crush of people around ration distribution; agitated crowds demanding improvements in their conditions sometimes surrounded aid workers.[5] The desire of refugees to return home, and their need for the food and goods they had left behind, led many to undertake the very dangerous journey across the armistice line. These facts were fundamental in shaping police practice and police relations. Such crossings in violation of the armistice agreement no doubt prompted the Khan Yunis meeting.

Refugees were the new majority in Gaza, but the area's native population also suffered the losses of 1948. The vast majority were dispossessed of property, which lay in territory thereafter occupied by Israel. Their homes, towns, and remaining agricultural land were crowded with displaced people from other parts of Palestine. They found themselves in the position of at the same time offering hospitality and assistance to refugees—people who were sometimes their relatives and friends with claims of kin and community—and being in need themselves. In his memoirs, Abu Iyad (one of the founders of Fatah) describes a common scenario. His family came to Gaza from Jaffa and took shelter with an uncle "of humble circumstances" where his family of seven crammed into a small room. Both hoping to return and lacking funds to move elsewhere, they stayed this way for two years, "until my uncle told my father that he was unfortunately unable to keep us any longer."[6] Stories I heard from people in Gaza about the early days after the *nakba* make clear that even as hospitality was widespread and genuine, so too were hostility and worry about the long-term impact of the influx of refugees on Gazan lives.[7] Sorrow about the past and worry about the future were defining experiences for everyone in Gaza.

Sharqawi's demand for participation in policing was made in a language of certainty—"the line is known to you"—that in some sense belied Gaza's unstable reality. But this language also was a key way in which the new condition of place and people was established. The call for participation named a set of relations, obligations, and subject positions, and in so doing (and backed by the threat of coercive power) helped produce and stabilize them. In his statement to the mukhtars, Sharqawi stressed, "If the people cross the armistice line, they put themselves in danger from one side and put the Egyptian side in a position of non-compliance with the armistice conditions from another. I do not think that you [the mukhtars] will accept this because such a phenomenon would place the Egyptian army and the administration in a position of not controlling affairs in their lands." He placed direct responsibility for compliance on the mukhtars: "I consider you responsible for making the people understand what is required of them to respect the armistice conditions and not cross the armistice line under any circumstances. It is your obligation to guarantee the implementation of this condition by informing us about each violator of these regulations immediately, so that he can be given the strongest punishment."

He then went on to explain the system of daily border patrols being set up in agreement with Israeli forces (the patrols would include personnel from the Palestinian police), and he further told the mukhtars that they were responsible for passing this information along to the population and for telling them not to shoot at these patrols, whether Egyptian or Israeli. Underscoring this point, Sharqawi stated, "From now on each mukhtar will be considered responsible for any incident that occurs in his area and is required to present the perpetrator or he will be taken himself." According to the record of the meeting, immediately following this threat he restated the call for participation in more positive terms: "I await, from each individual in the area where the Egyptian army is now, sincere cooperation so that the Egyptian army can devote itself fully to its primary mission: to protect you until your problem is solved in a manner that is to your benefit and which returns to you your rights." Sharqawi's language gestures to the multiple means of addressing Gazans: as citizens, as population, and as security threats. It invokes the language of rights and duties that is the purview of citizens. It uses the language of protection, which is often a frame for managing population. And most clearly, it emphasizes the possibility that Gazans could pose a threat to Egypt and the stability of its rule, positing Palestinians as security problems who need to be controlled.

Conditions of Suspicion

The Egyptian entry into Gaza was marked by a rhetoric and practice of mutual support and a climate of suspicion and recrimination. This condition was experienced both within the new population, as refugees and natives worked out their relationship to each other, and between Gazans and their new Egyptian governors. Circulating suspicions about threats to stability, to the nation, and to moral community both created the need for expansive policing and were mobilized to generate participation in this work. Suspicion underlay procedures for control of the border, the management of politics and behavior inside Gaza, and the prevention of crime. Police officers had to acquire a professional suspicion of the criminal, the traitor, and the dissident, and to learn proper techniques for utilizing their suspicions in interrogation and interdiction. Gazans were encouraged to turn generalized fear and uncertainty into grounds for joining in the police project through informing, self-policing, and control of others in their community.

Suspicion is a regular feature of security practices. Not only does it promote an expansion of police presence; in many circumstances it provides a mechanism for targeting and controlling particular persons and populations, very often defined in racial terms.[8] For example, in the

United States young black men are often the suspect category.[9] In France it is equally persons of North African descent who are targeted.[10] In Israel Palestinians are the most frequent sources of suspicion. As Juliana Ochs describes, suspicion is presented to the Jewish Israeli public as a security technique that they can adopt to protect themselves and their nation.[11] The identification of categories of concern often goes along with a discourse of moral or social panic that justifies this attention. Stuart Hall famously linked fear of mugging in England to moral panics that were driven more by media coverage than by any increase in crime rates.[12] Teresa Caldeira shows how the "talk of crime" in Brazil organizes the physical and social landscape (e.g., "don't go there," "fear those people") and obscures analysis of the underlying causes of violence.[13] By focusing on crimes as isolated actions, but also identifying particular groups of people as prone to criminality, crime talk is a depoliticizing language with significant political effect. In each of these instances, the category production that is key to suspicion operates as a mechanism of exclusion: identifying certain groups as threats to community and other groups as members of that threatened community.

In Gaza suspicion operated slightly differently. Certainly the elaboration of categories of persons was important in this space. And, yes, people expressed fears through category differences, but those differences were not generally racialized.[14] Many of the relevant category differences in Gaza were ultimately connected to the condition of statelessness: citizenship and its absence, dispossession and its consequences, displacement and its effects. Gaza was not alone in having displacement at the center of so much of its experience. In the years after both World War I and World War II, statelessness was a global problem.[15] Hannah Arendt described a Europe ever more starkly divided between privileged citizens and utterly disenfranchised stateless people, the latter treated as "the scum of the earth."[16] In Gaza, in contrast, the population distinctions were never so sharp. The loss of Palestine in 1948 meant that all Gazans were technically stateless. And, especially in the later years of the administration, Egyptian commitment to the at least rhetorical defense of Palestine meant that all Gazans were governed to some degree as Palestinian citizens. Neither "statelessness" nor "citizenship" was a stable category in post-1948 Gaza, and both were sources of security problems and central to structuring relations within the population and between Palestinians and Egyptian administrators. Ultimately, suspicion was attached to every category of person, circulating across these differences to identify "the people" as the dominant collectivity of concern for the police.

Simply being Palestinian made people a source of possible threat, so no behavior choice could render people free from surveillance and suspicion. At the same time, being Palestinian also made people objects of compassionate care, and therefore subject to the government's gaze through another, though not unrelated, lens. The fact that everyone in Gaza was a subject of concern (as both potential threat and object of protection) did not mean that police viewed all their activities in the same way. But it did mean that no activity was outside police jurisdiction. It should also be remembered that being in the police force did not ensure that one was beyond suspicion.

Membership in a political party, active political organizing, and even political talk were matters of special concern to the police. And involvement in any of these activities could make an individual a specific target for control. Staying away from active politics did not, though, ensure that police gaze would not come your way. Applying for a job as a teacher, establishing a social club, and traveling abroad were all activities that generated investigation and report.[17] One's comportment, dress, and social interactions might all be noted by police observers.[18] The intertwining of social uncertainty and state security concerns was a key feature of security talk and practice in Gaza.[19] So in some sense, security talk in Gaza worked in a different direction than the crime talk Caldeira has described in Brazil. Rather than depoliticizing, the discourse of concern in Gaza expanded the range of actions, behaviors, and events that could be understood as political threats. This expansion, in turn, supported a project of widespread participation in policing.[20]

Border Control, Political Containment, and the Palestinian Threat

The very circumstances that led to the Egyptian presence in Gaza were a source of suspicion. Although both Egyptians and Palestinians highlighted Egyptian efforts to defend Palestine in the 1948 war, this positive rhetoric did not entirely define the dynamics in Gaza. Gazans, upon learning more details of Egypt's largely failed war effort—such as the stories about the defective weapons with which the army fought—developed a certain amount of skepticism about Egyptian involvement.[21] And in the early days of the administration, Egyptians were quite distrustful of the Palestinians in Gaza. Egyptians accused Gazans of spying. Gazans remembering these accusations generally attributed them to a desire to deflect responsibility for Egyptian failures in the war: "One always looks for a scapegoat. So, they said 'the Palestinians cheated us. The Palestinians were conspiring with the Jews against us.' When the Egyptian army was routed, they started to say that the Palestinians were collaborators with the Jews. They blamed us for their defeat."[22]

Although it might seem implausible that Palestinians who were displaced and dispossessed by the establishment of Israel would spy for Zionist forces against Egyptian interests, implausibility is no guarantee against accusation. In this instance, the very fact of connection to lost places and communities in Palestine seems to have fueled the charges. The unauthorized border crossings (usually done to bring food from homes and fields occupied by Israel or to steal from nearby settlements) that occurred in the first years after 1948 were met with great suspicion.[23] A Gazan refugee from Beersheba, a farm worker, told me, "Anyone they caught they considered a spy." Still, the same man insisted to me, "This thing with the Egyptians did not last long, for about one year or less. When they really knew us, they became good with us."[24] Still, as late as 1954, at a moment when Egyptians were considering Gazan demands to be permitted to organize military units to fight for the liberation of Palestine, they were concerned about the dangers of allowing such border crossings: "This will help the Jews to use some of the soldiers to work for their benefit. The mixing of Palestinian soldiers with their relatives [inside] will help the Jews acquire detailed information about our forces and our locations in this Strip."[25]

Border control was, thus, an imperative for Egyptian administrators for at least two reasons: concern about violating the armistice conditions and possibly provoking an Israeli response and worry about Palestinian character and the political threat they might pose. In the first years after 1948, Egypt's primary concern was to avoid conflict with Israel, and hence any Palestinian attempt to cross over, whether for personal or for political reasons, met a harsh response. The effort to halt the crossings confirms how complicated the participation of Palestinians in the policing project was.

Before 1956 border control was managed by a force of Palestinian border guards operating under Egyptian command. According to Yezid Sayigh, the officers and most noncommissioned officers were Egyptians. He further notes that the force was "inadequate or unwilling for the task,"[26] and that infiltration across the border continued. He quotes Mustafa Hafiz, head of military intelligence in Gaza and later commander of the fedayeen (guerrillas), as saying that "entrusting Palestinian soldiers with this task will not further that aim [of stopping crossings], because they encourage infiltration and repeatedly conduct attacks."[27] The concern expressed about Palestinian police was about more than their failure to implement official policy on border crossing, although that was a significant concern in itself; it was also that their loyalties might remain too closely allied with their community and not their professional responsibilities. Even the forces who were supposed to help manage border security were themselves possible security threats.

In 1955, in part in response to Israeli attacks on Gaza, Egyptian policy shifted to support the establishment of fedayeen units to launch operations across the line. By legitimizing some border crossings, the creation of these units alleviated some of the problems with Palestinian personnel, but the fact that Egyptian security planners and Palestinian security personnel might have different agendas and connections was an enduring concern. In 1955 and 1956 fedayeen pursued a number of significant infiltrations into Israel.[28] Along with the Egyptian nationalization of the Suez Canal, these attacks contributed to increasing tensions between Egypt and Israel. These tensions culminated in October 1956 in an attack on Egypt by Israel, Great Britain, and France, and Israel occupied the Gaza Strip. This occupation once again transformed the nature of border control.

After a four-month occupation, Israeli forces withdrew under international pressure. The Egyptian Administration, but not its army, was permitted to return to Gaza. UN peacekeeping forces entered the territory and took responsibility for controlling border crossings. Until the 1965 establishment of a new Palestinian military force, the Palestine Liberation Army (PLA), these foreign soldiers were the primary military personnel in the Strip. Egypt continued to control the local police and intelligence apparatus. The police force, which continued to be largely staffed by Palestinians, generally cooperated with the UN Emergency Force (UNEF). This cooperation ended in 1967 when Egypt ordered the withdrawal of the force. In the June war that followed, Israel then invaded and occupied Gaza, along with the West Bank.

Among its other consequences, the brief Israeli occupation of Gaza produced new Egyptian suspicions about Palestinian police personnel. When UNEF forces surveyed the "police situation" as they found it upon deploying to Gaza in 1957, they noted that of the 500 or so Palestinian police working in the Strip, Egyptians were preparing to fire up to 190 of them for having worked with Israeli occupation forces. To make up for this shortfall in staffing, the administration had set up a training school in Gaza and hoped to train one hundred new police a month for at least the following two months. In addition, the police force was absorbing three hundred former members of the "Palestinian Brigade" (the fedayeen force) who, they said, "are now wearing police uniforms and are engaged on guarding roads, check posts, bridges, and railways."

In addition to making personnel changes within the Palestinian police, Egyptians increased the non-Palestinian security presence. The Palestinian police chief was replaced by an Egyptian, and, the report went on, "all the senior local posts are said to be held by Egyptian personnel."[29] According to "popular rumour," forty new Egyptian Criminal Investigation Department officers had also been brought to the Strip. The UNEF report commented, "The CID has been more active in recent weeks and have paid close attention to the local and UNEF personnel and their associations. It is also thought that the CID have resorted to the old practice of telephone line tapping." The Egyptians also introduced a new contingent of sixty to one hundred Egyptian Sudanese police, precisely because they felt that "they could not rely on the local Palestine Police, particularly as some had worked for the Israelis." Trying to define what sort of force these Sudanese were, the report noted, "They have been held in reserve and are not seen conspicuously around the town. They are thought to be here primarily as a preventive measure and it is not known whether they are army or police or both. . . . The feeling is that they are police." The change in professional oversight and the presence of these outside forces confirms that the local police were themselves subject to policing.

These forces were concerned not just with border control but also with internal security, especially the management of independent political organizing and unregulated expression. The UNEF report indicated that the Sudanese unit was meant to be available to contain such political activity and that it had already stopped a demonstration outside the administration's central offices. Even as Egyptians did not entirely trust the Palestinian police when it came to politics, they could not do without them. The project of participation entailed not just public involvement in policing but also the continual cultivation of police professionalism to ensure that Palestinian police officers would act against Palestinian subversives.

The key unit for internal security policing, as well as crime investigation, was the Mabahith al-'Amma (the CID). This unit was largely staffed by Palestinians under Egyptian command. The CID's jurisdiction included surveillance, information gathering, and criminal investigations. It was divided into four units: internal security, crime investigation, administration, and the secretariat.[30] Internal security included surveillance of students, foreigners (UN Relief and Works Agency for Palestine Refugees in the Near East, or UNRWA, and UNEF personnel, as well as hotels and international mail), syndicates, printing houses, and organizations (clubs, Arab nationalists, Muslim Brotherhood, communists, and Ba'athists). This unit also had responsibility for telephone tapping and press censorship. The secretariat was responsible for the gathering and maintenance of dossiers on individuals and different areas in the Strip. As significant as political control was to CID work, it is important to remember that its personnel were also responsible for responding to complaints of ordinary crime and disorder. CID employees were beat cops, detectives, and undercover agents. Crime investigation included smuggling, drugs, and forgery. And the administration unit was charged with personnel matters.

Control of political activity was always a crucial CID mission. Parallel to practices in Egypt proper, the Muslim Brotherhood and the Communist Party were the organizations of greatest concern. The Muslim Brotherhood had particular support in Gaza because members of the Egyptian organization had fought for Palestine in the 1948 war. Despite being banned by the Egyptian government after the war, the organization continued to be active.[31] The 1952 Free Officers revolution, which ultimately brought Gamal Abdel Nasser to power in Egypt, produced a brief period of the group's legalization. Until a 1954 assassination attempt on Nasser by a Muslim Brother led to its repression again, the Brotherhood was able to operate publicly.[32] The Communist Party was given some space for activity in the mid-1950s, but the Iraqi revolution of July 14, 1958, and the increasing rivalry between Nasser's Egypt and the communist-supported regime of 'Abd al-Karim Qasim led to a crackdown on communists.[33] These crackdowns certainly limited the membership of both organizations, but they never eliminated their presence entirely.

As part of their mission to control political activity, CID personnel reported regularly—daily, weekly, and monthly—on conditions in the various parts of the Strip. They attended meetings and gatherings of all sorts, tracked public opinion, and observed people's activities and behavior on the streets. Even as Egyptian administrators had concerns about how far they could count on Palestinian police to pursue their agenda, Palestinians who were active in politics viewed local CID personnel as working against their own community. Mu'in Basisu, a Gazan poet, teacher, and communist activist who was a harsh critic of the administration, saved his sharpest criticism for Gazans who worked for the CID: "Perhaps for one second in five years the Palestinian secret policeman pauses to remember that he is a Palestinian, but then he resumes writing his reports against Palestinians."[34] Even as Egyptian administrators worried that Palestinian police might be too directed by their nationality, Gazans worried that they might be too allied with their jobs and with the security directives of the administration. Categories of suspicion were never fixed.

Managing Suspicion Within the Community

Just as Egyptians viewed Palestinians at once as potential threats and as people requiring care, so too did Palestinians approach each other with a mix of suspicion and support. The emerging distinction between refugees and natives was a key structuring framework for these tensions. These were humanitarian categories that then mapped onto and shaped people's experiences in Gaza. One thing they did not do, however, was determine people's exposure to security practices and police forces. Policing was an area of service responsibility that was not shared between the administration and UNRWA (unlike education, health care, and housing). UNRWA had no security responsibility or authority: the same government force patrolled the refugee camps as did the cities.[35] Nonetheless, these differences mattered, and they continue to matter today. They decided whether people received assistance when in need, which administrative apparatus managed their daily lives, and what relationship people had to Gaza as a place.[36]

Having been dispossessed of much of their property, with the local economy entirely disrupted, native Gazans had little to cling to as a means of preserving their dignity. That they remained in their homes was one of the few things that distinguished them from the masses of people who had poured into Gaza. According to many refugees, with the loss of Palestine still fresh, native Gazans accused them of being traitors to their country for having left their land in the midst of war.[37] Some went further and accused refugees of collaboration with Zionist settlement. Refugees answered with their own charges, sometimes suggesting that large landowners among the native population may have been involved in selling land to Zionist settlers, arguing that staying put—what later came to be described as *sumud* (steadfastness)—was not sufficient on its own but required other political values to be made meaningful:

> They [the natives] used to say that we sold our land and came to ruin theirs. They accused us of being spies. But they are the ones who sold land to the Jews in Hebron. They used to say to the donkey, "your face is like the refugee's." The relation was good in the first weeks. We were guests. They thought that we would stay for a limited short period, but when they realized the situation, tension increased and they started differentiating between a citizen and a refugee.[38]

Calling someone a spy or traitor was, of course, a moral as well as a political charge, suggesting a betrayal of the most fundamental bases of community. At the same time, the mutual recriminations seem clearly rooted as much in people's difficult living conditions—and the threat that others posed to one's already-tenuous survival—as in abstract evaluations of ethical right and wrong.[39]

The tensions between refugees and natives were expressed in charges about the past, and they created potential security problems in the present. As one person told me, the police were quick to intervene: "The government prevented this nonsense. For example, if a native made a mistake and said that 'you are a refugee' or 'your face is like this,' the government caught, imprisoned, and beat him."[40] The possibility that a quarrel between individuals could escalate into a conflict between categories of persons was certainly something security forces wanted to forestall. The record, not just of policing but also of administration policies more broadly, suggests that the government often worked to lessen distinctions around refugee status. Even as humanitarian practices produced and maintained these categories, Egyptian procedures made some effort to diminish their significance, including housing policies that created neighborhoods in which natives and refugees lived together, employment practices that ensured that people worked together, and the creation of civic obligations that affected everyone. The category of "the people" included the entire population of Gaza.

Even as police worked to control tensions across demographic category differences, security practices stoked suspicions within the population on other grounds, most especially behavior. Gender relations, particularly interactions between unmarried men and women, were a frequent subject of both police surveillance and public comment.[41] People were directly encouraged to report to the police about political talk or action. They also clearly came to view the police as an appropriate audience for complaints about social misbehavior. The schools were a frequent source of complaints to the police about others' behavior. For instance, a complaint by a student at the teacher-training institute about the behavior of other students was sent to the police for redress.[42] And the police responded, noting both the poor morals of some of the students and the general importance of morality for a good educational system.[43] Even more common were student complaints about their teachers.[44] As a result, the schools were a frequent target of police intervention, generally via a sternly worded letter to the headmaster.

The willingness of the police to intervene in conflicts between neighbors and within families is evident in the records of interrogations.[45] Even as these records are not always helpful in tracking the full contours of a case, they provide important accounts of the dynamics of the policing relationship in Gaza. The records often include questioning of multiple witnesses and suspects, even about matters that seem relatively inconsequential. They frequently record mutual recriminations, sometimes about crimes and sometimes about relationships. Almost never do these files indicate the outcome of the investigation. They provide clear evidence of police activity and interest but little information about arrests and prosecutions. Unlike surveillance reports—which members of the population knew existed in principle but had no direct access to—interrogation records describe a relationship that was clear, direct, close, and interpersonal. The records themselves bear the mark of that close relation, as both parties signed each page of the transcript (see Figure 2). Also, in distinction to the generalized surveillance that cast a wide net across the social field to capture any relevant information that might come along with the detritus of everyday activity, interrogation was motivated by a specific event (e.g., a theft, a report) and sought information about that event. That such information was not always forthcoming—"I don't know" being a common response to police questioning—did not render these encounters less significant for shaping a sense of public security, in part through public confidence that the police were on the case.

One interrogation about a family conflict was prompted by a complaint by a Gazan that his nephew had threatened him in a conflict over money. The interrogator thus began his questioning of the nephew (Amin) having already heard a version of the events. The questions both drew on that account and sought to generate a possible alternative account from Amin's perspective. The officer asked open-ended, fact-seeking questions, such as "What is the conflict between you?" and "What is the story with this money?" He also asked questions drawn from the complaint, creating an opportunity for rebuttal: "You have not threatened your uncle by saying 'beware of yourself'?" and "You did not go to your uncle on the first night of Ramadan, pushed by your brother Mahmoud?" Amin denied all the accusations that he threatened his uncle, and he responded to other questions by providing the details of a conflict over the sale of

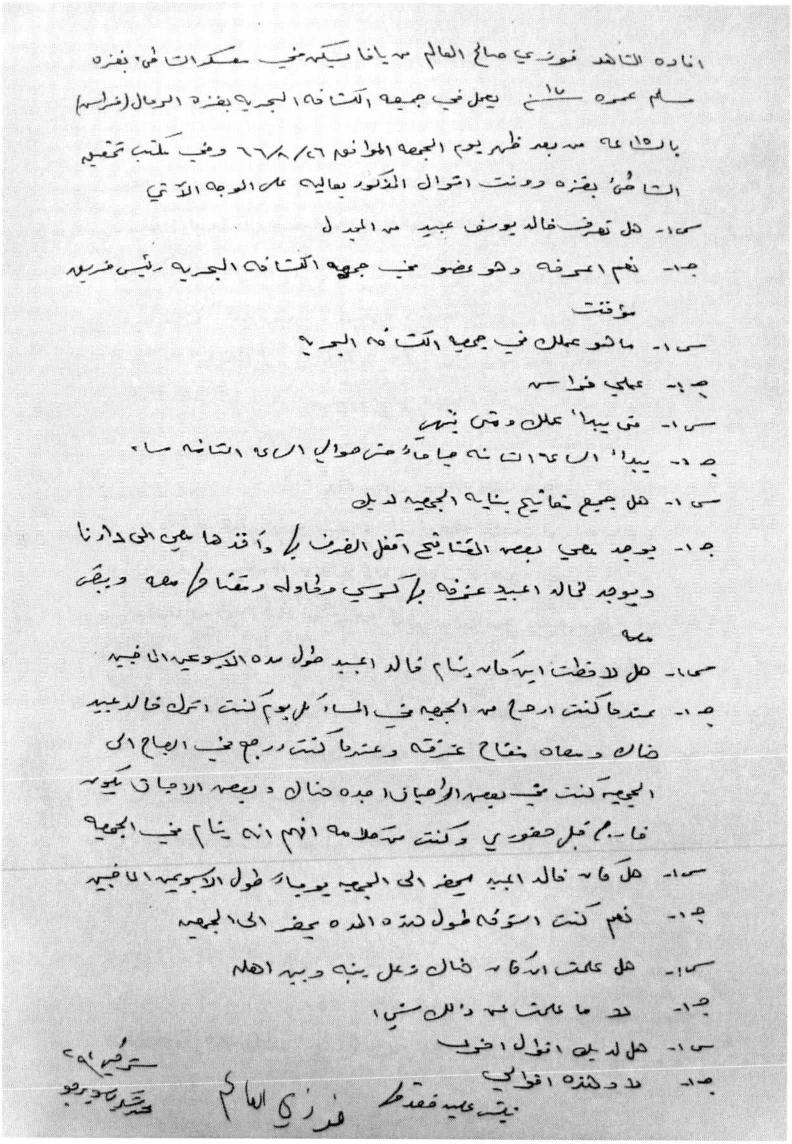

افادة الشاهد فوزي صالح العالم من يافا سكنه في معسكرات الشاطئ بغزة
مسلم عمره ١٧ سنة يعمل في جمعية الكشافة البحرية بغزة الرمال (مراسل)
بالساعة ٥ من بعد ظهر يوم الجمعة الموافق ٢٦/٨/٦٦ وفي مكتب تحقيق
الشاطئ بغزة دونت اقوال المذكور بعاليه على الوجه الآتي
س١- هل تعرف خالد يوسف عبيد من المجدل
ج١- نعم اعرفه وهو عضو في جمعية الكشافة البحرية رئيس فرقة
مؤقت
س١- ما هو عملك في جمعية الكشافة البحرية؟
ج١- عملي فراش
س١- متى يبدأ عملك ومتى ينتهي
ج١- يبدأ الساعة الثامنة صباحاً حتى حوالي الساعة الثامنة مساءً
س١- هل جميع مفاتيح بناية الجمعية لديك
ج١- يوجد معي بعض المفاتيح اقفل الغرف بها واخذها معي الى دارنا
ويوجد لخالد العبيد غرفة بها كرسي وطاولة ومفتاحها معه ويبقى
معه
س١- هل لاحظت ايه حالة ينام خالد العبيد طول مدة الاسبوعين الماضية
ج١- عندما كنت اروح من الجمعية في المساء كل يوم كنت اترك خالد عبيد
هناك ومعه مفتاح غرفته وعندما كنت ارجع في الصباح الى
الجمعية كنت في بعض الاحيان اجده هناك وبعض الاحيان يأتيه
قادم قبل حضوري وكنت من علامه افهم انه ينام في الجمعية
س١- هل كان خالد العبيد يحضر الى الجمعية يومياً طول الاسبوعين الماضية
ج١- نعم كنت اشوفه طول هذه المدة يحضر الى الجمعية
س١- هل علمت ان كان هناك زعل بينه وبين اهله
ج١- لا ما علمت شيء ذلك شيئاً
س١- هل لديك اقوال اخرى
ج١- لا ولهذه اقوالي
تلي عليه فصدق فوزي العالم

FIGURE 2 *Transcript of the police interrogation of a seventeen-year-old resident of Al-Shati refugee camp, 1966. Source: Israel State Archives.*

a family property. Toward the end of the questioning the interrogator put his own kind of threat on the table: "What if there is proof that you threatened your uncle? Are you ready to bear the responsibility and the consequent punishment?" To which Amin answered, "I am ready to bear all responsibility." The interrogation transcript is followed in the file by a commitment from Amin not to threaten or interfere with his uncle, to obey the law, and to accept any punishment that would be his due if he violated the commitment.

Interrogation had multiple effects. Not only was it a sign of police responsiveness to people's concerns—in this case a private conflict among family members, in other instances more public problems—it also provided an opportunity for ongoing expansion of police access. By signing the commitment, Amin ensured that he would have an ongoing relationship with the police (one that could be distant if he behaved). Other interrogations ended with the subject's promise to inform the police about anything he learned about the case.[46] Even the utterly banal questioning of people (often youth) who came to the police to report a dog bite let those youth know that the police had an interest in and responsibility for a broad swath of life.[47] This was an important lesson. Not only did interrogation bring Gazans into close encounter with police; the form of the questioning often reminded them that the police were paying close attention to life in the Strip. Going to the police with complaints about the behavior of members of their community was another way that Gazans took up the call for participation in the police project.

Ordinary Crime and Professional Suspicion

Crime control involved prevention, interdiction, and rehabilitation. Surveillance was crucial for the first, investigation for the second, and imprisonment for the third. In their pursuit of criminals and their efforts to halt crime, police officers need to develop skills of professional suspicion. These skills and this arena of police activity were not wholly separate from the management of politics and propriety that also concerned security personnel. The widespread surveillance that was necessary for tracking patterns of possible political organizing produced records and registers that were helpful in identifying criminals. The largely successful cultivation of public participation in information gathering and the frequent willingness of people to invite police into private domains aided in criminal investigation processes. The cultivation of police professionalism was necessary to make best use of this assistance.

The methods of crime-scene investigation used by the police were neither remarkable nor unique to Gaza. Directives in police files about how to proceed with these investigations indicate the guiding imperatives. Guidelines led detectives step-by-step through the appropriate course of crime-scene investigation—from making sure that the "incident bag" contained all the tools needed for the investigation to using the proper powder for illuminating prints. Instructions about how to lift difficult prints—such as sunken footprints or those left in sand—were provided.[48] Detectives also had to question the responding officer, area residents, and anyone else who might have seen the crime to determine how it was committed. From there they could determine the best course of investigation. "If a closet or door to a room was opened," for instance, "it is logical that the criminal touched the handle or near it. His own folly will ease the investigation."[49] By his own "folly," therefore, the criminal could unwittingly inform on himself. The emphasis in these recommendations was on teaching police to use their knowledge and expertise to outwit criminals. Police work demanded not simply a toolbox of skills but also clever thinking and sharp minds. These traits could be encouraged by training and developed through experience, but they ultimately depended on the capacity of individual policemen.

This sense of personal capacity, and the pride that it engendered, was conveyed to me by a retired police detective who told me stories of his work. Ismail Suleiman was first hired into the British Mandate police force, and he remained in the force when the Egyptians took over. He rose to the rank of sergeant in the CID.[50] When I interviewed him in Gaza in 1999, he spoke with great pride about his work during both periods. A story he told about solving a theft of cement from an UNRWA truck highlighted clever thinking as a key to investigative success. From the beginning Ismail was convinced that the truck's driver was the culprit, but proving it required a range of skills. The driver, he told me, loaded the truck from the storehouse on Saturday, for a scheduled Monday delivery to a camp:

> He sold [the cement] on Saturday, and parked the truck in the UNRWA garage. On Monday they found out that there was no cement. They questioned him and he insisted that he had parked it inside with the cement in it. How could it be proved that he sold it? They phoned us. Kamal [the prosecutor], three policemen, and myself went to the place and examined it. The UNRWA director sent for us. He talked with Kamal in English, and I pretended that I did not know English. Kamal translated for me. He told him to tell me that he knew the power of the CID, and if I wanted to find the cement I would find it, and if I did not want to find it, it would never be found. I told Kamal to tell him that we are not prophets, or diviners, or astrologers, but God willing, good will happen. I went to my policemen and explained the situation, and told them that I wanted the load. They said to me, "But we are not prophets." I said, "No, but it is easy to find." They asked how. I swear I told them: "This truck was unloaded, and who unloaded it? Porters. So I want you to slip among the porters." I chose one of them. Just three hours later, he came and told me that the driver sold the load. We arrested the driver.

This story illuminates a number of things about investigative practice and about policing more generally. The UNRWA director's comment speaks to the reputation and presumed power of the police, and especially of the CID: if they wanted to find the cement, it would certainly be found. I suspect that the comment may have referenced brute power more than skill, but Ismail emphasized the latter. I am not certain why he pretended not to speak English (or whether in fact he did speak it). Perhaps it was to put a distance between himself and the UNRWA director—ensuring that any complaints would go to Kamal, not to him. Or perhaps he sought an advantage in understanding more of what was being said than the director would realize. Whatever the goal, he was clear that it was a deliberate strategy. In underscoring the limits of police capacity—"we are not prophets"—he may have been seeking greater acknowledgment of the accomplishment of solving the crime. His report of his interactions with his staff is without doubt a tale of his own cleverness. Solving the crime was easy for him, but that was because he was so good at what he did. Success in investigation required the capacity to understand all the actors around the crime: perpetrators, police, victims, and so on. It further required utilizing that understanding to good effect—knowing how to get what you need out of each actor. Investigation, Ismail indicated, was all about relationships and about developing a properly calibrated sense of suspicion.

Imprisonment and the Production of Fear

It was not only police whose personae were molded in the work of crime control; so too were those of the criminals who were the targets of that activity. Imprisonment was a key technique in shaping these subjects. In the European instance, Michel Foucault showed how, despite the attention to rehabilitation, imprisonment and the continual work of prison reform operated to produce the delinquent as a subject category.[51] In Gaza there was a similar emphasis on rehabilitation in prison policy discourse and a similarly more complicated set of effects of these procedures. Delinquency may have been one product of imprisonment. Even more than the work of sorting subjects into positions of legality and illegality, though, policing and imprisonment under Egyptian rule seemed to operate to remind everyone of their vulnerability to security control.

The question of reform ran through discussions of prisons and prison conditions. A 1953 report from the Refugee Affairs Department described some of the problems with existing prison structures, especially the difficulty in separating petty criminals from more serious offenders. Noting that most of the cases its Social Affairs Department confronted involved petty theft (that year there were 790 cases), the report stated that the fact that these culprits served their sentences among more serious criminals meant that they were suffering harsh punishment rather than being rehabilitated. The report argued that it was imperative to set up a reform school so that such individuals could be "returned to society as good citizens."[52] This language about society underscores the extent to which imprisonment was understood as part of the broader field of policing and the production of good order.

When they made claims on their own behalf, prisoners emphasized their rights. Pushbacks against police procedure were part of broader efforts to change governing policy and practice. A record from a 1959 meeting of a government antismuggling committee makes some references to prisoner activism. In response to a hunger strike in one prison by prisoners sentenced for drug smuggling the committee proposed a series of reforms. A hunger strike created the threat of political crisis around prison conditions, so some response was necessary. The reforms seem intended to accomplish multiple goals, both to alleviate some of the complaints that led to the strike and to enhance the effectiveness of imprisonment as a tactic against smuggling. The proposals were as follows: (1) to free all prisoners who had been held for more than four years; (2) to limit the period of imprisonment to no more than nine months, "which creates an opportunity for rehabilitation and to return them to their life in society. If they return to their prior activities they can be imprisoned for a longer time"; (3) to separate prisoners who were from different places; (4) to separate smugglers from other criminals and security prisoners; and (5) to say a word to each prisoner who is released to let him know that a smuggler will always have "the sword of imprisonment hanging over his neck."[53]

The adoption of these recommendations was tabled until the following session, pending further study. In that next meeting the committee affirmed the importance of having adequate mechanisms to respond to the smuggling problem.[54] For this reason it rejected the recommendation to set a limit to prison terms, arguing that it was vital that the authorities have the power to imprison smugglers for as long as they posed a danger to society. It did recommend granting parole to some prisoners—according to criteria that would determine their degree of danger—under very strict conditions. They were to have limited freedom of movement, to be required to check in with the police regularly, and to be put under surveillance. At the end of the report it was noted that the representative from the Gaza Strip to the meeting stated that there were no prisoners being held in Gaza for longer than a year and that the governor-general, under his authority to imprison and to release prisoners, checked in on the status of prisoners on a regular basis. The recommendations—and their revision—were clearly intended to ensure that imprisonment continued to be an efficacious "weapon against smuggling." Even as these policy discussions were specific to smugglers, the cultivation of a sense of fear, an awareness of "the sword of imprisonment hanging over his neck," constituted a much broader effect of policing and imprisonment.

Fear was both a product of the insecurities produced by social, economic, and political conditions and a direct tactic of policing. It seems clear that Egyptian administrators sought, on occasion, to actively promote a sense of fear. For Sharqawi's threats to the mukhtars to be effective, for instance, there had to be some sense that serious consequences might arise from refusal to cooperate. The use of physical force by police against detainees was one means of producing fear. How exactly this violence was deployed in police practice is difficult to know: In which circumstances was it used? How much injury were police willing to inflict? It is not surprising that the answers to these questions do not appear in the police files I have. In fact, there is no mention of police use of force. That force was used, and used regularly, was mentioned in interviews I conducted with Gazans.

The most extended discussion I have encountered about police use of force against prisoners is in the memoirs of Mu'in Basisu, *Descent into the Water: Palestinian Notes from Arab Exile*.[55] Basisu, along with other Palestinian communists, helped organize among the population, produced a secret communist periodical, participated in demonstrations, and spent time in prison in Egypt. His memoirs provide a vivid account of the range of violent tactics deployed in prison. In addition to regular beatings, Basisu recalled unsanitary conditions and the insufficient provision of food and water. He describes the force used in questioning: "And the interrogation began. 'Your name.' 'K.S.' And the whip landed on his face. 'Say "Sir!" you son of a bitch.' And after he gave his name and said 'Sir,' another lash landed. 'I am a teacher, sir.' And the guard raised his voice: 'Teacher? That means Communist you son of a bitch.' And the lashes began to land."[56] He described one particular torture device called "the bride," because it looked like "a woman with her arms opened. Each arm had an opening in it through which the prisoner inserted his hand, and a hole in the head through which he put his head." Once the prisoner's shirt was removed and he had "married" the bride, the whipping began: "The first strike felt as if it tore out a rib. As if you had been struck by hot wire. The strikes continued and by the tenth you felt as if you had fallen into a sea of ants. Some of the students who were with us were no more than seventeen years old, and they received twenty lashes."[57] Basisu describes a relationship between police and public marked by violence, and one of the effects of that relationship was fear.

Palestinian prisoners in Egyptian jails reported these conditions to their families and communities, and the fear of being subjected to such punishment was no doubt a strong incentive for many people to stay away from political activity and to participate as requested in the policing regime. In my interviews in Gaza I heard often that people were afraid to engage in political activity. This fear is also evident in much of the informing activity that was prevalent during this period. There is nothing unusual about the Egyptian use of fear to seek control over a population or about the particular techniques the police used to generate this fear. It is important to note, though, that here, and in other places, this fear did not succeed in entirely shutting down politics, public expression, or the making of demands of government. The police use of fear as a technique of control is a reminder of the coercive component of the project of participation. The condition and cultivation of suspicion helped create conditions in which people would want to participate in policing. The production of fear helped make sure that they did.

Police practice that permitted, and encouraged, the use of force was part of a process that rendered suspicion and uncertainty fundamental to people's understandings of community, of their membership in it, and to the relations among the various actors in Gaza. At the same time, Gazans often cited this use of force by police officers as contributing to their everyday security. As one person put it, linking fear directly to feeling secure: "[Life] was better than today. There was fear; there was stricter rule and more respect. That is, the policeman or government was respected and people feared it, not like today."[58] Another Gazan echoed these comments, saying that people "were scared but there was security. One-hundred percent." Making a further connection among participation, suspicion, and fear, he went on to describe witnessing a theft on the street. The people, he said, went after the thief, and "they beat him up on the street until they really hurt him—the people. Then they [the police] took him and imprisoned him for two years. Just for the theft of a bag. So the situation for security, it was tough."[59] And this, in his view, was positive.

The pairing of suspicion and support that structured Egyptian rule in Gaza and shaped Palestinian attitudes about Egyptian rulers was fundamental to police practice. Each motivated and shaped that practice.

Both, in tandem with police practice and other government work, helped define political and social community in Gaza. The relevance of police practice to community dynamics and everyday life is evident in the project of participation called for by Sharqawi and in ordinary Gazans' turning to the police for redress. The wide and deep policing deployed in Gaza both provided people with "a powerful token of their membership [in] a political community in ways that afford them the material and symbolic resources required to manage, and feel relatively at ease with, the threats that they encounter in the setting of their everyday life"[60] and promoted insecurity as a fundamental condition of that everyday life. The attitudes and affects that were produced in this process were then deployed against a range of behaviors and crimes, and operationalized in police techniques such as surveillance and informing. The cultivation of fear and the promotion of a feeling of safety, the encouragement of both suspicion and participation, were aspects of a single policing process.

2

Uses of Surveillance and Informing

IN JANUARY 1967 a police officer in the Criminal Investigation Department (CID) in Gaza filed his daily activity report. According to this report, he had observed nothing unusual during his tour:

> On the 25th, at exactly 11 a.m., I passed by the Household Cooperative Society, the Center for Youth Protection, and the Price Control Council, and everything is calm there. At exactly 1:00 I passed by the [UN Relief and Works Agency for Palestine Refugees in the Near East, or UNRWA] clinic, where they are giving injections and medicine in an orderly fashion, and things are calm. I passed by the provisioning storehouse and they were distributing rations with considerable order. At exactly 2:00 I went to the Bir Saba secondary school and asked one of the students about whether there was any lack of teachers or teaching materials, and he told me that there was nothing negative and education is well ordered. There is nothing happening that is contradictory to public order.[1]

The policing files of the Egyptian Administration are filled with reports such as this: policemen reporting back on their hours spent in surveillance during which nothing happened, of the completion of their rounds during which no troubling activity occurred. These reports were products of the condition of expansive policing and the effort to document any possible political, criminal, or immoral activity. No space or moment was deemed beyond the interest of the police; all aspects of people's activities, speech, and opinions were relevant to their mission.

Given this expansiveness, it was inevitable that as often as not, surveillance provided little or no information about either criminal or political activity—it produced, that is, reports of nothing.[2] Even when they contain little evidence of public activity, the reports are replete with information about how suspicion and participation were operationalized in police work. Surveillance was an exemplary form of suspicion operationalized as a technique. Informing was another important technique of suspicion, as well as a key form of public participation in the police project. Both surveillance and informing worked within, and contributed to, a context in which not knowing where one stood and not knowing what the police knew were widespread conditions. The frequency of reports of no activity, even among subjects who were known to have political affiliations and attachments, provide evidence about the nature of policing during the Egyptian Administration and its success. Though never absolute, this expansive police project did succeed in constraining, containing, and derailing political organizing, criminal activity, and socially improper behavior. This chapter focuses on surveillance and informing to investigate not just the ways they were used by the police but also how their effects circulated through the space and population of Gaza.

Perhaps counterintuitively, one of the effects of these techniques of suspicion[3]—both reliant on and productive of wariness among persons—was the mobilization of the collective category of "the people" as an object that required protection and that could be a source of threat.[4] Even as both surveillance and informing undermined certain expressions of community (e.g., popular political organizing, comfortable social relations) the claim that these policing techniques were necessary for the collective good posited the people as that collectivity. To a certain extent, this category was an alternative proposed by governing authorities to potentially more challenging collectivities of citizens or political partisans. At the same time, this articulation of a comprehensive unitary category meant that even apparently small-scale threats to moral order, propriety, and national security were seen to risk infecting the entire social body.

In its reliance on surveillance and informing Gaza's security order was like, rather than distinct from, other security systems around the world. David Lyons has described security conditions in Europe and the United States as constituting a "surveillance society," one that is increasingly high tech but that, he emphasizes, preceded recent technological developments.[5] The extensive use of surveillance (justified in slightly different terms) appears to be a feature of policing in almost any political system.[6] Even if nearly universal, the effects of these techniques are not identical across time and place. And in this, technological differences matter. The discomfort and uncertainty produced by people's knowledge of the fact of surveillance is a cross-technological effect, but in low-tech human surveillance, relations among persons are a crucial requirement and product of this work. This relationality is a striking feature of the surveillance and informing landscape in Gaza. Another is the extent to which these techniques did not only, and sometimes did not primarily, differentiate among persons (as categories or as individuals) but also relied on and helped shore up the idea of the people as collectivity.

Surveillance and informing depended on a range of relationships: the public's participation in policing that was demanded by authorities, the popular commitment to social control that underlay concerns about propriety, and the local knowledge of policemen that was necessary to read a social landscape and provide accurate reporting. Even as relationships were a necessary precondition for the success of surveillance and informing, these techniques were themselves a site and form of relationship. This relational quality was in one aspect concrete and direct: surveillance of people's activities required the police to be in proximity to them; reports about these observations of often mundane activities made them relevant to governing authorities; informing both produced a direct connection between informants and police and called out particular individuals for police attention. Along with these direct relations, surveillance and informing also participated in a more conceptual relational field, which shaped people's understandings of the character of their connections. Uncertainty, suspicion, and therefore a degree of isolation were key features of these relationships: within the population and between population and police. So too, though, were solidarity and attachment, a reminder that repression was not the only result of these practices.

Even as I consider ways these policing techniques worked to control and to inhibit, I am also interested in what was enabled through these forms. What sorts of actions were, and are, possible in a security state? In what ways might techniques whose primary purpose was to constrain the population also create opportunities for expression and influence? It is clear that people often can and do act even in circumstances of tremendous control and repression, and it is certainly clear that people sometimes did in Gaza. Surveillance reports show that the administration was interested in, and in fact responsive to, not just what people did but also what they said and thought. People's capacity—and I mean neither to overstate this capacity nor to dismiss it—to effect government policy and procedure was sometimes a result of moments of organized dissent, and it also emerged out of police attention to everyday talk and rumor. The generation of avenues for influence and effect—not just through claim making, but simply through everyday living—was another result of these techniques of suspicion. This is a central feature of security society. The instruments of police control can also be mechanisms for popular politics, even if the room for political maneuver remains quite constrained. Surveillance and informing provided, without any intention toward this end, a limited opportunity for Gazans to influence government, to—in fact, as Hannah Arendt puts it—make their "opinions significant and actions effective."[7]

Uncertainty as a Technique

There is no doubt that Egyptian authorities would have viewed a book that justified the 1956 Israeli attack on Egypt as a threat. So it makes sense that the possession, in 1960, of such a text by a student was reported first to his teacher by a classmate, and then reported by the teacher to the principal, by the principal to the police, and by the police to the director of the CID. Perhaps more surprising is the fact that the possessor of this material and the first informant were eleven years old.[8] That children would participate in informing confirms how widespread the practice was. Although this instance was a report of "something," informing, just like surveillance, was just as apt to offer "nothing."[9] Whether or not the reports provided any information, they confirmed the participation of the public (in the case of informing) and the fulfillment of professional obligations of police officers (in the case of surveillance) in the security project. They also contributed to a condition of uncertainty.

The importance of uncertainty as a prevailing condition and an instrumental technique of control is evident in both the action of reporting and the products (reports) of that action. Even as reports of no activity were of limited immediate use for police investigation, they participated in describing and shaping the contours of public life. People's awareness of the persistence of surveillance as well as the collection and circulation of the reports from that activity helped shape life in Gaza. The production of uncertainty was especially central to surveillance's effectiveness. Observing and recording everyday activity was of great importance in expanding the range of things about which people might feel unsettled, uncertain, and therefore worried. Concentrating so much police attention on behaviors that did not evidently cross the boundaries of permitted conduct gave even the apparently acceptable a taint of illegality. By making any possible action a "case" and by turning each event into a "report," surveillance helped produce a space of indistinction even between the everyday and the extraordinary. If any word, any deed, *could* signal subversion or crime, then no word or deed could be entirely perceived as ordinary. The citizen could easily become the criminal, perhaps even without awareness or intent. This vagueness injected uncertainty—and sometimes fear—into the most mundane of activities, as one could never be wholly sure what those activities might turn out to mean.

Surveillance targeted individuals as a means to understand, and thereby control and contain, a collective category. As a practice of expansive uncertainty, surveillance approached the population horizontally.[10] Everyone, that is, was in the gaze of observing personnel (see Figure 3). Even as some individuals might be subjects of particular interest on the part of police (most notably political activists and major criminals), everyone in fact could be captured by surveillance. This was a relatively undifferentiated police practice. In surveillance the people appear as a generic possible threat. Informing worked slightly differently: it identified specific, supposedly actual, threats to this general category, persons as threats to the people. Where surveillance was largely general and horizontal, informing was particular and differentiating. It was particular in the sense that specific individuals or specific actions and events were the subjects of informing. It was differentiating in that, whereas surveillance made everyone a possible suspect, informing sought to distinguish the

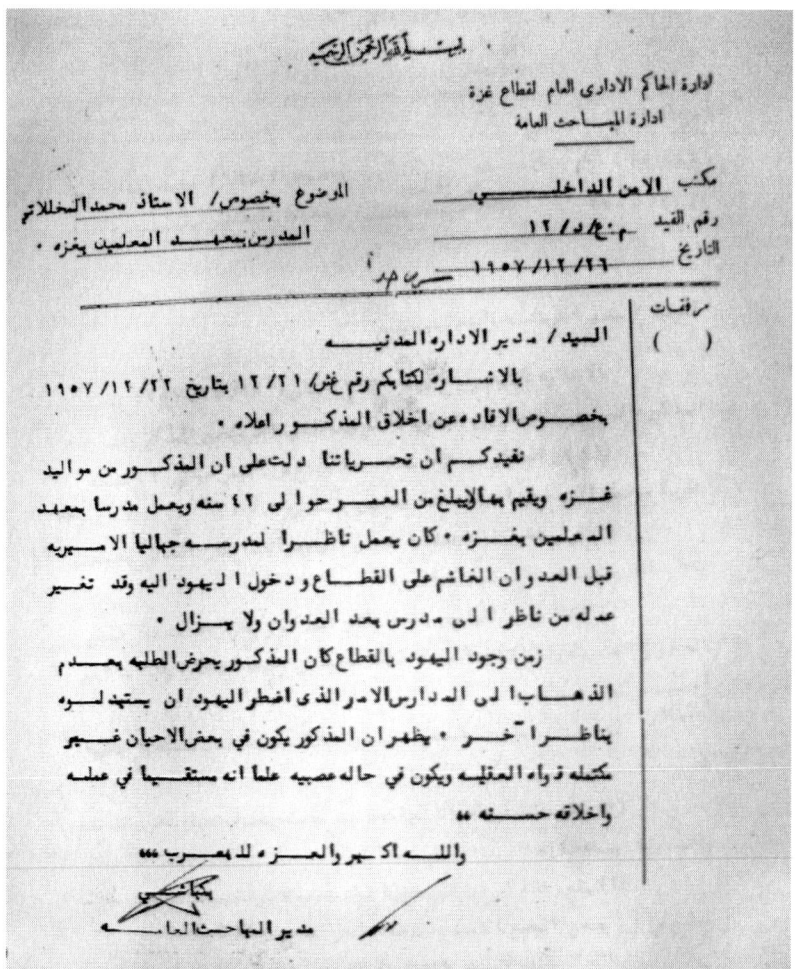

FIGURE 3 *Report from the CID director to the director of civil administration on the morals and character of a teacher, 1957. Source: Israel State Archives.*

informer (as innocent, as civic participant in the maintenance of order) from the informed upon (as criminal, agitator, deviant). Through this differentiation people sought advantage, sometimes defined as a particular outcome (e.g., an asked-for job or money) and sometimes as a more general condition of not being a suspect.

Although police personnel conducted surveillance, informing was often citizen initiated. There is no doubt that some of this informing was a result of the prevalence of surveillance. If one might have been observed picking up a political leaflet in the street, there was a heightened imperative to inform the police about what was found, lest one be accused of involvement in the matter. Informing is a kind of preemptive engagement—responding to surveillance and seeking to avoid interdiction. When Gazans informed on their fellow citizens, they participated in police work and also partially assumed the role of police themselves.

The existence of widespread surveillance and informing had a range of effects. By promoting distrust and insecurity in relations among people, it created barriers to connection, and it clearly inhibited political organizing and community. At the same time, it also worked at the level of collectivity. It was certainly shared by all, and it shaped everyone's experience of community and place, albeit not in identical ways. Many accounts of security states highlight their isolation effect, the way, as Hannah Arendt describes it, "a neighbor gradually becomes a more dangerous enemy . . . than are the officially appointed police agents."[11] Life in Gaza was not, though, entirely defined by isolation. Certainly, surveillance constrained public life and relationships in important ways, but people were also engaged in a variety of networks of relation, some more explicitly political than others, many apparently not political at all, but each potentially able to have an effect on government policy. Some people, though a small minority, were involved in overtly political movements. They were targets of police repression. Family ties, religious affiliations, and associations of various kinds all kept people ensconced in relations that worked against isolation to some degree. And these forms and sites of relation were themselves objects of police interest.

Surveillance of Political Life

Much of the impetus behind the broad surveillance practice was concern about possible political activity among the population. In both Egypt and Gaza dissident political activity, and indeed any independent political organizing, was opposed both as a source of specific challenge to the governing order and as a more generalized threat to the unity of the people. This general threat posed by political parties was described as factionalism.[12] One mechanism for combating factionalism was the creation of successive single national parties to represent the entirety of the people. Another was the close surveillance and control of independent organizing. It is no surprise that police files are replete with references to tracking political affiliation and activity. Lists of supporters of various political parties were regularly compiled; in addition to communists and Muslim Brothers, Ba'ath Party affiliates were tracked. Even in these efforts to differentiate the population, however, the recording of everything meant that uncertainty remained a crucial mechanism. The files include many reports of police officers following people to meetings, noting who was there, how long they talked, but often saying nothing about the content of their conversation.[13] That is, even reports that were ostensibly about politics were often reports of nearly nothing.[14] In this context, the fact that there was nothing to report was an indication of some success of the policy of repression, although the fact that people could still be identified as members of these outlawed organizations also indicates the limits of that success.

In a typical series of reports on Nuseirat camp (one of a group of refugee camps in the middle of the Strip), police described their surveillance of known communist sympathizers. On January 4, 1960: "The persons I was asked to watch did not have any meeting yesterday. They did not meet at the barber's place as usual. I have seen some of them walking alone, or talking to others not from the same group."[15] The next day's report indicated: "This is to inform you that after watching the barber's shop, we observed that some people from the Communist Party visited him but did not stay for long. The party does not yet have obvious activities."[16] Another police officer reported: "This is to inform you that the supporters of the Communist Party met at the school, and then everyone returned home. Two of them walked back and forth in the street, then went to [so-and-so's] house where they stayed for half an hour, and then each went home."[17] The file continues in this vein.

The fact that the Communist Party had little activity in the Nuseirat camp was itself noteworthy for the police. For them, that is, this information wasn't exactly nothing. Even more interesting, though, are the possible effects of this extensive surveillance on the population under scrutiny. The thing about this kind of surveillance is that everybody knows that it is happening, but they can't always pinpoint exactly when or by whom. That people knew these files existed but could never see them, could never know for sure which of their activities or words were recorded, without doubt contributed to their power. These effects are difficult to determine with precision, however. That people were afraid of the police seems clear, but it is equally clear that this fear did not eliminate political activity and indeed may have promoted activism on some people's part.

People in Gaza indicated to me that much of the population was hesitant to engage in organized political activity. As one person told me, describing conditions among government employees, "The civil servant was afraid. . . . Other than teachers, most civil servants did not participate in political activities, but teachers did. They were active with either the Communist Party or Muslim Brotherhood."[18] The many reports in police files about teachers' political affiliations and even political talk in the schools confirm this view.[19] Even widespread reticence to engage in formal politics should not be taken to mean that Gazans were wholly apolitical in public. Police reports indicate, in fact, that among ordinary folk there was considerable political conversation on the street and in other public spaces.

Police were aware of this conversation in part because the imperative to observe political activity required that surveillance extend beyond those actually active. So while people could certainly reduce their risk of arrest by not affiliating with political organizations, they could not escape police scrutiny. The reports from Nuseirat describe known suspects doing very little that was suspicious; other reports describe a similar lack of activity among people who had no known political ties. A case in point is a report on a Palestinian woman who had moved to Gaza from Baghdad when she married a Gaza resident. While it was no doubt her residence in Iraq that provoked interest in her, she was not otherwise a suspicious person. And, according to the report: "No harmful activity has been observed since she arrived until this date."[20] The government's demand for such a breadth of surveillance in the service of control meant that its targets, and its effects, regularly exceeded the immediately instrumental.

Surveillance as Social Control

The considerable police concern with propriety makes these broad effects clear. Improper behavior was a common topic in police reports, as were the range of actions taken to stop such transgressions. The reports also indicate the extent to which policing propriety was a matter of public interest. If, in general, the police sought the public's participation in policing work, propriety was an arena in which this participation seems to have been eager. People often actively demanded police involvement in matters of propriety, thereby extending police reach into seemingly private matters. The morality claims in concerns about propriety made this a ripe terrain for articulation of both the idea of the people and anxieties about threats to this whole.

One police report on social misbehavior described the interrogation of a photographer, Hussein Sharif, who had been observed photographing women. Police frequently relied on rumor, gossip, reputation, and other somewhat vague sources to guide their investigations, and this instance was no different. Hussein was reported to be known for flirting with women and to have a bad reputation.[21] The particular incident that provoked his questioning was a report that he had taken a picture of two teenage girls with a boy. In Hussein's statement he insisted that although he did photograph women he only did so "within the general morals."[22] He denied this particular accusation, saying that when it became clear that the boy wanted to be in the picture, he had refused to take it. Following the questioning, further reports were compiled. One suggested that he had admitted to other people that he had taken the aforementioned photograph. Another indicated that there had been complaints about his behavior in the past.

Despite Hussein Sharif's insistence that he had done nothing wrong, being brought in for questioning was enough to enable the police to extract from him this declaration: "I the undersigned, photographer Hussein Sharif, hereby undertake not to take any photograph that does not go with our morals, customs, and traditions or that can affect the reputation of the Gaza Strip." This statement, and the repeated references to acting only within "our morals," constitutes a promise to not harm the people (as a whole) and a recognition that the misbehavior of individuals could do severe damage to that whole (indicated here in the reference to the reputation of the Gaza Strip). Whether his denial of misbehavior or the subsequent report of his guilt was the truth of this case did not matter to the control of social behavior through police surveillance and intervention. Hussein was willing to promise not to do anything wrong, even as he denied having done so. The questioning itself was an effective means of control and did not require any formal adjudication. It was in part the very condition of expansive policing—and the uncertainties that were part of this practice—that lent it this power.

The control of social behavior by the police intersected with its control by the population itself. And this dynamic is certainly not unique to Gaza. This kind of control is precisely why Hannah Arendt expressed concern about the emergence of "society": a space between the household and the polis, blurring the distinction between public and private. For Arendt, society poses a threat to politics by privileging behavior over action: "society expects from each of its members a certain kind of behavior, imposing innumerable and various rules, all of which tend to 'normalize' its members, to make them behave, to exclude spontaneous action or outstanding achievement."[23] Police files offer clear evidence of Gazans working to make other Gazans behave, and of the police using this interest in behavior for their own control purposes. But they also provide evidence to suggest that it was not only by breaking out of the realm of behavior—returning to the public and action—that people could exert political influence. Propriety, and society, have more complicated effects than Arendt perhaps credited.

Pierre Mayol's exploration of propriety as a key feature of the neighborhood as a social space captures some of these multiple effects.[24] Naming other people as transgressing norms of good behavior is a powerful mechanism of social control. But as much as propriety provides a means for controlling others, for shaping their behavior, understanding the rules of propriety is also a way of getting things done for oneself. Being seen as proper, as respectable, can help one accrue social capital of considerable value.[25] Mayol's exploration of propriety in the neighborhoods of Paris focuses on the residents alone. In Gaza the policing of propriety was a key site where the police and public came together as agents of surveillance and control. And in this arena, as in others, the relationship between police and public was never equal.

The social policing of behavior is described in police reports about the behavior of *shabab* (young men) in the Shati camp, next to Gaza City. A police officer reported in January 1967 that he had seen a group of young men harassing girls on the street. In this instance, the police did not intervene to stop the behavior, although the report described the efforts of other people to do so. At least one observer chastised them, saying: "Shame on you, *shabab*, each of you has a sister or a mother. Protect the honor of people, as it will reflect on your own honor." The report concluded with a list of the young men's names, each also identified by his town of origin in Palestine. This attention to detail underscores that it was neither lack of interest nor absence of concern about stopping this behavior that led the police officer to take an observer position in this case. A follow-up report from a month later indicated that there had been further intervention from the public. People had spoken with the young men's families, who exercised their influence, and the harassment had ceased.[26] Clearly, surveillance did not only come from the police. Just as clearly, control of the social domain did not only come from the people.

One cannot say with certainty why the photography incident demanded an active response, and the second simply reporting. Perhaps it is because the first seemed a more serious violation of proper norms, whereas harassment, even though clearly frowned upon, was a common feature of social life. Or perhaps it was the readiness of members of the public to take on this policing task with the young men that rendered police involvement unnecessary. These possibilities remain speculative, however. What is significant for my purposes here is the importance of propriety as a security concern and the range of actors involved in its policing.[27] The policing of behavior underscores the ways that security practices both utilize and transform existing social practices. These practices rely on existing concerns about proper behavior as a mechanism, to encourage public involvement in policing, and also expand the power of social control, to the extent that police were willing to get involved in such efforts. Even as both police and the public participated in the management of behavior, they did not do so equally. Without diminishing the significance of social opprobrium and reputation management to people, police had significantly greater coercive powers at their disposal.

Informing

Just as police surveillance of people's activities shaped the relationship between the public and the government, so did the informing practices of private citizens. Even as informing was a more direct encounter between police and population than surveillance was, its biggest effects may have been on relations within the population. The preemptive engagement of informing police about activities in one's neighborhood, crimes by one's colleagues, or political organizing by one's compatriots further worked to shape relations among the public itself, as it broadened the circle of suspicion and concern.[28] Informing was another means of public participation in policing work, but one that was more fraught than the public shaming that often characterized the policing of propriety. People informed about a variety of ideas and behaviors—from "subversive" political activity to "ordinary" criminal conduct—and the motivating factors for such informing were equally multiple. The broader conditions that I have already discussed provide a general context for understanding informing and how it came to be such a widespread practice. Each instance, of course, was also propelled by a more particular motivation or motivations. Fear, duty, and personal advantage all seem to have been reasons for informing, often all at the same time.[29]

In one report to the police, Musa ʿEid, a refugee living in the Nuseirat refugee camp, described how he had happened upon some communist publications. In his statement on April 15, 1960, he said: "I went out to use the public toilet at 10:30 in the evening. When I reached there, carrying a flashlight, the light shown on a paper. When I looked at it I found out that it was a publication for the Communist Party. Then I found two more papers three meters away. So I went to my teacher's house and told him, and then we came to the police."[30] The police also took a statement from his teacher, who confirmed Musa's story and also added that "he [had] noticed that the writer [of the pamphlet] is not educated, because the publication is full of grammar mistakes."[31] This statement about grammar could be part of the effort of teacher and student to distance themselves from the publication. In the ensuing days, investigation into the question of who distributed these publications continued—apparently on the part of the police and the residents of Nuseirat. One resident of the camp was brought in to provide a handwriting sample to see if it matched that of the publications. Shortly thereafter, a teacher at the Nuseirat school provided the police with the names of the people who, he claimed, wrote the pamphlets. According to the teacher, the authors "claim that the Egyptian government does not work for the good of our country, and that we should kick them out of the Gaza Strip" (see Figure 4).[32] What action the police may have taken against these people is not included in the file, but the information seems to have brought the investigation to a close.

Informing is one of the clearest examples of the success of the project of participation. Not all informing involved naming names. In fact, in many of the reports about finding "seditious" materials, which were the most frequent subject of informing in the files, there is no mention of possible authors.[33] The materials themselves were viewed as security problems, and people's informing the police of their (always declared to be accidental) encounters with them seem an effort to inoculate themselves from being identified as particular security threats. People's uncertainty and discomfort are on display in these instances of informing. As one person (Khalil) declared to the police when he made his report: "While going back home after visiting my cousin, I found an envelope on the street. I opened it and found that it was written against the government, so I burnt it, because I was afraid. I do not remember any of the words and I do not suspect anyone particular of being the author."[34] Another person (Hassan) making a statement about the same pamphlets declared: "While going home in the night, I found five envelopes. Since we were told by the police to notice any paper or envelope thrown on the ground, I took them and brought them to the station. I did not look at the pamphlets because I am illiterate. I do not know their author; I do not suspect anyone."[35] Hassan's reference to "being told" to notice any materials indicates the extent of both police concerns and the demand for public participation in policing. Awareness of the concerns and the demand had clearly circulated widely.

Whereas one statement emphasized fear and the other duty, the two sentiments appear clearly linked. The apparently greater fear on

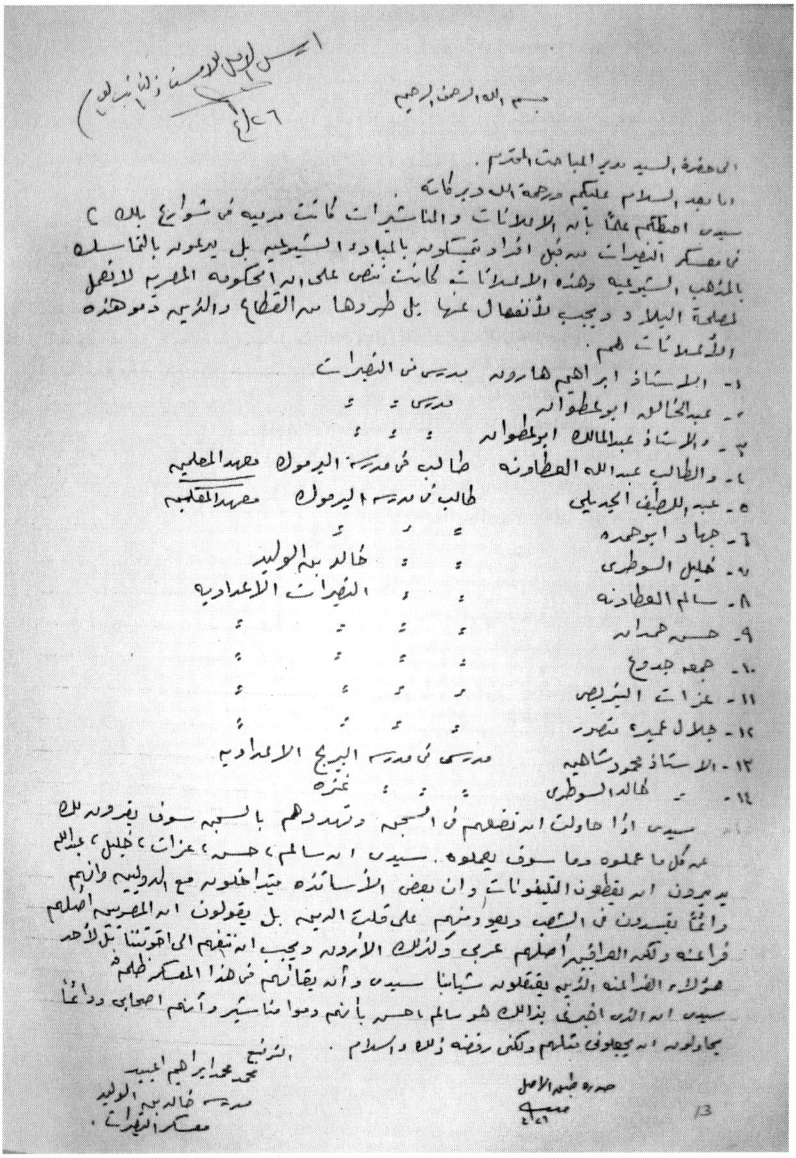

بسم الله الرحمن الرحيم

الى حضرة السيد مدير المباحث المحترم.

وبعد السلام عليكم ورحمة الله وبركاته

سيدي اطلعكم علما بأن الاعلانات والمناشيرات كانت مرمية في شوارع بلوك C في معسكر النصيرات من قبل افراد تشتكون بالمبادئ الشيوعية بل يدعون بالمذهب الشيوعي وهذه الاعلانات كانت تنص على ان الحكومة المصرية لا تعمل لمصلحة البلاد ويجب الانفصال عنها بل طردها من القطاع والذين قاموا بهذه الاعلانات هم:

١- الاستاذ ابراهيم هارون مدرس في النصيرات
٢- عبد الخالق ابو مطاوع مدرس " "
٣- والاستاذ عبد المالك ابو مطاوع " " "
٤- والطالب عبد الله القطاونة طالب في مدرسة اليرموك معهد المعلمين
٥- عبد اللطيف الجديلي طالب في مدرسة اليرموك معهد المعلمين
٦- جهاد ابو حمده " " "
٧- خليل السوطري " " خالد بن الوليد
٨- سالم القطاونة " " النصيرات الاعدادية
٩- حسن حمدان " " " "
١٠- جمعه جدوع " " " "
١١- عزات البزايعة " " " "
١٢- جلال عيد منصور " " " "
١٣- الاستاذ محمود شاهين مدرس في مدرسة البريج الاعدادية
١٤- خالد السوطري " " " غزة

سيدي اذا حاولت ان تفصلهم في السجن وتهددهم بالسجن سوف يقرون لك عن كل ما عملوه وما سوف يعملوه. سيدي ان سالم، حسن، عزات، خليل، عبد الله يريدون ان يقطعون التلفونات وان بعض الاساتذه يتداخلون مع الدوليين وانهم دائما يفسدون في الشعب ويعودونهم على كلمة الدين بل يقولون ان المصريين اصلهم فراعنه ولكن العراقيين اصلهم عرب وكذلك الاردنيين ويجب ان تنفيهم ... هؤلاء الفراعنه الذين يقتلون شبابنا سيدي وانه بقائهم في هذا المعسكر ظلم سيدي ان الذي اخبرني بذلك هو سالم احسن بانهم وزعوا مناشير وانهم اصحابي ... يحاولون ان يجعلوني مثلهم ولكني رفضت ذلك والسلام.

محمد محمد ابراهيم الجبيد
مدرس خالد بن الوليد
معسكر النصيرات.

صورة طبق الاصل

13

FIGURE 4 *Letter from schoolteacher to CID director providing the names of persons he claimed had written pamphlets denouncing the Egyptian Administration, 1960. Source: Israel State Archives.*

Khalil's part may have had to do with his closer contact with the danger-ous material. Not being able to read, Hassan was perhaps more insulated against contamination by the subversive materials. Even Khalil, who had read the pamphlets, tried to downplay his contact with them by stating that he did not remember their content. Still, both were careful to stress that they had no knowledge about where these pamphlets had come from and could not venture a guess as to their authors.[36] Both cases appear to have been an informing of self-preservation. Neither Khalil nor Hassan seem to have sought to enter into a more generalized relationship of in-forming with the police or to gain anything particular from having come forward. Rather, each was compelled to tell the police what he knew but no more. Instances such as this, when people informed without being "informers" in a classic sense (regular sources of information, possibly on the payroll), further indicate how widespread the practice was.[37] Anyone might, on occasion, be compelled to participate in the gathering of police knowledge.

Other instances of informing—in which people were more expansive about the knowledge they provided and sometimes more explicit about the rewards they expected—do suggest a willingness to take on the per-sona of informer. In one case, in 1949, a Palestinian living in Egypt offered to provide information about "conditions in Palestine" if the Egyptians would provide jobs for his two sons. The director of military intelligence was amenable, and indicated that, if the man's information proved valu-able, the son with a bachelor's degree in science could be offered a job "in the Health Ministry as a technical assistant or as a lecturer, or in the War Ministry. The second can have any clerical work."[38] Detailed information offered without such a clear quid pro quo was often presented as a form of service by the informer. In one such instance, a Gazan living in Saudi Arabia offered information, in his words, out of national duty: "Whereas it is the duty of every citizen who feels loyalty to his nation to work for the good of that nation, I am obliged to offer you all the information I have about activities that are harmful to that nation."[39] In a six-page letter, he detailed the activities, including members' names, of an association of Palestinians established by the Saudi government. The police responded positively to the letter; the inspector who received it described it as hav-ing been written "in defense of his nation, because it provides a lot of detail."[40] The informer had access to this detail because he was a member of the founding board of the organization. The Egyptians were certainly suspicious of this Saudi-sponsored association—believing that its aim was to embarrass and damage the administration—and may very well have taken what action they could against its members.[41]

In addition to politically connected informing, there was also considerable informing about criminal activity. In one such case, an anonymous letter was sent to the CID accusing three people from Khan Yunis of operating a smuggling ring. "I ask you to search their house," the letter advised, "and I assure you that a large amount of money will be found." Upon investigation, however, the accusation proved false. The report on the investigation indicated that the accused "have nothing to do with smuggling. We think that [so-and-so] sent the letter because he is in dispute with the aforementioned three persons."[42] Such accusations were no doubt meant not only to create trouble with the police but also to damage people's reputations in the community. This kind of false informing seemed to happen a great deal, especially in regard to crimes like smuggling.[43] Still, there were plenty of occasions when information about criminal activities proved accurate, although the reasons for providing such information were no less complicated for its being true.[44]

The use of informants is an important part of police practice in almost any setting.[45] And in almost all circumstances people become informers for multiple, sometimes contradictory reasons.[46] In the expansive policing environment of Gaza informing seemed to be a means to make distinctions, in a field that was shaped by indistinction, and therefore to shield the informer from some of the effects of uncertainty as a policing tactic. Whether the immediate motivating cause was financial gain or protection from suspicion, by naming names, informers sought to locate themselves clearly on one side of the line between legal and illegal, between criminal activity and proper behavior. These efforts were not always successful, and in fact police reports about false information often turned to focus on the informer's misbehavior—sometimes criminal, sometimes just contemptible.[47] Further, given how central uncertainty was to police practice, even accurate information could not assure people of a protected location. The prevalence of informing did ensure that suspicion would remain a central feature of Gazans' relations with one another.

"On People's Tongues": Surveillance, Circulation, and Possibilities for Civic Effect

While widespread informing and the public policing of propriety helped create a public space in which everyone seemed to be watching everyone else, other aspects of policing produced a much more opaque public. In fact, one effect of surveillance was to constitute a public sphere to which the public did not have unfettered access. One of the central features of public life is the circulation of talk and opinion. This is why the press, the coffee house, and the public square are sources of such interest for people exploring the contours of the public sphere.[48] These things certainly existed in Gaza. In addition, however, and in many ways just as significantly, police surveillance of talk and attitude produced another mechanism for the circulation of talk.

To a considerable degree, it was the severe restrictions placed on public and political expression that gave both the observation and the circulation of talk by the police its particular importance in Gaza. The sanctioned means of expression that did exist in Gaza—for instance, the government-sponsored Arab National Union and the Legislative Council, which were established in the latter part of the administration—were not exactly opportunities for independent political action.[49] It was perhaps a recognition that these forums did not really provide satisfactory avenues for political expression that so much police attention was directed to tracking opinions expressed in other spaces.

Reports produced by the police about public opinion, about meetings, about gossip and rumors, circulated this talk far beyond its immediate domain, giving it life and significance that it might not have otherwise acquired. This circulation of everyday talk illuminates ways that social life could be a mechanism of civic effect. In some ways, this is the other side of the coin of the social control discussed earlier. Even as aspects of social life were constrained by heavy policing, this life could have an impact on the civic order. To be sure, most members of the Gazan public did not have access to these reports and could not even know for sure that they existed.[50] They were nonetheless significant in shaping the contours of public life, in part by shaping government policies, in part by functioning as a spectral presence around this life.

The surveillance of everything was in many ways a separating experience, interfering with people's direct and comfortable relations with one another. At the same time, even as people were isolated in some ways, they remained embedded in a variety of other webs of relation, with both political and social import. Action, in Arendt's sense, was still possible here, and not only in those moments when people explicitly challenged the political isolation of surveillance.[51] There were, to be sure, moments throughout the administration when people did join together to engage in organized political activity, when the potential inherent in human action transformed into a clear political endeavor. So it should not be imagined that repressive policing completely precluded such possibility. My focus here, though, is on the more tenuous possibilities for action and effect that emerged even among those who were not activists. What kind of web, which sorts of relations, can we identify in the collection and circulation of Gazans' everyday talk in police reports?

One site at which police tracked Gazan talk was the meetings (*nadawat*) that were an important part of civic life in Gaza, providing formal, and social, opportunities for the expression of opinion and, as it turned out, sometimes dissent. They were organized by associations and clubs, and sometimes by the government itself.[52] Government authorization was required for any *nadwa*, so the events were by definition legal. They were also the targets of regular surveillance—a CID officer was supposed to attend every meeting—indicating the police's awareness that these "social" events could very easily have political import. Participants could not see the reports police produced about the meetings, but they were certainly aware of police presence. The clear orders for surveillance of public meetings also make it easier to identify some of the failures of this practice. Although it is impossible to know what casual talk police officers missed, there are records of meetings not attended. Sometimes this absence was due to a mistake by the police—in one case the police officer assigned to go to a meeting was late and missed the lecture around which the event was organized. Seeking to minimize the significance of his mistake, in his report he assured the inspector, "According to what I heard about the lecture nothing happened, and the number of attendees was very small."[53]

Other, much rarer, occasions indicate clear resistance to police presence. In these cases surveillance itself became a site of contestation as people attempted to create and protect spaces free from observation. The police clearly identified refusal of their presence as a threat to their authority and to the police project. A report on a cinema owner's refusal of admittance to a police officer emphasized not only that such actions "obstruct our work and harm our reputation" but also that the owner was trying to "exert his personal authority even over government employees."[54] The implication is that the owner, from the Dajani family, was trying to throw his social weight around. But he formally challenged the entrance on procedural grounds, saying that the police officer needed a permit from the governor-general to enter the theater. This, according to the police report, was not true: "he has permission to enter all public places."

In another such instance, police officers were prevented from entering an organizational meeting of a medical association by the convener (Haidar Abdul Shafi). The policemen reported to the inspector that Dr. Abdul Shafi "prevented us from attending the meeting, saying that he was not told that someone from the police would attend. He told us that the meeting had nothing to do with politics."[55] Of course, Dr. Abdul Shafi did not really have the right of refusal, but his personal stature (he was a member of the Legislative Council and a respected local leader) probably intimidated the (no doubt) low-level personnel who were sent to monitor him.[56] The response to Abdul Shafi's refusal, confirms both how widespread surveillance was and how difficult it could be to challenge it (very few people had either his status or strength of character).

In addition to organized expression, police records are filled with data on ordinary talk. In the monthly reports that inspectors compiled for headquarters from the information submitted by police, there was a section for public opinion. Police investigators searched for this opinion in everyday talk—"on people's tongues" (*ala alsinat al-nass*).[57] The police tracked discussions about politics (whether regional Arab affairs or Egyptian positions) and government policy, about civil service salaries and UNRWA ration distributions.[58] They also recorded the mundane frustrations of everyday life. The concern with tracking everyday talk, and the ways that simple grumbling could turn into something else, highlights another aspect of uncertainty in policing. Uncertainty was not only a security tactic that could make people afraid of the possible meanings behind other people's talk and action (was an apparently mundane statement really a political threat?). Uncertainty about talk was also a social fact. Casual talk among people about everyday problems could develop into awareness of shared concerns and even possibly into organizing to make demands. Whether talk was banal or important often could not be determined with any certainty by anyone.

This uncertainty meant that everyday talk could sometimes produce a civic effect without ever being articulated as a direct challenge. In 1965 and 1966, for instance, there was a crisis surrounding the dearth of *fakka* (small change) in circulation. A police report from January 1966 noted, "There is a lot of complaining about *fakka*. This is especially a problem in relation to taxis. It is said that the money does exist to solve the problem."[59] Another report from later the same month elaborated on the problem, and the talk: "Everyone is wondering why there is this shortage, what has created it and what the role of the government is in this problem that is harmful to social and economic life in the Strip."[60] There was no suggestion in the reports that anyone was organizing around this issue yet—and there was no direct petition to government to solve the problem—but the possibility of talk leading to political action was clearly concerning. There is evidence that public opinion was not only gathered but also, sometimes at least, acted on. In the case of the absent *fakka*, even as public frustration was being recorded, government efforts were under way to address the problem, although they do not seem to have been the most efficient of efforts.

In October 1965 the director of finance and economic affairs wrote the director of internal affairs and public security asking him to intervene in this matter. According to the former, there was clear evidence that people were manipulating the availability of small change for their own financial gain, and he asked that the police investigate this matter and bring the culprits to justice.[61] A few days later, the governor-general wrote to the director of internal affairs and public security telling him to ask the director of finance and economic affairs to talk to the banks about this problem.[62] In November the CID director also wrote to the director of internal affairs and public security telling him, "The people of Gaza are complaining about the lack of small change. Please be in touch with all the banks and ask them to put a lot of small change—5, 10, and 50 mils—into circulation."[63] The repetition and circularity of these requests for action may explain why, in January of the following year, there was still "a lot of wondering among the people who are waiting for the government to take an active role."[64]

What is significant here is not the efficiency of government response but the fact of it. The surveillance of talk and public opinion produced a governmental awareness of a potential social and political crisis, and clearly mandated a response as well. The surveillance of everyday talk enabled the administration to exercise control, and it enabled the public to exert influence. The surveillance of talk had the effect of lending that talk a power it might not have had otherwise. Not only did surveillance operate as a vector for its circulation; it lent this aggregated talk a weight that its repeated individual articulations did not have. In conditions where there was limited opportunity for citizen involvement in the policies of governing, the surveillance of everyday talk actually created such an opportunity. Even without a clearly petitioned demand, this talk came to be a means of having an effect on government.

Unlike instances of refusal of entrance to a police officer, the *fakka* case is not a case of resistance but rather highlights the potential of ordinary life, lived in its immediacy, to affect the civic order. It is, to return to Arendt's terms, a case of "potentiality in being together,"[65] a potentiality that in this instance was brought to life and made effective precisely by surveillance. The circulation of talk illuminates a civic practice that did not depend on formal clarities and that was not always fully evident to the public. The fact that people would not necessarily have been aware of the effects of their talk renders this an admittedly strange version of public life. They certainly knew that what was "on their tongues" might be recorded, but that record was not available to them. They could not know for sure what use was being made of their words. To be sure, the record of government is never entirely transparent, nor can people ever be sure of the impact of their opinions; Gaza represented an extreme condition of opaqueness in this regard. Nonetheless, this capacity to influence government illuminates the potential of surveillance not only to control politics and expression but also to create limited opportunities for it. Uncertainty produced fear, and sometimes possibility.

Widespread surveillance and use of informants is a key part of police practice in any security state (and perhaps every state is, to a certain degree, a security state). That these techniques would create fear, uncertainty, and mutual suspicion is not surprising. Perhaps more unexpected are the ways that this expansive observation also provided mechanisms for people to influence government and to make changes in the conditions of their lives. Sometimes these opportunities were highly individualized, as when people offered information to seek direct personal advantage. Sometimes the opportunities were focused on the moral order, as when people's mutual surveillance operated as a mechanism of social control. Yet other times the opportunities may not even have been known to the participants, as when the recording of everyday talk produced a governmental response without any direct petition or demand.

The practices of surveillance and informing show how the key instruments of security society operated both as mechanisms of control and as means of action. To be sure, action is the minor part of this scene and the kind of action that was possible through these techniques was heavily circumscribed, but it was significant nonetheless. Not only could generating suspicion about other people be a means of getting things done for oneself; the government's concerns about the population and the threat it could pose made it responsive to some of the desires that circulated among that population. Influence and effect can and do happen in the space of security society, and they happen not just (and maybe not primarily) through declared opposition to security practices or government policies. The mechanisms of control, and the fear and uncertainty that they both mobilize and produce, also serve as pathways for action.

3

Reputation, Investigation, and Criminal Interdiction

THE INTERDICTION OF ORDINARY CRIME, the pursuit of regular criminals, and the investigation of everyday disruptions were a big part of what the police did in Gaza. In every area of crime control there was more at stake, and a wider set of effects, than the simple reduction of illegality. These effects are evident in the detailed records of crime control, which include numerous transcripts of interrogations, reports on investigations, correspondence among police personnel, and policy directives and instructions. Criminal investigation required tremendous attention to detail: the crime scene, the behavior of witnesses and suspects. Interrogation was a site of close relation between the police and members of the public. Arrest and imprisonment entangled Palestinians in the full coercive powers of the regime and had radiating effects on the wider population's view of the Egyptian Administration. Similarly, police misbehavior, whether due to corruption, negligence, or even policy, influenced the public's perspective on the police.

The work of everyday crime control is important for understanding the centrality of policing in shaping relationships in Gaza. It also brings to the fore an additional set of security concerns: the desire of the population for security of person and possession. Here personal concerns and state concerns were closely related, as a population that did not feel secure on a day-to-day basis might be more likely to challenge the governing order. The techniques of crime control were similar across the spectrum of illegality. Whether petty theft or political subversion, police used the same kind of expansive observations, intrusive interrogation styles, and deployment of fear as a means of controlling criminal behavior. Although in some contexts and moments this expansive, intrusive, and fear-promoting policing worked to create distance (between Egyptians and Gazans, and within the Gazan population) the policing of ordinary crime shows how it could also have the effect of bringing people into closer relation. Crime control underscores the double work of producing closeness and distance through policing, especially between the governors and the governed. The challenge of calibrating governing relations, a challenge made especially acute by the uncertain status of Gaza, involved seeking a balance precisely between distance and closeness.

This calibrated relation, and its complexity, is evident in the ways that Gazans remember policing. The promotion of everyday security, giving people a sense of personal safety, produced a positive evaluation of Egyptian rule. It made people feel, at least in this context, that Egyptians governed on their behalf and did not simply impede or constrain them. When I talked with Gazans in the late 1990s, many praised Egyptian authorities precisely for the absence of crime and the protection from threats to persons and property. Abu Nizar, a onetime fedayee (guerrilla), drew a contrast between the past and present: "You want the truth, the days of the Egyptians were better than these days. . . . People respected and loved each other, and no rights were lost. There was a government that controlled the situation well, so nobody could assault another. Nowadays, however, there are assaults and government does not interfere."[1] Yusra, a retired teacher, mentioned the provision of security—along with education—as one of the administration's greatest achievements: "The Egyptians had a great role in security; people used to sleep with their doors open. I remember when we were doing maintenance work on our house, we used to leave the doors open—nobody entered. There was security and education, both of which were very important from the economic point of view."[2]

In addition, police methods brought individual police officers and members of the public into direct and close relation with each other. To be sure, this closeness was not necessarily pleasant or positive. Interrogation was an almost intimate encounter, although of course it was an intimacy achieved across a broad power divide. The surveillance of, and collection of information about, criminals as a category provided a starting point for interrogations. This surveillance meant that the police had detailed knowledge about many individuals that they could mobilize as circumstances required. Abu Said, a Gazan who worked as a cook in the police department during this period, highlighted some of these dynamics in his praise of the effectiveness of policing: "There were thieves, but if someone's shop was robbed, the thief was caught within twenty-four hours, because thieves were registered in the government files. If a jewelry or dress shop or something was robbed, they investigated and they would bring in ten or fifteen people; they would beat them to get them to tell them who did it."[3] Police willingness to use force in their encounters with these subjects was understood as a way to use their preexisting knowledge about them to acquire specific information about the crime in question. Of course, considerable research shows that torture is not a generally effective way to gain accurate information, but people who told me about beatings in connection with policing understood it to be. The effectiveness of ordinary policing depended on, or at least fully utilized, the expansive coercive policing techniques of the security state. These were not the only techniques deployed, to be sure. And they were likely not those most commonly deployed. They are, though, those that are most remembered by Gazans, both negatively and positively.

Police methods of crime interdiction in Gaza shared a great deal with police practice elsewhere, in the Middle East and beyond. To understand their local significance, it is necessary to look not just at their form (though this remains important) but also at their content. What were the sorts of infractions that the police went after? What kinds of complaints did Gazans make? What were the limits of police purview? The answers to these sorts of questions show how security society was not simply imposed on Gazans; it was sometimes also actively pursued by them, even as the expansive police presence in Gazan life had significant negative consequences for freedom of expression and organizing. The records of crime investigations generally do not follow the cases to their end, but as stories of crime response they offer a window into crucial moments in policing work. Police responses to crimes such as smuggling, petty theft, "honor crimes," and police corruption illuminate an array of practices that brought the police into close relation with Gaza's population and that also sustained a degree of distance. In the process of searching out criminal behavior and stopping crime, reputation proved a crucial factor.

The importance of reputation in crime control further confirms the centrality of uncertainty in this work. Even as crime control aimed for precision—to catch and prosecute criminals, to discourage criminal activity more generally, and to provide protection and redress for victims—it made use of the same kinds of techniques of suspicion that were the focus of the previous chapter. Reputation—what was "on people's tongues" about other people—can be an unstable thing. As evident in the cases described in this chapter, it did not always provide a solid basis for criminal interdiction, but it certainly had significant effects on shaping people's relations. The use of reputation as an investigation technique is an important part of any police toolbox, but its effects are variable. A report on a suspect accused of breaking and entering stated that he "has a bad reputation among the people in his area and he was caught many times breaking into houses."[4] In another investigation, in this case of a shooting, a suspect who was ultimately released for lack of evidence was brought in for questioning precisely because "he has a bad reputation and is known for hanging around with criminals."[5] People's reputations regarding political activity and affiliation were also a frequent topic in reports. In these cases a good reputation meant no evident political leanings, and therefore permission to teach, preach, travel, and so on.[6]

People's social reputations also figured prominently, especially those involving familial conflicts. At issue here was talk about moral propriety and gender attributes. Masculinity was a repeated concern, as in one case in which a husband was unable to keep his estranged wife from going to stay with another man because "his personality was weak,"[7] or another in which it was stated of a recipient of a threatening letter that his family "hates him, because he is completely under his wife's control."[8] In another case, in which concern was expressed about possible "immoral behavior" or "activity against public security" in the frequent visits of a Brazilian UN Emergency Forces (UNEF) soldier to a Rafah man's house, the worry may have been about homosexuality. In this instance the man's reputation was vigorously defended by the administrative governor of the Rafah area, who declared, after investigation, that the man had no regular visits from a UNEF soldier, that "he has good morals and a commendable reputation," and that the accusations levied against him were false.[9] This investigation, like many others, confirms the intersection of criminality, social propriety, and political threat. It also confirms the instability of reputation.

Reputation was mentioned in nearly every investigation of an individual, whether that person was targeted as a suspect or a witness to a crime, or whether the report was part of the general surveillance system. People's reputations could make them suspects, make them vulnerable to crime, and sometimes protect them. Following Foucault, considerable attention has been given to the ways that modern states operate to both totalize and individualize. The policing of ordinary criminal activity was one site at which the latter operation was evident in Gaza. In this work the collective category of the people was disaggregated, in part through the identification of distinct behaviors and subject positions. The criminal and the victim are obviously central subjects in any crime-control operation. Consideration of the range of crimes police went after shows how multivalent those categories could be. And reputation was a key mechanism by which particular acts of criminality or impropriety were identified as fundamental to a subject's persona and personhood.

Border Crimes: Smuggling Interdiction

Cross-border smuggling, especially of drugs and money, engaged all these matters. The conditions of suspended war and political uncertainty that prevailed in Gaza during the Egyptian Administration (and still today) made border control especially concerning, even when the illicit movement was of a purely commercial character.[10] Egyptian officials went to great pains to control this criminal activity, although there is also evidence to suggest that some officials were themselves involved in smuggling.[11] People's knowledge of these efforts, and of the serious punishments for smuggling, made smuggling a subject of reputation talk and likely contributed to the extent to which charges of smuggling were a focus in informing. This tactical value also led to false accusations, which accounted for a significant portion of the informing cases.[12]

In general, smuggling was pursued as a serious crime, with considerable resources directed toward its interdiction, though not always all the resources that the police wanted. Concern about smuggling to and from Gaza, especially of drugs, was as much a concern about its impact on Egypt and Egyptians as it was about law and order in Gaza. For this reason, unlike the other criminal activity considered in this chapter, smuggling received the attention of high-level officials in Cairo. A committee established under the auspices of the Egyptian War Ministry to oversee the antismuggling campaign included high-ranking military officers from the Coast Guard, customs, border defense, and antidrug unit, as well as a representative from the Gaza administration.[13] In the September 1959 meeting the committee discussed a report about the state of smuggling interdiction in Gaza, which concluded that "the imprisonment of drug smugglers working in the border, coastal, and interior areas had a major effect on limiting smuggling activity and drug trafficking in the Strip, and in reducing these smuggling activities to individual unorganized ventures."[14] The committee supported continuing this broad arrest policy, recognizing that "arrest is a productive weapon against smuggling."

At the same 1959 meeting, the committee discussed a request from Gaza that camelry units be dispatched from the Egyptian border defense to patrol the Rafah border, as had been the practice before 1956. Referring tantalizingly to an earlier meeting (whose minutes are not in the files), the Gaza representative commented, "The guard force is now composed of members of the Palestinian police, which is a force that cannot be relied upon, for reasons outlined at the meeting on July 14, 1959." What these reasons were, we can only guess. Were the local police too likely to indulge in the opportunity to do some smuggling themselves? Or to accept bribes to look the other way? The representative of the Egyptian border defense expressed his regret that he could not offer the services of his department, as it was faced with too many other responsibilities. Despite this apparent setback, by the June 1962 meeting, the Gaza representative was able to report considerable success in the campaign against drug smuggling: "All the smugglers have left Gaza and have transferred their activities to Beirut. Drug smuggling has been almost entirely eradicated in the Strip."[15]

The response to smuggling shows how policing both worked with and produced a set of spatial relations that, in turn, helped further define population relations. It is not surprising that cross-border crime would have a spatial effect, and this is one reason that border control has been of great interest to scholars.[16] Because Gaza was such an unsettled space—with provisional borders, unclear international status, and an uncertain future—responses to smuggling had a heightened role in defining spaces and people's relations to them. Egypt insisted that it governed Gaza as a foreign territory: that Gaza was Palestine and not Egypt. At the same time, even in policing, Egyptian officials claimed a close connection of care and concern for Gaza's population. Responses to cross-border smuggling were one way this dual condition of distance and closeness was articulated. Two stories of quite different responses show these dynamics in action.

In the first case, Egyptian officials in Gaza reacted to an instance of unlawful import of money into Gaza by interceding on behalf of the violators: in the name of compassion and with a declaration about the suffering of Palestinians and Egyptian responsibility to care for them. In 1959 customs officials at the Gaza-Egypt border seized money from five Gazans who were caught bringing in amounts above the legal limit. The governor-general interceded with the Egyptian Ministry of Finance, asking that the money be returned:

> Given that the intention of these people was not to smuggle this money, or to break the financial laws, but rather their intention was to help their unfortunate families, and since we have given these people strong commands to follow the legal channels in bringing in money from outside—given all that we have explained, we ask that you reconsider the decision to seize these funds and to release them to the people that are so desperately in need of them.[17]

This intervention is a clear instance of Egyptian advocacy, in this case to other Egyptian officials, on behalf of Gazans. To secure the release of this money, the governor-general linked the individual cases of money smuggling to the broader political and social conditions in the Strip, suggesting that the cause of this violation was "the difficult circumstances facing the people of Gaza, especially after the Israeli attack upon them [in 1956], which has left the people of Gaza in difficulty. This has led people who are outside of Gaza to send money to their family in the Strip after their liberation." At issue here was not just the reputation of individuals in Gaza but also that of Gazans as a group. The governor-general argued that the absence of criminal intent should warrant excusing this instance of illegal activity. There are two messages in this request: caring for Gazans should be a matter of concern to all Egyptian government officials and Egyptian administrators with direct responsibility for this territory and the population would work to ensure that law and order were maintained, thus minimizing the future need for compassionate pardons. So this statement brought Egypt close to Gaza, for care and control. At the same time, the law that regulated currency movement across the border and the punishment imposed for its violation underscored the administrative distinction and distance between the two places.

Another smuggling case, this one of gold smuggling in 1964, generated a significantly different response, but it too produced both distance and closeness between Gaza and Egypt.[18] As with many police investigations, the file on this case does not record its conclusion, but it contains the details of interrogation. This case involved eleven kilograms of gold that were smuggled from Gaza to Egypt and a charge of attempted bribery of a police officer. There were eight suspects, each of whom was interrogated by the police in Gaza. The reports on the interrogation of each suspect followed a similar style: each was given the opportunity to make an initial statement on the matter; each was then further questioned about his relationship to the other suspects, his knowledge of the car, the gold, a plan to smuggle, and the attempted bribery. The Criminal Investigation Department (CID) inspector, an officer, and the suspect then signed the bottom of each page of the report.

Four suspects were arrested in Egypt and later released to return to Gaza. The others were suspected of connection with the crime within Gaza. The basic facts of the case were as follows: Ibrahim (a taxi driver), Said and his nephew Ahmed (a student at Cairo University), and another man also named Said each went to Cairo. There were two cars among them. The police came upon them, with the two cars, stopped on the side of the road leading to the airport. When they searched the cars and passengers, they found eleven kilograms of gold in one car and Ahmed was carrying 250 Egyptian pounds. This much is clear. Everything else was disputed among the suspects, including who rode in which car.

Ibrahim said that Said offered to employ him, in Said's car, on the Gaza-Cairo taxi route. Said denied ever having purchased the car and even knowing Ibrahim. Ahmed said that he had gone to Egypt only to learn the results of his exams and that the money was to support his studies. The second Said claimed that he had stopped his car just to assist what he thought were stranded motorists. Ahmed's father, Abdullah, and another uncle, 'Eid (among the Gaza suspects), denied involvement in the purchase of the car as well as any knowledge about smuggling. The seventh and eighth suspects, however, were the car's seller and someone who brokered the deal. They both said that Said and 'Eid participated in the purchase but denied any involvement in smuggling themselves. No confessions were made, and the number of competing and contradictory claims in the interrogation records makes them somewhat difficult to follow. It is impossible to determine from these transcripts what actually happened. The case report does not provide the police determination of the truth of the matter, although presumably it was recorded elsewhere.

Even without a record of the outcome, this case suggests some interesting things about policing in Gaza in general and the control of smuggling in particular. The four suspects who were arrested in Egypt were held for a few days, then released without fine or bail. They then made their way back to Gaza, some immediately, some a few days later. It was in Gaza that they were interrogated. This sequence seems to underscore both the distinction of jurisdiction between Egypt and Gaza (distance) and the deep entrenchment of expansive policing in Gaza (closeness, though here more in terms of coercion than compassion). That procedures appear to have called for Gazans to be policed in Gaza reinforces the territorial separation that was maintained throughout the administration, even as Gazans had increasing opportunities to study and work in Egypt. That the suspects were left to return to Gaza on their own may have been connected to the degree of police confidence in their surveillance capacities and records of the population, which would have made it unnecessary to keep the suspects under direct control as they made their way back to Gaza. Control and punishment of smuggling not only contributed to shaping conditions in Gaza; it helped define the relations between Egypt and Gaza as spaces.

Petty Crime

A significant portion of police time and energy was spent in the investigation of petty crime—small thefts, insignificant altercations, minor insults. The files of local police stations were filled with reports about lost or stolen wallets, IDs, and money. There are numerous reports about dog bites, apparently following a regulatory requirement that all such bites be reported to the police.[19] On occasion more unusual objects were noted in the files, such as the instance in April 1966 when an eight-kilogram turkey was reported missing. This loss prompted a serious investigation, as the police questioned five possible witnesses in a seemingly unsuccessful effort to determine the fate of the turkey.[20] Response to these crimes, each relatively insignificant on its own, was central to defining police practice and the security landscape. The importance of reputation in structuring police response and investigation is especially evident.

In a somewhat more typical case than the missing turkey, Yusuf Khalil reported in February 1966 that he lost his wallet in the course of a crosstown bus ride in Gaza City (from the main town square in the eastern part of the city to the sea at the west).[21] The documents on this case include records of the questioning of the victim, a suspect, and witnesses; a report of the responding officer; and correspondence among police on the case. Key features of this investigation included the alacrity and breadth of response, an apparently wide acceptance of police intrusions, and the extent of weight placed on witness statements. This case did not raise political security concerns. It did not present any risk of instigating a crisis. Nonetheless, the same kinds of surveillance and informing practices that were developed with such security concerns in mind seem to have shaped how police conducted themselves in the everyday realm. There is no doubt that police distinguished different kinds of crime, but their methods of investigation and interdiction appear similar across the field of criminality.

Yusuf first reported his loss to the bus driver, telling him that he suspected a passenger had stolen the wallet. Upon hearing this, the bus driver immediately stopped at the Rimal police station. A policeman boarded the bus and, according to his report, "questioned the passengers to see if any of them had taken the wallet. I asked to inspect all of them and the bus to look for the wallet. Nobody objected and I inspected all the men and boys, as well as the bus. I didn't find the wallet."[22] This initial response indicates both the broad reach of police, as well as some of its limits. Without objection the police officer was able to search passengers without any particular suspicion of guilt, but he limited such a search to the male passengers.

As the investigation continued, suspicion centered on one Salem Faris, who Yusuf's brother Ahmed thought might be the culprit. According to the police report, Ahmed told the police, "When he got home [from making the initial report], he started thinking about the matter and remembered that he saw Salem standing on the sidewalk by the taxi stand. He doesn't know if Salem rode the bus but does know that he has been suspected in thefts, so he suspects him."[23] Ahmed's knowledge of his suspect was pretty vague. Asked if Salem had stolen from someone he knew, Ahmed responded, "No, but I hear from people that he is a thief." Asked what Salem did when the bus departed the taxi stand, he said: "I don't know if he stayed on the sidewalk, or rode the bus." And as to where he lived, Ahmed was only able to report: "I know he frequents the Daraj quarter café."

In a security society where suspicion was everywhere and reputation a key marker of a subject's propriety, Ahmed's vague concerns were enough to have Salem brought in for questioning. Salem denied the charges, offering a credible alibi for his whereabouts at that time. As it turned out, at the time of Yusuf's loss, he was with a police officer, pursuing a suspect in another wallet theft.[24] He spent the rest of the afternoon in a café in the Tuffah quarter. Witnesses corroborated both statements. Further, when he was brought in to identify Salem, Ahmed himself decided that he was not the person he had seen. Instead, he said, he had seen someone who looked like Salem.[25] The police briefly considered the possibility that the other thief (in whose arrest Salem participated) might have stolen Yusuf's wallet, but he was already in jail by the time the theft occurred.[26] The documents do not indicate that, or if, an arrest was made in this case.

The willingness of the police to respond to a witness's fairly flimsy accusations is notable, although it fits with the culture of informing the police had fostered. Even the nature of Ahmed's suspicions about Salem seems to reflect the effects of this dynamic. His suspicions were based on things he had *heard* from people, on the *talk* about Salem, on Ahmed's general *knowledge* about him. This is exactly the sort of information that police were collecting all the time about Gazans: their reputations, their actions, their patterns of behavior. But the investigation did clear Salem of suspicion, so informing talk and suspicious character was a starting point, but not necessarily an ending point, of investigation.

The fact that so much police energy was directed toward the recovery of a lost wallet (and there are many similar stories in the files) tells us something about both what police were able to do at this time and what they were expected to do. The police-population relationship was about fear, and also about participation in the establishment of a secure public domain. As the Gazans I quoted at the outset of this chapter noted, everyday security was something they valued in Egyptian rule. This value let people see some positive valence in the frequent reliance on coercive policing techniques. Everyday security was accomplished, in part, through people's willingness to be included in the information gathering practices of the police. The practices may not have been very different from those deployed in the pursuit of political control (surveillance, reliance on informants, interrogation of a wide circle of persons, imprisonment under harsh conditions), but when directed toward everyday criminal activity, they appear to have added to people's feeling of security.

"Customary" Crime and the Pursuit of Justice

Petty theft and smuggling are different sorts of crimes, but the relevance of both kinds of activity to the police was self-evident. The crimes might be difficult to solve, but they were easy to identify as criminal activity. Other sorts of activity—that which might be called customary crime or, as John Comaroff and Jean Comaroff term it, "cultural policing"[27]—was not always so easily described and pursued. The same action might be called a (customary) crime from one perspective and (customary) justice from another. In the Middle East the most spectacular and oft-talked about form of customary justice or crime is the "honor killing"—the murder of women at the hands of relatives for perceived violations of norms of propriety, and therefore the besmirching of family honor. International attention to these crimes has increased considerably in recent years—Lila Abu-Lughod tracks the interest to the late 1990s.[28] The other sort of cultural policing that is attributed to Middle Eastern cultures—particularly in their tribal expressions—is the revenge killing. Such killings are one possible outcome of an interfamily dispute and an outcome that indicates the failure of other, equally customary, lines of response. Given the frequent focus on women as objects of concern and justifications for interventions of various sorts, it is no surprise that revenge killings have not received the same level of international attention as honor killings.[29] Gender, and gendered propriety, though, is crucially important in both sorts of crime. Frequently, it is anxiety about masculinity that seems to be at the heart of the matter. The records of policing in Gaza during the Egyptian Administration include references to both sorts of crimes or justice.

A range of tactics was required to deal with these sorts of crimes. In some cases, especially those involving the potential for revenge-motivated violence, the police were party to customary means of dealing with customary crime: here I reference the "reconciliation" (*sulha*) as a means of bringing conflict to an end. When they participated in the practice of *sulha*, where responsibility was discharged, restitution was made, and the matter was resolved outside the realm of formal law, police supported an acceptable alternative form of justice. In the regular police reports on conditions in various parts of the Strip, there was frequent mention of reconciliations among feuding families. These events seem to have been generally well attended, thus suggesting their importance to Gazans.[30] Even as such events were, in a formal sense, private affairs, they took place under the watchful eye of the police. In one reconciliation that occurred in 1963, the two families had been in conflict since 1955, when a member of one had accidentally killed a member of the other. The reconciliation was attended by "notables, sheikhs of Al-Azhar, and a large number of citizens."[31] The conditions of the event itself were typical. The offending family paid the victim's family 150 Egyptian pounds, "whereupon they abdicated all their rights, considering the incident settled." By abdicating their rights—a key part of any reconciliation—the aggrieved parties redefined the original event as not a crime. Justice was served and public order maintained, here not through a direct police action, but rather through a managed parallel procedure for ensuring public security.

The challenge of how to engage, manage, and sometimes halt alternative policing mechanisms has been a key question for many police orders. In colonial policing the management of customary law and justice (including both alternative court systems and "popular" policing) was a matter of great concern.[32] This management has also emerged as a problem for postcolonial nation-states interested in promoting what they consider modern justice. Much has been written about efforts to curtail sati in India, witchcraft killings in Africa, and amok in Indonesia.[33] In analyzing the policing of "occult-related violence" in South Africa (violence against those understood to be witches), the Comaroffs identify the situation as a "confrontation between legal universalism and cultural relativism."[34] They describe a tension between the postapartheid South African state's commitment to the rule of law and universal justice and its recognition of and respect for cultural particularity within the polity. This tension—one found in many more places than South Africa—does not seem to have defined the situation in Gaza.[35] There is no discussion in the record of either local barbarity (as has been key in discussions about necklacing in South Africa and sati and hookswinging in colonial India) or the need to modernize the people.[36]

The files also include no discussion of whether the police had the authority to intervene in these areas. It is possible that these discussions took place in other contexts. Investigation reports might not, after all, be the primary place for such judgments (although there is plenty of editorializing on other topics in these sorts of reports). I have no way of knowing either how frequent such killings were or how many of them were pursued by the police, but the records include instances of police responses to such events that deal with them as criminal matters. Indeed, insisting on this criminality appears to have been a strategy in police response. Even if the police were certain they had jurisdiction over these reputation-related crimes, the public's acceptance of that authority still had to be acquired. The very fact of these crimes was, in fact, a challenge to police authority. In contrast to instances in which people asked the police for help in managing propriety problems, honor and revenge killing represented a claim that the perpetrator could take care of the problem on his own.

Even as public participation in policing was a central feature of the security apparatus in Gaza, truly independent policing could pose a threat. What was asked for was participation, not vigilantism. Private, parallel, police practices had to be contained and controlled. This question of authority may in part explain the apparent lack of "moral panic" around these morally inflected crimes.[37] In other areas, around other crimes, the language of moral threat provided a mechanism for deepening police involvement. In these cases, the language of propriety could be mobilized, in fact, to keep the police out. Responding to these matters within the strict category of crime may have been a strategy for avoiding a jurisdiction challenge. Here the naming of the action as a crime helped make police presence possible.

Honor killings bring two features of the security field into conflict: the interdiction of crime and the claim of propriety. These crimes occur with a claim that the victim has violated the boundaries of proper social and moral behavior, and the killing is a means of protecting that order and providing redress to those (her relatives) who have been "victimized" by this breach of propriety.[38] A police response that treats such killings as crimes claims a hierarchy of both authority and value. One police file contains the records of investigation of two honor-related crimes, one a murder and one an attempted murder in which the surviving victim of the attack was able to speak about it, name the perpetrators, and challenge the accusations leveled against her. In both cases the police claimed authority to enter into the domain of customary crimes. In the second they seem also to have engaged with the terms in which such attacks occurred.

The first case involved Fatima Ahmed, who was strangled in her parents' home in Khan Yunis on April 29, 1965. On the day of the murder, her father and mother had gone to Gaza City to visit a son, and her two sisters who also lived in the house were working.[39] Thus, Fatima was alone at home when the murder took place. The crime was discovered by her sister, who found the body when she returned home from her teaching job. The police were immediately inclined to believe that the killer knew Fatima and her family. Upon investigation, they discovered that several women neighbors were witnesses. These neighbors identified some of Fatima's relatives as the perpetrators. They saw two of them climb the garden wall into her house, and they heard another say that he intended to kill her because of "her immoral behavior."[40] Acting on this information, the police brought dogs to identify the assailants. The dogs picked only one of the accused, Fatima's brother, Hussein, and he was the only one arrested. The others, upon denying the charges and without the corroboration of the dogs, were released "for lack of evidence."

What was the "immoral behavior" that prompted this attack on Fatima? According to the police report, two years prior she had gotten pregnant out of wedlock. Although she married the man in question, "their married life was full of conflicts and problems that forced her to return to her father's house." Without the protection of her husband, Fatima was left vulnerable to familial punishment. Different members of the family had different reactions to both her behavior and her murder. Her sister reported the crime to the police. Her mother, though, after the arrest of Fatima's brother, seems to have attempted to provide an alternate explanation for the murder and thereby to save her son. She complained to the police that money and jewelry had been stolen from the house, trying to suggest that the murder was part of a robbery. The police dismissed this complaint, noting that the mother did not report the robbery until May 8, whereas the murder took place on April 29. This report, the police concluded, "had no basis in truth, and was intended to misdirect justice in the murder case."[41] In this case, the police response to the murder did not engage the question of the validity of the charges of "immorality" against Fatima. Killing her was murder, whatever the justification.

In the second case, an attempted murder, the claims against the woman became an object of attention. This may have been because Hamda Musa survived her attack, thereby rendering her vulnerable to further attack if the accusations stood. In addressing the question of the truth of the accusations, police took a position not just on the punishment meted out by her family but also on the social judgment that had led to this action. On June 14, 1965, when Hamda was treated in the Khan Yunis hospital for a serious stab wound, she accused her father and brother of trying to kill her.[42] The police investigation into the crime and the accusation determined that Hamda had been charged by her husband with having an affair, and she had been sent home to her family.[43] Her father and brother stabbed her and left her buried in the sand to die, but she was found by people who then took her to the hospital.[44] Her father admitted that upon hearing that she had engaged in "bad conduct," he had attacked her with a knife; her brother denied the charges.[45] The final report in the file on this matter concluded, in a somewhat remarkable analysis, that the accusations against Hamda were entirely false: "She is very good from the moral aspect and is ugly in shape. She could not have had an affair because she is not at all beautiful."[46] The whole trouble started, the report concluded, because someone had stood near her during a harvest, and another person had taken it upon himself to pass along the gossip to her husband.

In this case the prevalence of social policing appears to have made an innocent person vulnerable. Even though Hamda's innocence or guilt in relation to matters of propriety was not a matter for formal police adjudication, its importance to the case—and to society—made it relevant in police investigation. Although the logic of the police conclusion that Hamda *could* not have had an affair is flawed, their statement that she *did* not may have offered her a form of protection from future attack and could have helped reconcile her with her husband. Their response indicates that the police recognized that successful control of these kinds of crime demanded that they sometimes engage with the terms of the crime, with the cultural system within which it occurred.

Just as understanding the causes and course of honor killings demanded considerable knowledge of the social activities of the parties involved, so too did the investigation of revenge killings. Ismail Suleiman, the retired police detective discussed in Chapter 1, underscored the importance of local knowledge when he told me about investigating one such crime. Further, just as in honor killings, this case had gendered relations at its heart: here masculinity was highlighted, and of course masculinity was an issue in the attacks described already as well. Concerns about masculinity proved crucial to the crime and to its investigation. On Ismail's fourth day of assignment in Rafah, a family was attacked with explosives while eating dinner at home.[47] The mother and child died, and the father lost his eyesight. Ismail's investigation was hampered by his unfamiliarity with the local community and their desire to keep the matter away from the judicial machinery, but he got lucky:

> There was an old man . . . who said, "Let me tell the CID officer." People told him, "Shut up old man." They knew the perpetrator; they knew that it was a revenge killing. I took the old man to my office and closed it so nobody could interrupt us. I asked him to tell me the story, which he did: Once the wife of the perpetrator went to bring water, and she had a clash with the dead wife. The latter kicked her in her belly, and made her miscarry. Afterward, though, the doctor stated that she had not been pregnant and the case was closed. Nonetheless, the wife kept pushing her husband, accusing him of not being a man and not having self-respect until he took an explosive and threw it at the family.

Had Ismail been posted to Rafah longer when the crime occurred, he would already have been aware of the conflict between the two families, and he would have had suspects from the outset. In the event, he was fortunate that at least one person was not satisfied to let customary justice run its course and wanted to help the police pursue their justice.

Acting on this information, Ismail had the man arrested and his quarters searched. The police found a detonator similar to the one used in the attack. Under questioning, however, the suspect denied responsibility. Ismail told me that rather than responding to the stonewalling with force, he once again used his cleverness to outwit the suspect:

> I did not beat him, because I was going to be a witness in court and if I was asked if I beaten him, I did not want to lie. I entered his room and said to the police: "What are you doing? Untie him. What do you think he is, a man? No he is not. He thinks that his bomb could cause harm? He does not know that it exploded in the air." Then the man said, "If that's true I will keep following them till I finish them off. I will throw four bombs at them." And then he told me the story. We took his statement and he signed the confession.

In this instance Ismail used the language and logic of honor and revenge to provoke a confession from the guilty party. It was a challenge to his manhood that prompted the crime in the first place, and another such challenge made him confess. This was an instance of police manipulation of custom and culture in order to achieve their security purpose. Having gained a confession, and prepared himself to be a good witness, Ismail's work was still not done. He said that he had to convince the prosecutor to raise the case without any delay, for fear that the guilty man would retract his confession. He told me that his perseverance paid off, and the man was convicted and sentenced to death, a sentence later reduced to life imprisonment.

The importance of gender in all of these crimes and their investigation is apparent. Ideas about masculinity, male pride, and male honor were at stake. And in each case, women threatened this male pride, whether by engaging in illicit sex or by challenging a husband's manhood. And claims about femininity, female propriety, and women's honor were at issue as well, both in the social and familial regulation of sexual behavior and in the police response to women. Police investigators did not accord women's statements the same weight as men's; recall that some of Fatima's alleged killers were released when the police dogs did not corroborate the statements of female witnesses. This imbalance underscores the fact that although police did not accept private claims to govern gendered propriety outside the realm of the law, nor did their interventions seek to alter the gender relations that underlay some of these claims about propriety.

Policing the Police: Corruption and Negligence

In November 1965 an anonymous letter—signed in the name of a "social reformer"—was sent to the CID director about the state of affairs in the Khan Yunis police station. According to the letter, the station was functioning not so much as a police station but rather as a crime center. The letter writer accused a number of the police officers at the station of corruption, of interfering in investigations as well as in rations distribution.[48] This complaint was apparently taken seriously, and the next document in the file was a letter from a police officer to a CID inspector indicating that this was not the first complaint about the station, but that the changes that the inspector had recently instituted in staffing were likely to take care of the problem.[49] This complaint and the response to it are a window into another arena of personal security: the professionalism and competence of the police themselves. Public opinion about the police was an area in which personal security and regime security met, as a population that did not have confidence in the police to keep them safe in a reasonably uncorrupted manner might turn to other means to ensure that security, including possibly seeking a change of regime.

Complaints about the police are present, but not especially prevalent, throughout the policing files of the administration. Sometimes complaints were investigated and deemed fraudulent, such as the case of a man who complained that his mother was manhandled by the police when they searched his store for sugar being sold for more than its allotted price.[50] He also claimed that he did not have much sugar in stock and so the search itself was a mistake. A police report to the CID inspector concluded that both claims were false: a large amount of sugar was found on the premises, and no one had harmed his mother.[51] Not all complaints were so personally motivated, and not all complaints were false.

One such complaint about police misbehavior further highlights the intersection of concerns that were relevant to security matters. A March 1963 police report on "rumors and public opinion in the Middle Area [of the Strip]" included a report on the public's opinion about a guard in Bureij. According to the report, people were saying, "Instead of being wary of criminals, we have to be wary of the patrol. This harms all the police in the area." Apparently, people didn't limit their talk to complaining about this malpractice; they also offered a possible solution: "Poverty impacts everything. If this guard received a sufficient salary, he wouldn't engage in activities that harm the government."[52] People wanted crime to be controlled, the police to have good standing in the community, and (apparently) for everyone to earn a decent living. Complaints like this describe a set of expectations about police involvement and comportment. They suggest an awareness of the multiplicity of factors that shape any professional relationship and that affect reputation.

Judging from the relative frequency of these complaints, Gazans were more concerned with police negligence than police aggression. A 1963 report from a police officer to a CID inspector about conditions in the Jabalya refugee camp is a case in point. The officer reported that people in the camp were complaining that the police were not active enough in ensuring that goods were being sold for their proper price: "the people are asking themselves if the police work at all." This specific complaint produced a more general commentary about the state of policing in Jabalya: "It is known that the local police station is always closed after 2 p.m. There is only one officer in the station in the afternoon; if there is a crime he closes the office and goes to investigate. As for the rest of the personnel, after 2 p.m. they go back to Gaza City, because most of them live there. The village police office is the last one to learn of what goes on in the village area."[53] This sort of complaint suggests that Gazans expected police involvement in the daily life of the place and that, when not forthcoming, it was a cause for complaint.

Claims of police misbehavior sometimes resulted in the same kinds of interrogations to which other citizens and suspects were subjected. In one case four police officers were questioned about an accusation of improper payment for evicting residents from some land near Jabalya.[54] The accuser was another police officer (Khalil) who was himself being accused by someone he arrested of having extorted money from him. The file does not say explicitly that Khalil offered information on the other officers in exchange for leniency or release from the charges against him, but it seems likely. According to his accusation, a sergeant and two police officers were dispatched to support an officer of the court in removing residents from land recently purchased by the mukhtar Ahmed Ayyash. After the task was finished, Khalil averred, the mukhtar gave the sergeant five pounds and each police officer one and a quarter pounds. Khalil claimed to have reported the incident to the officer in charge. He also reported hearing that similar payments were made in other instances.

On the basis of this accusation, the sergeant and officers were brought in to the CID for questioning. All denied the charges entirely and each claimed that Khalil "has terrible morals. He has a lot of problems with people. Many complaints were registered against him at the village police station." The interrogators appear to have believed the accused, closing out the interrogations. Whatever the facts of this case, it was without doubt an instance of misbehavior on the part of a (or some) member of the police. That the charges were investigated to the degree they were suggests that the CID took such cases seriously. Part of what is evident in this case is that the discourse of propriety that Gazans often mobilized in their relations with one another was also relevant to their evaluation of the police. Propriety was not an alternative language of control but a strand in a network of ways of talking about suspicion and threat, about security and confidence.

The use of a range of techniques in the control and interdiction of ordinary crime further indicates the complicated and sometimes contradictory relationships that developed between Egyptian authorities and the Gazan population, and also within that population. These relations were defined by both protection and threat. They spoke to matters of both public order and private behavior. They shaped a social field and a political domain. Everyday policing required that police delve into people's affairs and that people bring things to the police. The practice of crime control depended to a considerable extent on Palestinians seeing the police as a proper and adequate space of redress. It was, therefore, the reputations of the police as well as of the people that were at issue. This need is not unique to Gaza; it is a crucial feature of crime work anywhere. In the United States, for example, widespread distrust of the police in many cities frequently leads people to refuse to participate in this work (to refuse to "snitch"). Although one cannot suggest that participation in police efforts to stop crime in Gaza was wholly voluntary—one very well might not have been able to refuse to answer questions when approached by a policeman—the fact that many Gazans went to the police with criminal complaints indicates that participation also was not wholly coerced.

In each of the sorts of crimes that police investigated and interdicted, and in each of the methods they used in pursuit of these goals, a broader effect than the management of crime was achieved. Crime control was a meeting point of a range of ways of thinking about security that circulated in Gaza, with protection of persons and property intersecting with concerns about propriety and sometimes politics. It was a key space in which people invited the police into their affairs, as well as a key mechanism through which the police extended their jurisdiction over propriety. Everyday police work shaped the relations not only between police and the broader Gazan public but also among Gazans themselves. The work of crime control illuminates with particular clarity how the details of police practice brought police and public into close relation. And in this, reputation—of people and of police—was central. What people think can make someone vulnerable, to both the public and the police. It can also offer a degree of protection, and can sometimes counter accusation. The widespread feeling of security from crime that Gazans reported was not a counterpoint to their subjection to expansive surveillance and control. Both were part of the same network of security practices and field of security concerns.

4

Managing Protest and Public Life

EGYPTIAN AUTHORITIES MADE a range of demands of Gaza's population: participation, compliance, acquiescence. And as previous chapters have explored, those demands were often satisfied. But it was not only the authorities who made demands. Over the course of the twenty-year administration of Gaza, Palestinians put a number of claims to Egyptian authorities, claims that were directly connected to the security field. Palestinians demanded that Egypt govern in their interest. They first insisted it not be "colonial" like the former British Mandate government (this rhetoric appeared in arguments for changes in the tax system, press freedoms, the ability to move),[1] and later argued for permission to develop independent Palestinian institutions. Foremost among these demands was for the right to fight for the liberation of Palestine. The administration was faced with the challenge of how to both respond to and contain these demands. That is, with how to create outlets for Palestinian public and political expression without losing control of the political field. What developed in response to these sometimes competing imperatives was a highly policed public sphere. In each area where Palestinians sought expanded freedoms—often couched in the language of rights—Egyptian authorities worked to limit the range of expression—often using the language of duty in imposing these barriers.

As this reference to "rights" and "duties" suggests, both Palestinian demands and Egyptian responses to them were sometimes explicitly framed in the language of citizenship, a conceptual category that remained important in Gaza, even as on its face it might seem out of place in a condition of formal statelessness. Security dynamics in Gaza provide a window into two aspects of particular, even unusual, citizenship dynamics. In Gaza citizenship was distinguished by the fact that it remained a relevant political category even though it was not an existing legal category and intersected in specific ways with the categories and forms of action of security society. As a significant body of scholarship on citizenship in practice shows very clearly though, the instances in which citizenship requires a qualifier and deviates from a supposed standard model may in fact be more usual than cases where it does not.[2]

The continuing relevance, even centrality, of citizenship as a category of governance and rights claims was connected to the Egyptian position that it governed Gaza as a caretaker, preserving and protecting the space and its people for its future as part of an independent Palestine.[3] Even as this stance was in many ways an empty rhetorical position (meant to forestall possible Palestinian opposition to Egyptian rule and to distinguish Egypt from Jordan, which had annexed the West Bank), it had significant effects on how Egypt governed the territory. Not only did the language of citizenship run through the discursive terrain of expectations between Palestinians and the Egyptian Administration, a Gazan legislative council was established in 1957 and a constitution for Gaza was promulgated in 1962. The practical authority of these institutions was limited, but their form was of the government of citizens. The language of citizenship also played a part in Palestinian nationalist address to other Palestinians.

Gaza helps clarify the expression of citizenship in conditions of formal statelessness, and it also offers a view into its experience within the constraints of security society. These dynamics imposed limits on rights claims when those claims ran up against "security concerns." Confrontations between rights and security are a general (perhaps even universal) feature of governance, no less relevant to democratic governance than authoritarian rule. The form of this confrontation varies. In Gaza's security society the limits imposed by security concerns were frequently expressed through the language of the people as a unit. In these instances the concrete, but general, category of "the people" was identified as more fundamental (to security, to society) than the abstract, but individuated, collection of citizens.[4]

In addition to imposing limits, security society also shaped the forms and mechanisms through which people sought to affect government policy and practice. To return to the three dominant categories of governance ("citizens," "population," "people as security threat") and their concomitant modes of action (civil society, political society, security society), it can be broadly said that citizens make rights claims, populations engage in practices that change facts on the ground (e.g., building without permits, stealing electricity), and people as security threats work to change calculations about security concerns. Public speech and political protest—which are obvious venues for citizens to make rights claims—also provide opportunities through which people can change the threat calculation of security forces. These actions can change the answer to the question of whether the best means of containing threat is to respond to a demand or to crush the protest. This change in calculation is often only very partial and perhaps temporary, and Gaza's experience underscores these limits, but it is a real factor for security and politics.

This chapter explores three key arenas in which the struggle over public life and political action occurred in Gaza: the circulation of ideas, the opportunity for protest, and the possibility of organized armed resistance to Israel. Control over the circulation of ideas was largely about the control of reading and writing, press censorship being its most prominent form. It also included the surveillance of readers of books and other written materials. Police always surveilled protests, as they did any meetings and gatherings, even those without political intent. When security forces identified a protest to pose an actual challenge to Egyptian authority, they invariably arrested and imprisoned participants. Military action was one of the trickiest issues for Egyptian authorities to manage. They had entered Gaza with the promise to defend Palestine. Despite their failure at this mission in 1948, they ruled with the claim that they stood in support of the liberation of Palestine. They were nonetheless generally very reluctant to embark on or permit military activity that would invite a response from Israel. Balancing the multiple security concerns posed by Palestinian insistence on the opportunity to fight for Palestine was a challenge throughout the administration. Speech, action, and organizing were all identified as security problems and therefore had to be controlled. At the same time, and for the same reasons, these were the same arenas in which the administration had to be most responsive to people's demands. A careful calibration was required to create an outlet for expression and a sense of a public, political space, without creating a truly free space that might actually threaten government control.

Claim making and control came together to shape a relationship not just between Egyptian authorities and a Palestinian public or within the Gazan population, but also with the territory of Gaza and Palestine. The displacement and dispossession of 1948, the loss of Palestinian territorial integrity (what had been one country became three separate territories), and the concomitant cutting off of (easy, legal) access to much of Palestine necessitated a new relationship of Palestinians to this territory. For the new refugee majority of Gaza's population, that meant developing a new kind of connection to Gaza and coming to a more distant relationship with the places that had been "their" Palestine. Gaza's natives did not have to learn to be connected to this place, but they did have to come to terms with its new configurations, both geographic and social. For everyone, it was in part through the balance of claim and control that new sorts of relations to Palestine as a whole entity (the past and future country) were worked out. And at each moment the different relationship that Palestinians and Egyptians had to these territories was also elaborated. Contestations over the public life of past and future citizens in a space that was governed as Palestine-in-waiting required a multiplicity of forms.

The Press, Censorship, and Public Order

The importance of the press, in its variety of forms, for mobilizing public opinion and dissent is well known. The press is a key site, as Benedict Anderson noted, for the production of a sense of belonging in a shared community.[5] When "everybody" is talking about some event or another, whether it is a minor scandal involving film stars or major shifts in geopolitical arrangements, the everybody that is constituted in that talk is often more significant, and frequently has more lasting effects, than the event under discussion. The press serves as a forum for the articulation of a national opinion. It both didactically educates people about what *they should* think about different matters, and it subtly inculcates a sense of what it is that *we do* think. In the same way that the wide circulation of rumors lends their content an aura of facticity, the repeated expression of opinion in the press contributes to its status as the views of a broadly construed public. Certainly, the Gazan press presented itself as the effective mouthpiece of the Gazan public.

It is no surprise, therefore, that the press was a site of concern for Egyptian security personnel. In this they were no different from British Mandate officials who preceded them, and who had imposed heavy censorship on the press.[6] They were also no different from the Israeli occupation forces that followed, or myriad other security states in the region. Although it used to be newspapers that were the focus of most concern and control—as was the case during the Egyptian Administration—in many Arab security states today the Internet is a key focus of attention. In the fall of 2012, as small but regular protests occurred in Jordan, for example, the monarchy moved to impose limits on the Internet. When protest erupted in Egypt in January 2011, the regime took the extraordinary step of shutting down the entire country's Internet. But as the ineffectiveness of that move in stopping the uprising confirmed, public life and political expression, even today, do not take place only over the Internet and in virtual spaces. Old-fashioned forms of public expression remain crucially important.

During the years of Egyptian rule in Gaza, the administration sought to control, direct, and contain public expression through the press. It monitored a wide range of written materials. And it was at the same time responsive to matters brought up in the press. Each of these interventions highlights the careful negotiations over public expression that characterized this period. There is no doubt that Egyptian authorities had the upper hand in these negotiations, but it is also clear that they could never wholly dictate the public landscape.

Newspapers

During the British Mandate, Palestinian newspapers were generally national ones, published in places like Jerusalem and Jaffa but read across the country. The 1948 war and the creation of the new entity, the Gaza Strip, also occasioned the emergence of a new specifically Gazan press and a new Gazan public. This new press began immediately to make a call for additional freedoms, and it very quickly confronted the limits of those freedoms. Some newspapers, such as *Sawt Al-'Uruba* and *Ar-Raqib*, began publishing shortly after 1948 (the first issue I have seen is from October 1949). From the start, these papers self-consciously positioned themselves as representatives of the Gazan public. In complaints about conditions and policies, the papers spoke as the voice of the people, directed at the powers that be, whether Egyptian authorities, other countries, or occasionally local leaders.

Even as formal citizenship had disappeared with the end of the British Mandate and the subsequent splitting of historic Palestine, newspapers spoke in a language that evoked the claims of citizens. Among the early demands made of the new administrators was that they permit freedom of the press. In February 1950, *Sawt Al-'Uruba* published an open letter to the Egyptian government describing the denial of the rights of the press during the "odious Mandate era" and urging that the Egyptians recognize "the necessity of complete press freedom for giving the people hope."[7] Comparing Egyptian practices to those of a colonial regime was a technique to bolster claims for greater liberties, but Egyptian concerns with maintaining security and managing dissent ensured that censorship continued unabated.[8]

That Gazans did contest censorship is made clear in police records. In November 1957, for example, the publisher of the newspaper *Al-'Awda* was sent a letter of reprimand by the censor (who was also the Criminal Investigation Department [CID] director) for having printed an issue with certain articles blacked out. By blacking out the articles, the paper made the general fact of censorship, as well as its details, visible to the reading public. Such a gesture would seem to be a protest against the censorship of the articles. It may also have been an attempt to increase the credibility of the paper among the public, to suggest that it was a vehicle of public opinion, not "government lies," and that the press was

therefore of the public. The censor certainly appears to have understood
Al-'Awda's action as a form of protest, and he told the publisher that this
action "raises doubts and makes me certain that you are not following
the publication laws as they relate to the press." The letter warned against
any further such disregard of the law: "You will be held responsible if in
the future I see any blacked out article in your newspaper." To ensure
that this order would be followed, a copy of the letter was also sent to the
company that actually printed the newspapers.[9]

In his memoirs the poet and communist activist Mu'in Basisu described both what he saw as the effect of such censorship on the main-
stream press and opposition efforts to evade it. The press, he said, was
made up of "newspapers that lie sixty seconds of every minute."[10] But
Gaza's Communist Party produced its own noncensored, nonauthorized
journal that it circulated by hand:

> I gave one of the workers a copy of *The Spark*, a periodical we printed about
> the Party. He returned it to me the next day—we always wanted copies back
> so they would not make their way into the hands of the police—and said:
> "You must like the workers very much. It scared me just to read this, let
> alone to write and distribute this as you do." Paper was difficult to secure
> because bookstore owners had to report to the police all quantities of paper
> sold. However, comrades in the schools began sending us paper, pens, carbon
> paper, and ink from the Agency's [UN Relief and Works Agency for Palestine
> Refugees, or UNRWA] warehouse.[11]

Through its journal and its organizing, the Communist Party sought to
create a "counterpublic"[12] to the one sanctioned by the administration,
but its capacity to do so was limited by the intensity of government regulation and control.

It should be emphasized that the administration's aim vis-à-vis the
press does not appear to have been simply one of suppression. Rather, it
tried to harness local opinion and demands to shape a public. And there
were occasions when government officials responded to calls made in the
press for changes to policies or practices. For instance, an article published
in *Al-Tahrir* in June 1960 prompted the director of interior and public
security to ask the CID director to respond to a complaint about public
propriety.[13] In addition to being an occasion for government responsive-

ness to public demands, the article highlights how security threats around national interest and social propriety sometimes came together. It also shows the press, at least indirectly, asking for some form of censorship.

In this article, *Al-Tahrir* complained about the prevalence of violent and sexual films in Gaza's cinemas, saying that they were introducing the youth of Gaza to "strange matters" that were dangerous for morals. The article reminded the cinema owners that when they had opened the theaters they had claimed to do so "to contribute to the national battle," and they asked, "Have you forgotten this promise and were these just words?"[14] In immediate response to this article, the director of the interior asked the CID director to come to an understanding with the cinema owners that they cease showing those movies that had such a negative impact on morals. The owners, the director suggested, should "take responsibility as citizens." This instance indicates the capacity of the press—even one so heavily regulated and policed—to have an effect on the police as well as on the public. In this case, the police and the press spoke in a similar language of moral exhortation, reminding the cinema owners of their duties to national community. As allies in a campaign for public decency, the press and the police both participated in the process of defining, producing, and delimiting public order.

Interrogating Readers

It was not only press production that posed a security concern. Reading was one of the activities that could bring a Gazan to the attention of the police. Among the interrogation records of the administration there are many reports of people being questioned about their reading material: whether publications received through the mail, accidentally encountered in the street, or sometimes borrowed from libraries. A frequent pattern in such interrogations was the subject's disavowal of any connection to the material. In 1960, for example, two people made statements to the police about Communist Party publications they had received in the mail. Each denied any knowledge of the sender, saying that the publications must have been sent after their addresses were published in a newspaper when they won a contest. Both proactively reported the receipt to the police.[15] In other cases, police records describe the presence of Egyptian newspapers (particularly *Jumhurriya*) lying around in public and recount people's disavowal of knowledge of the papers.[16]

In 1967 a Gazan who was completing his master's degree at Cairo University was called in to explain his relation to a book he had borrowed from Dar al-Kutub (the National Library) in Cairo. The tale he offered was somewhat complicated, and it also highlights the complex circuits of surveillance and informing that marked policing in Gaza, and in Egypt, at this time. On February 5 Abdullah sent a telegram to his professor in Cairo asking him to send the book within a week—"because I am in a dangerous situation," he said—and asking for the professor's telephone number so he could explain further.[17] He was immediately called in for questioning. When he was interrogated on February 7, he explained that he had sent the telegram because the police had given him one week to turn over the book, titled *Palestine: The Reality*, which he no longer had in his possession.

The police, he said, accused him of having smuggled the book to Israel. That accusation, in turn, was based on a report from the director of Dar al-Kutub to authorities in Gaza that the book was an "international political document" that Israel was seeking to destroy. But, Abdullah averred, the book was in fact an "ordinary historical" book that was published in 1938 and that defended the position that King Faisal took in the 1919 Paris Peace Conference. Furthermore, he said, the book was then in Egypt, not Israel. He proceeded to tell a winding tale of the book's passage: he borrowed it originally and then lent it to another student, who gave it to his brother to translate, who eventually sent it back to Egypt so his professor could check the translation.[18] It is no surprise that a book perceived as political would arouse suspicions. That the director of Dar al-Kutub was providing reports to authorities in Gaza about Gazan borrowing habits indicates how comprehensive the surveillance system was and how many people were called on to participate in it. The policing of both readers and writers, the public and the press, underscores the importance attributed to these activities by the police.

Protests and Political Expression

A clear and key goal of police practice was to impede independent political organizing and expression. The widespread surveillance of political talk and organizing was intended to stop any threatening political action before it started. Just as in the realm of the press and the public sphere, work to control political life not only involved efforts to halt independent politics but also entailed the establishment and support of sanctioned political organizations. In the latter part of the Egyptian Administration this included the creation in Gaza of the Arab Socialist Union, a counterpart to the Egyptian organization of the same name,[19] followed by support for the new Palestine Liberation Organization (PLO). When Nasser spoke in Gaza in the same year he identified support for Palestinian national political rights as a duty incumbent upon all Arabs: "In 1948, we, the Arabs, were responsible for the disaster; we were also responsible before 1948. . . . You paid a high price to draw our attention to the menace and to awaken the whole Arab nation. The Arab nation, hence, has a duty to fulfill in the restoration of your rights and the realization of your goals and aspirations in Palestine."[20]

The text of the 1962 constitution was explicit that it "shall continue to be observed in the Gaza Strip until a permanent constitution for the state of Palestine is issued."[21] The constitution was replete with the language of the people—criminal "sentences shall be passed and implemented in the name of the people of Palestine"; the oath of office for members of the legislative council was to "take full care of the interests of the Palestinian people." Even as the people as a unitary entity was defined as the foundation of rule, the text also identified citizens, as a collection of individuals, as having certain rights and duties: punishment was to be "personal" and "private freedom" guaranteed. Further, "Palestinians have the right to address general authorities in writing and with their signatures. Public authorities may not be addressed in the name of groups except by organizational authorities." This last clause indicates the careful balance that Egyptian authorities sought between creating opportunities for and defining the limits of expression. It also suggests the different work that the categories people and citizen played in these efforts.

The combined work of surveillance, detention, and the provision of limited sanctioned outlets for political expression was largely, but never entirely, successful in controlling the political terrain. Most people were clearly afraid to engage in independent politics and especially afraid to be members of eventually banned political organizations like the Communist

Party and the Muslim Brotherhood. Some people did choose the more dangerous path, though, and engaged in such political activity. Further, even beyond the realm of the highly committed and organized, occasions arose in which people protested and demonstrated—exactly the sort of action that Egyptian policing sought to curtail—sometimes on matters of national import (against a proposed resettlement of refugees, for a right to fight for Palestine) and sometimes on more local, bread-and-butter issues (staffing in a hospital, municipal council appointments). Even when such protests did not get out of control, they indicate that there were limits to Egyptian capacity to wholly constrain the public landscape.

Local Protests

Egyptian authorities were clearly attuned to ways that even protests that posed no apparent challenge to Egyptian rule could spark wider political engagement. Police did not generally arrest and imprison participants in these sorts of demonstrations, the way that they did those involved in overtly political protest, but they did carefully observe them and made efforts to contain them. A case in point was a 1959 demonstration by nurses in the Bureij hospital.[22] The cause of the disturbance was the possible transfer of a much-beloved doctor from the hospital. The file on the subject includes numerous reports of investigations and interrogations about the events, their cause, and their consequences. There are several references to actions by the prosecutor, but these are not specified. The issues in this demonstration were extremely local—personnel matters in the hospital—but even in such a case the potential for wider import was evident. In addition to demonstrating in the hospital, nurses wrote to the governor-general asking that he intervene in the matter (and at least one expressed her intention to write to Nasser). Some people invoked the "laws of the republic" in arguing that there was no grounds for transfer. The situation was unstable enough that the governor of the Deir al-Balah area (where Bureij is located) felt compelled to go to the hospital himself to calm the situation. Despite his efforts, tensions remained among the staff. The relatively high-level attention the demonstration garnered, even as it did not have any specific political purpose or import, indicates how careful the administration was to contain action before such possibilities could emerge.

But of course, politics could not be entirely controlled, as evidenced in another localized protest. This instance, in 1964, involved a conflict over the appointment of Khan Yunis's mayor. Although the problem was in its origin a struggle between two families for power in the area (a member of the Al-Astal family was appointed mayor, and the Al-Farra family complained) as it developed, the terms of people's claims became more explicitly political. Administration authorities had made the appointment and it was to its offices that complaints were addressed. Both sides mobilized supporters to send telegrams to the governor-general. One text in the telegrams read: "Elections are the only thing that the people accept. We refuse the appointment of Al-Astal."[23] Members of both families (and of a third powerful family) went to the area governor's office and to the CID office. According to a police report to the CID director, rumors in the Khan Yunis area were that a member of the Al-Farra family cursed the Khan Yunis governor when he was told to leave the office and said to him: "You leave. This office is our office and this country is our country and you are leaving it."[24] It was further rumored that the Al-Farras had contacted authorities in Egypt to press their case and that their favored candidate would be appointed. Finally, the officer reported there were rumors that the district governors in Gaza were going to be replaced by Palestinians.

A memo on this matter from the CID director indicated that when the Al-Farras went to the police office to complain about the appointment, they demanded elections for the mayoralty.[25] Khan Yunis's administrative governor told them that the appointment was part of the jurisdiction of the governor-general. According to this report, when told to leave the office, Qassim al-Farra said, "This is the people's office and I will not leave." The next event in this sequence of protests was the posting of signs around town refusing the appointment of Al-Astal and insisting that "elections are the realization of democracy."[26] The remaining documents in the file report on the discovery and interrogation of the people responsible for the signs. The actual writer was a high school student from the Al-Farra family who was asked to make them by three other members of the family. All confessed their involvement. According to the

CID inspector's report, "The matter was turned over to the director of the interior, who said the record should be kept in case they do something like this again. The four have been warned not do anything against public security and not to write anything against any person."[27]

This protest is interesting in several respects. It shows how a struggle over power and influence among Gazans could express itself as a political claim against the administration. It indicates the availability of a vocabulary of citizenship and representativeness, and even representative democracy, in the landscape of protest ("elections are the only thing that the people accept"). It suggests that nationalism, or nativism, was sometimes deployed against Egyptian authority ("this country is our country"). The fact that nobody was arrested in these protests, despite the direct challenge to the authorities, further indicates the careful calibration that such protests required. The influence of powerful families in Gaza may have been a specific inhibiting factor in this case (better to stop the activity than motivate further opposition), but in all cases in which Gazans made demands for public and political expression and for freedom of action and organizing, the administration had to find a way to contain the threat posed by those demands while also appearing responsive to them.

National Demonstrations

Even as the authorities worked hard to curtail political organizing and demonstrations, and even as most people in Gaza were generally afraid to engage in overt politics, there were occasions when people took to the streets. Sometimes these demonstrations were prompted by regional political affairs, such as the 1959 attempted coup against 'Abd al-Karim Qasim in Iraq.[28] Most such protests, even when they had political themes, were quite limited in their actual political threat. There were, though, a few times when popular opposition to either Egyptian or UN policy led to more significant demonstrations. In these cases the police responded quickly and harshly, arresting leaders and stopping the protests. The most significant such protest was initially sparked by Israeli attacks on Gaza—leading to demands for supporting armed Palestinian resistance—and widened into a critique of both the UN and Egyptian authorities. A history of UNRWA operations published in 1982 described the challenge posed by these demonstrations: "Normally the Gaza authorities managed to maintain order. An exception occurred in February 1955, however, when for several days draconian measures had to be taken by the Egyptian authorities to control outbreaks of mob violence directed mainly against United Nations property by refugees and others."[29]

On February 28 Israeli forces attacked an Egyptian army camp north of Gaza, killing nearly forty Egyptian soldiers and a Palestinian boy.[30] In the wake of this attack, Gaza erupted into demonstrations against Egyptian authorities and UNRWA officials.[31] Two key policy changes emerged in the aftermath of these demonstrations: the establishment of Palestinian fedayeen groups to launch attacks against Israel and the abandonment of a proposed Egypt-UNRWA project to resettle refugees in the Sinai. Neither change was acknowledged to be a response to Palestinian protest. Nasser described the first as a response to the Israeli attack itself.[32] He argued that the attack proved the futility of a conciliatory policy: "After the Gaza attack it was incumbent upon us to respond, and we decided to increase the number of *fedayeen* . . . organized on the basis of small groups."[33] Palestinians had been pushing for permission and support for efforts to fight for Palestine from the early years of the administration.[34] And some people did launch attacks across the armistice line even without Egyptian authorization. Until the 1955 attacks and demonstrations, however, the administration not only did not support such activity; it actively sought to curtail it, arresting people who crossed the border, even if they were not engaging in military activity.

In their protests, Gazans made demands about both these matters and identified clear links among the raid, resettlement, and the need for self-defense. Hussein Abu Naml argues that Gazans felt that the attack was designed to "bring Gazans to their knees, to push them to accept resettlement and reconciliation."[35] As Mu'in Basisu, who was a leader of the demonstrations, put it: "It was as if the Israelis wanted to say: There is no one to protect you from the Sinai project. But they were wrong."[36] He recounts the slogans used in the protests: "No settlement! No relocation!"[37] The leaders of the demonstrations were arrested, but in contrast to earlier arrests of opposition figures, this time Gazan public opinion was mobilized in support of the prisoners.[38] This widespread support, Abu Naml argues, compelled Egyptian authorities to be responsive to the demands of the population, thus signaling the beginning of a new phase not just in Egyptian policy toward Israel, but in relations between the people of Gaza and the administration.[39]

Basisu described the demonstrations and the confrontations with Egyptian authorities: "The demonstration had to advance or be broken like an egg on a steel helmet. We marched to within 20 meters of the [military] truck, which stood in the middle of the street obstructing the demonstration—10 meters—5 meters. Then the order was given, and we were sprayed with bullets from behind the truck and the orange trees."[40] A demonstrator was killed in this shooting, and in response, according to Basisu, the demonstrators burned the truck, after which the police fled. The demonstrators, who included "students, teachers, workers, and peasants,"[41] then continued on to the police headquarters in the Rimal quarter. The threat that authorities saw in these demonstrations is captured in Basisu's description of the assembling of personnel from all parts of the government to meet them at the police station:

> At the entrance to the station . . . the policemen, including those from the secret police, gathered. With them were members of the Gaza Municipal Council, the religious judge, the Rimal *mukhtar*, a member of the Muslim Council, a school principal, the director of Intelligence, and the director of the secret police, Sa'ad Hamza. Hamza, who was also the administrative governor of Gaza, shouted: "Go back to your schools!"[42]

According to Basisu's account, there were two different sorts of response to the demonstration: one repressive and one conciliatory. The communist leaders of the uprising were arrested, and a curfew was then imposed to inhibit further organizing.[43] And, Egyptian authorities changed their policies to meet Palestinian demands.

Basisu ascribes these policy changes directly to the demonstrations, describing a proclamation by Hamza stating that "the Sinai project was no longer of substance" and that "the camps would be armed and general military conscription would be declared soon."[44] Conscription did not in fact come until 1965, but the arming of fedayeen did follow these events.

Egyptian documents do not acknowledge the link to the demonstrations in either policy change. The same proclamation that promised these policy changes also made promises that were honored in the breach:

key among the broken promises were that the protest leaders would not be arrested. These demonstrations and the response to them were a clear instance of Gazans successfully changing the security threat calibration. Even though the guarantee of "the freedoms of Gaza residents" (another part of the proclamation) was not achieved and people did not have the full protection of the rights of citizenship, Egyptian security calculations did mandate a response to their demands. This case confirms both the possibilities of influence when acting through security society and the very clear limits to such influence.

Threat Calculation and the End of the Sinai Resettlement Project

The trajectory of the Sinai project shows the complexity of such security calculations. Although people mobilized first in response to the Israeli attack, the fact that the demonstrations quickly focused on the Sinai resettlement project highlights how difficult it could be to contain, and certainly to direct, political claims. The uncertainties and suspicions that were endemic in Gaza, and were promoted by security practice, made people wary of each other and of the intentions of their governors. Even as Egypt claimed to govern Gaza on behalf of Palestine, its willingness to consider and possibly support a project to resettle refugees outside of Palestine threatened to undermine that claim.

The Sinai project, the subject of extensive discussions between Egyptian authorities and UNRWA and backed by considerable research, proposed to develop portions of the Sinai desert and resettle some of the Palestinian refugees living in Gaza in this territory. Water was the first concern, of course, but there were a range of technical complications that had to be worked out before such a project could become a reality. According to a draft agreement between the agency and the Egyptian government, the purpose of the project was to "without prejudice to resolution 194 . . . result in the achievement of self-support and removal from ration rolls of refugees residing in the Gaza District."[45] To that end a feasibility study was undertaken that concluded that with proper irrigation it should be possible to settle 12,500 refugee families—approximately 62,500 people—in northwestern Sinai.

Despite the fact that the preamble to this project averred that it was not meant to undercut Palestinian refugee rights as outlined by UN General Assembly Resolution 194, refugees in Gaza saw it as a threat to exactly these rights. And the demonstrations rejected the plan. Basisu explains that members of the Communist Party in Gaza got their hands on a copy of the UNRWA report on the project. They made further copies that they then, on February 15, distributed throughout the Strip. When the Israeli raid took place on February 28, the demonstrations became an occasion to demand the end of the project. The threat of sustained crisis to the security of Egyptian rule in Gaza was averted when Egypt canceled the project.

The material on the Sinai project in the UNRWA archives does not reference this political crisis, and it is not mentioned in my archive of police files, but the UNRWA record does document a transition from apparent enthusiasm about the project on the part of the Egyptian government to hesitancy to commit. Concerns about resources began to be raised and delays introduced. The Egyptian government indicated, for instance, that it could not begin on the Sinai project until the High Dam was completed.[46] According to UNRWA's 1956 annual report, the Egyptian government retracted its approval for the project on the grounds that "it could not undertake to make water available for a project for refugees when it was obliged to restrict the amount of water used by its own citizens."[47] Even if this concern for "its own citizens" was not the primary reason for Egypt's withdrawal of support, this reference to its different obligations to Egyptians and Gazans is notable. Questions of citizenship rights and representative government were a part of Gazan relationships with Egyptian administrators.[48] This statement confirms some of the rhetorical limits (and there were plenty of practical limits) in such claims.

That there was more than simply a question of resources at stake in the ultimate decision to halt the project is made clear in an UNRWA memo reflecting on the question of agency responsibility for both "relief" and "rehabilitation." The UNRWA representative to Egypt quoted an Egyptian statement on this question: "Egyptian Government agrees to the development program as a temporary means of employing refugees without prejudice to their rights of rehabilitation and compensation."[49] Alexander Squadrilli, UNRWA representative to Egypt, interpreted this statement to mean: "We will not obtain a suitable agreement on the Sinai Project from the Egyptian Government unless their attitude changes to an acceptance of the ultimately permanent character of that project in terms of refugee resettlement, with or without a general political accord on the Palestine question." No mention is made of Palestinian opposition to the plan or the relationship of such opposition to Egyptian attitudes, but that there was such relationship seems certain. This episode highlights the difficult balance between concession and control that defined the policing of political demand.

The episode further illuminates the intersection of the multiple modes of governing Gazans. The planned resettlement project was part of a welfare practice that was concerned with meeting the humanitarian needs of the people. And the belief that they might go without complaint or concern for its political effects suggests that, vis-à-vis the project, they were considered a population with "needs" rather than citizens with "rights." The opposition to the project clearly utilized the language of rights and positioned Gazans as Palestinian citizens with rights to their nation. Running through both the project and its response was a set of security concerns. In the end, Gazans appear to have been able to derail the plan by making the security risk of proceeding greater than the security risk of maintaining an unsettled refugee population in Gaza.

Military Action: Fedayeen, the Palestine Liberation Army, and the Defense of Palestine

When Palestinians demanded the right of self-defense and the opportunity to fight for the liberation of Palestine, their claims for Palestinian national security came into potential conflict with Egyptian national security. When not responding to their demands seemed to pose a bigger threat than meeting them in a controlled fashion, Egyptian authorities changed their position. The relatively brief "war of the fedayeen," which was one of the outcomes of the 1955 demonstrations, ended with the Israeli occupation of the Gaza Strip in November 1956 (in the context of the Suez Crisis). Israel occupied Gaza for four months, departing only under US pressure and with the creation of a peacekeeping force, the UN Emergency Force (UNEF), to monitor the borders.

As a contributor to the tensions that culminated in this invasion and occupation, the fedayeen raids had a significant effect on the political and military landscape of Palestine and the region, but they also had more intimate effects on people's transforming relations with home.[50] When Egyptian authorities began to organize, train, and arm fedayeen groups in 1955, they defined as a collective national imperative what they had previously seen as individual, criminal (though still political) acts. In this process, the border crossings that had previously landed Gazans in jail became a credential in the recruitment drive for fedayeen. One Gazan remembered the transition:

> Before people were sneaking into Israel in order to steal. People would go to steal a pipeline or something like that and the Egyptians arrested and jailed them. Mustafa Hafez [the commander of the fedayeen] was clever. He came to these prisoners. He asked them if they knew places [inside] well. They would tell him that they knew, for example, Hamama, its roads, vineyards, and the settlements there. Mustafa Hafez told them: "Let's work together. Instead of being thieves, you will become fedayeen. And you will receive a salary as a member of the organization. But this time you will not go to steal; you will put a mine in the way of an Israeli patrol. You can explode a bridge, a factory, or a cinema to frighten the Jews."[51]

Fedayeen border crossings differed from earlier crossings to retrieve possessions or to steal from Israeli settlements in more than simply their objective. Gazans' relationship with their lands was reformulated as well. This relationship was removed from the realm of the immediate—the knowledge of home that enables one to collect one's things—and was reconstituted as political knowledge, a tool in a struggle.

Abu Nizar, a former fedayee, remembered: "They said to one fedayee, 'You are from Jaffa, so you go to Jaffa.' Someone from Askelon will go there. Someone who knows al-Faluja will go to al-Faluja—and so on. Anyone who knew a place would go to that place to attack the Jews there. The Jews, of course, inhabited all these places."[52] People's connection to their home villages was made to matter at a national scale. Knowledge of al-Faluja, of Hamama, of Majdal, became a node in a larger communal knowledge of Palestine. Both proximity and distance were crucial to this practice, which relied on the detailed knowledge of territory and home that could only come from closeness to these places. At the same time, it was precisely the confirmation of the loss of this home, and the consolidation of new social and communal relations within the boundaries of Gaza, that made possible organized national activity to attempt to regain that which was lost. As Abu Nizar recalled, it was the increasing realization that they were not about to return that strengthened the demand for fedayeen: "A long time had passed. People feared that their cause was lost. They said to the Egyptians, 'You have to [create fedayeen units] so we can fight these people and restore our homeland.'"

Unlike the earliest border crossings, fedayeen raids had to recognize displacement. But also unlike the earliest crossings, they made an explicit claim to their land. They were a statement of rights. As Abu Nizar told me:

> What made me a fedayee, and made me sacrifice myself, was that the Jews took our land and villages and we could not regain them. . . . This upset us and made us want to be soldiers to fight those people. We wanted to force them to recognize our rights and life. . . . We have rights the same as they have rights; we have dignity like them. This is what bothered us and made us fight them—they took our homeland, said that you are strangers and you have nothing, and expelled us.

An old man many years removed from his military service when I interviewed him, Abu Nizar continued to stress his right to fight for his homeland, even as he expressed his desire for a just peace: "The Israeli Jewish people should reconcile with the Arab Palestinian people and the whole Arab people in order for peace and safety to prevail; do not take my right and displace me out of my village and homeland and say that you have nothing."

As brief as the war of the fedayeen was, it had a profound effect on how Gazans understood their role in the struggle for Palestine and in their relations with their homes. Abu Nizar spoke with tremendous bitterness about the failure of the neighboring Arab countries to effectively defend Palestine:

> The Arab armies told the Palestinians, "You stand aside and do not fight the Jews and we will fight." . . . [F]ive months after the Arab armies had entered

Palestine they handed Palestine to the Jews and they then retreated. The Palestinians who were still in their villages said to them, "Where are you going?" They said, 'We want to withdraw from here.' . . . They handed all the villages, the rest of Hamama, Majdal, Askelan, Barbara, Burayr, Bir al-Saba, and all these villages to the Jews without fighting. The people, of course, were miserable and had nothing to fight with. The people relied on the army, but the army retreated.

Being a fedayee enabled Abu Nizar to feel that at least he was taking action on his own rather than relying on others for help that might not come. Crossing the armistice line as a soldier not only enabled dispossessed Palestinians to make a claim for their right to their homes; it enabled an active connection with that home, even if from a distance. By refusing to accept a position of passivity, to wait for others to facilitate their return, Gazans may have felt that they redeemed themselves for their failure to stay in their villages in 1948. Abu Nizar directly connected being a fedayee to the restoration of dignity, saying he was obliged to fight because "one cannot live in humiliation."

Fedayeen raids repeated—through practice—an intimate knowledge of home that affirmed its connection to community. They sought, further, to reintroduce security into the lives of Palestinians by taking action toward the end of reclaiming home. Still, even as being a fedayee offered people a source of pride, and even as it affirmed their claims to their occupied homes, the raids were also part of a process through which people came to terms with their dispossession, not accepting its legitimacy, but acknowledging its actuality and its tenacity. That fedayeen were unable to recover home also contributed to the recognition of displacement. Even as they claimed the "right" to home, both the passage of time and the transformation of practice introduced distance into people's relations with their homes.

Even as substantial fedayeen activity ended with the 1956 Suez War, the Egyptians continued to support and organize fedayeen units. UNEF intelligence reports describe recruitment, training, and activities of these units. According to one undated report, there were three primary recruitment methods: "Local mukhtars and beduin [sic] sheikhs are called to the Intelligence Bureau and asked to submit a list of "volunteers." Agents recruit Palestinians in the refugee camps. Criminal elements under arrest may volunteer under promise of release."[53] After training, fedayeen were sent on missions with three primary objectives: "Ambushes on roads and the laying of mines. Sabotage of installations (principally water installations), [b]lowing up houses in undefended localities." Echoing Abu Nizar's account, the report described the importance of personal knowledge of Palestine in what it called "Fedayeen Fieldcraft": "As they are chosen for their knowledge of the country, Fedayeen do not use navigational aids, such as maps and compasses. They move through deserted villages, using as memory aids small features, lone trees, orchards, wells, etc." Given that UNEF's presence in Gaza was intended to stop the kind of infiltrations that were the heart of fedayeen activity, it is not surprising that the report also noted this: "Some discontentment among the registered Fedayeens [sic] in this area have appeared lately. This is mainly due to the fact that a number have not been paid lately. But inactivity may also be a reason. It seems that a plan for their method of operation under the present circumstance is lacking."

Another UNEF report, this one dated February 22, 1960, indicates that a plan of some sort was worked out. According to this report there were five hundred to six hundred fedayeen in Gaza operating within the framework of the Egyptian National Guard, "in what is called the Battalion of the Palestinian National Guard."[54] This force was divided into two groups, one which was active in Gaza—patrolling, tailing UNEF personnel, staffing outposts—and one, Company 17, focused on intelligence missions in Israel. The report indicated that "at present men of this company are sent only on purely intelligence missions" but that they "are trained and capable of carrying out missions of sabotage inside Israel should this be required of them."

Fedayeen units existed throughout the remainder of the administration (to little effect) and in 1964 (in the context of the establishment of the Palestine Liberation Organization, or PLO), the Palestine Liberation Army (PLA) was established.[55] In 1965 universal conscription was declared in Gaza. Symbolically, this force represented both the fulfillment of Palestinian calls for opportunities to fight for Palestine and the recognition of Palestinian obligations to one another as citizens of a not-yet-realized state of Palestine. Military service is, after all, frequently described as the most sacred of citizenship duties, even as it is rarely one incumbent on all citizens.[56] In practical terms, Yezid Sayigh has detailed the severe limitations Egypt imposed on the PLA's ability to actually serve as an independent Palestinian military force.[57] Conscription was short lived, however. The Israeli occupation of 1967 brought an end to this period of Palestinian organizing.

Despite its limitation, the formation of the PLA was precisely what many Palestinians had been demanding for a long time, and to this extent it was a right of citizenship. At the same time, service in the army was also burdensome, and to this extent it can be seen as an obligation that citizens acknowledged but may not have liked. Among the files from the Egyptian Administration are indications that some people did go AWOL from their service responsibilities, although how widespread a problem that was, I cannot say.[58] CID reports on public opinion in Gaza indicate widespread support for military mobilization, one report insisting, "This isn't simply talk, but a real desire. The people are ready to send their sons to the army in anticipation of battle."[59]

Because there was not yet a Palestinian state, the declaration of Palestinian sovereignty was in part enacted by neighboring Arab countries, which were "pledged to backing the efforts of the struggling Palestine Arab people to assert its nationhood and substantiate its sovereignty over its homeland."[60] The law announcing the conscription policy clearly framed military service as a national duty: "military and national service is for every Palestinian Arab, an honour, a sacred duty and the honourable means of achieving the highest aims of the whole Arab nation in the liberation of Palestine." It further linked this service to the obligations of citizenship, noting that among the principles on which the conscription law was based was "equality of all citizens in paying the blood-tax to the homeland" through performance of national service. This not surprisingly somewhat hyperbolic language of duty and desire (which clearly did have a connection to Palestinian demands) was paired in the law with a description of concrete mechanisms for managing recruitment, service, exemptions, and penalties for evasion. The creation of the PLA and conscription to it are clear indication of the imperative to balance control and concession. From fedayeen to the PLA, each of the resistance institutions created in Gaza were directly responsive to people's demands to be allowed to fight for Palestine. Even as military conscription was talked about in the language of citizenship, its establishment was in significant part a result of Palestinians acting through the terms of security society.

The forms of public life explored in this chapter each marked a space of confrontation between the strict controls imposed by the security regime in Gaza and the demands of Gazans to have their political aspirations and collective demands acknowledged and met. In each of these areas, a primary aim, sometimes stated directly and sometimes simply enacted, was for opportunities to act autonomously and collectively. Palestinians have often made claims for redress and restitution, asking parties responsible for their plight (whether Israel or the international community) to support their rights and assist in their reclamation. These sorts of claims are evident in the political expressions explored in this chapter, but equally prominent are attempts to take control of their own fate. Palestinians wanted to organize militarily to liberate Palestine. They were willing to do so under Egyptian auspices but also, and increasingly, ready to go it alone. Public protests about matters both large and small were instances of refusal: refusal to accept the imposition of policies to which they objected, refusal to acquiesce to being simply objects of governance. Press demands were directed both at governing authorities and at the local community, and they served as a mechanism for the formation of a collectivity, the nation, which had roots in the pre-1948 Palestinian community but also had been dramatically reshaped by the *nakba*.

Like the surveillance of everyday life and everyday talk, the policing and control of public political life described here indicates the broad range of action that can happen in a security milieu. To say this is not to suggest that the population ever had as much, or even anything close to, the same power as did the police to assert their vision of public life, but to underscore that even in a highly undemocratic setting such as Gaza under Egyptian rule the power of the police was not limitless. In fact, accomplishing the aim of containing security threats sometimes required being responsive to political demands. Security society was both a means of governing and a way of acting politically. The arenas of the press, protests, and military action show how they intersect in struggles over collectivity.

5

Peacekeeping and International Community

IN THE SECOND HALF OF THE EGYPTIAN ADMINISTRATION— after the pullback of Israeli occupation forces in March 1957—Egyptian and Palestinian security personnel were joined by a new international peacekeeping force: the United Nations Emergency Force (UNEF). The presence of this force highlights the significant international concern with security matters in Gaza, the range of actors involved in policing this space, and the array of security problems identified in this practice. In turning to the work of UNEF, this chapter brings a different set of actors into the consideration of the security landscape in Gaza. The UNEF experience is a reminder that security society in Gaza was not produced only in negotiations between Palestinians and Egyptians. The space was always connected to an international and a regional field whose actors mattered at the local level. In UNEF's work we encounter these actors operating on the ground. The issues that loomed largest in Egyptian security practice—threats to national interest and to social propriety— continued to matter in UNEF practice (though not always in the same ways), and they were joined by additional concerns about threats to the full establishment of a robust "international community."

The previous chapter explored intersections between citizenship and security in Gaza's security society. UNEF's work in Gaza indicates how population and security came together in this field and, especially, highlights the crucial presence of the additional category of "humanity." Whereas Gazans made claims to Egyptian administrators as Palestinian citizens and as Arabs, when they were disappointed in their treatment by UNEF, they often used the language of "humanity" to express frustration and make demands for better treatment. UNEF soldiers and officials sometimes took up this language in their responses, but even more frequently they interacted with Gazans (when they interacted with Gazans) through the prism of population or security threat. Not only did UNEF soldiers take an interest in providing charitable aid to locals, approaching them as subjects in need and deserving of compassion; their descriptions of them as security threats (as when they crossed the border or got into conflict with UNEF forces) suggests a view of Gazans as, variously, an uncontrolled mob, a local culture group, and even primitives.

Whether seen as humanity, as population, or as threat, UNEF's interest in and ability to respond to Gazan demands was sometimes limited both by the structure of the force and by the perceived security problems that undergirded its practice. Where Egyptian administrators sought to control independent Palestinian political and military activity in the service of the national interest, UNEF personnel sought this same kind of control (insofar as such activity pertained to the border) in the name of regional stability. Containing the threat of military activity across the armistice line was the heart of the force's mission. Worries about social propriety were also key to UNEF's practice, but not because promoting propriety was part of their mission, as Egyptian officials might have argued it was part of theirs, but because violations of proper behavior could undermine the capacity of the force to pursue its aims of maintaining "international peace and security."

The Gaza Emergency and the Creation of UNEF

The immediate background to UNEF's creation was the invasion of Gaza and the Sinai Peninsula by Israel, Great Britain, and France in the Suez Crisis. Israeli forces occupied the Gaza Strip on November 2, 1956, seizing both military and administrative control from Egypt. Even as the international community widely denounced the attack, and the French and British quickly agreed to withdraw, Israel took a number of steps that suggested it intended to remain in Gaza for a long time to come. Within days of occupying Gaza, Israeli authorities announced plans to switch the currency from Egyptian to Israeli and to reopen the railroad link between Gaza and Tel Aviv.[1] Within weeks, a broader array of programs were approved: "the measures include the restoration of the local municipal government, full cooperation with United Nations relief workers on providing supplies to refugees, full restoration of fishing along the coast and free communication between villages."[2] These actions were seen as indications that "Israel plans to retain control of the Gaza Strip for a long period."[3]

As international pressure grew for Israel to depart from Gaza, and as the Israeli government objected to handing the territory back to Egypt, the idea of stationing an international force between the warring parties took hold. The product of already ongoing discussions, spearheaded by the Canadians, about the possibility of creating a "truly international peace and police force,"[4] UNEF was meant to represent "the determination of the world community to establish peace and order in this area."[5] Israel did not allow UNEF soldiers to be stationed on its territory, but it did agree to withdraw from Gaza and the Sinai when UNEF went into those areas. After Israel withdrew, Egyptian administrators (though not military personnel) returned to Gaza, staying until the 1967 Israeli occupation of the Strip.

Key to the UNEF deployment was the identification of an emergency in Gaza, and in the Middle East more broadly. *Crisis* and *emergency* are key terms for many humanitarian interventions and have become central to the conceptual vocabulary of peacekeeping.[6] In this case, naming the situation did not, as happens so often now, mobilize an existing mechanism but helped create one.[7] Naming the Israeli invasion and occupation of Gaza an emergency identified the situation's relevance to the UN mandate and enabled the development of a response. The idea of emergency therefore made it possible to create an institution (UNEF) that brought the international community into the space of Gaza.

UNEF was meant to represent the international community but, as the UN secretary-general noted in 1967, it was "an international force in only a limited sense."[8] Its soldiers came from India, Brazil, Colombia, Scandinavia, and Canada, and they were organized in distinct national units, each with its own command, its own uniform, its own kind of weapon, and its own menu (the issue of proper rations for the different nationalities was a subject of considerable discussion).[9] Soldiers also came to UNEF under different circumstances: some were volunteers, others were completing national-service requirements and had volunteered to fulfill that obligation as part of UNEF, and still others were personnel who had been assigned to serve in the force as part of their service.[10] The force was a "marriage of national military service with international function" whereby soldiers remained in their national service even as they came under the authority of the United Nations.[11] Although this arrangement introduced certain weaknesses into the UNEF structure (as language barriers sometimes created communication difficulties and commanding authority was not a robust as in ordinary military forces), the secretary-general expressed pleasure in how well the force functioned overall: "In the sense of maintaining quiet and preventing incidents [UNEF] was a most effective United Nations peace-keeping operation."[12]

There were several distinct groups of actors whose ideas, expectations, and actions helped shape the UNEF experience in Gaza: representatives of UN member countries who planned and promoted the force, UNEF soldiers, Gazans, and the Israeli and Egyptian governments. UNEF's planners were far from the field of action, putting in motion ideas about a UN police force to promote and protect international ideals without being part of the enactment of such ideals on the ground. It was these people who seem to have had the strongest commitment to peace-keeping: many UN members were deeply disappointed by UNEF's end. UNEF was actually put into practice by people who did not necessarily share this degree of investment in the ideal. Peacekeeping soldiers came from many countries and for a variety of reasons. Their behavior in Gaza, as has been the case with later peacekeeping missions, evidenced varying degrees of respect for the local population and its sensitivities. Gazans also had a range of opinions about UNEF and its presence: some objected to its presence as a form of foreign interference, some appreciated the work opportunities the force provided, and some expressed gratitude for the relative peace UNEF was able to maintain.

Later peacekeeping missions have often been motivated by a problem of "failed states," wherein peacekeepers have perceived chaotic situations.[13] This was not the case in Gaza. UNEF soldiers in Gaza confronted

a highly governed and patrolled landscape. Both the Egyptian Administration and the UN Relief and Works Agency for Palestine Refugees
in the Near East (UNRWA) managed large bureaucracies. UNEF did
not displace these apparatuses but, rather, joined them. The Israeli occupation disrupted the Egyptian security apparatus, but when Egyptian
administrators returned to Gaza in March 1957, so did their expansive
police practices. Cooperation with the police was crucial for UNEF operations; soldiers turned people they apprehended over to local authorities
and counted on them to keep internal order in the Strip. The conditions of cooperation were outlined in a UNEF memo: "Egypt will make
it known effectively to the refugees and residents of the Strip that it is
Egyptian policy to prevent infiltration across the Demarcation Line. . . .
A unit of the Palestinian Police will be designated specifically for duty
in the prevention of infiltration, and will co-operate closely with UNEF
in this function."[14] The memo further stated, "The announced policy of
Egyptian cooperation with UNEF will periodically be emphasized to the
population of the Strip." That is, UNEF was to be folded into the broader
policing project that Egypt had implemented.

It should also be noted that UNEF was a different sort of international body than UNRWA. Even as UNRWA is an international institution, authorized and governed from elsewhere, its staff is made up almost
entirely of locals.[15] The relationship between UNRWA personnel and the
rest of the Gazan population therefore was only partially international. In
contrast, UNEF hired some Gazans in support positions, but its soldiers
were all foreigners (see Figure 5). Both UNRWA and UNEF shared an
approach to Palestinians in Gaza as population, but for UNEF the possible security threat posed by that population was a more central concern
than for UNRWA (which is not to say that this concern was absent from
UNRWA calculations). Of the variety of UN bodies that were engaged
with the Palestine question, it was UNEF that most directly made the
international community an arena for relations on the ground in Gaza.
If emergency made this kind of engagement with humanity in Gaza possible, it also structured that engagement in ways that circumscribed relations. How UNEF soldiers could interact with Gazans was limited by
both policy and social difference, and these limits had important consequences for how UNEF was perceived.

FIGURE 5 *Observation post staffed by the Brazilian battalion of the UNEF on the Armistice Demarcation Line, 1959. Source: UN Photos.*

The Novelty of Peacekeeping

UNEF was the first UN peacekeeping force, though not its first effort to keep the peace, whether in Palestine or elsewhere.[16] In the immediate aftermath of the 1948 war, the United Nations sent a small staff of observers to the area. These personnel—members of the UN Truce Supervision Organization (UNTSO)—heard complaints from both Israeli and Egyptian officials (and other parties around other armistice lines) about violations of the armistice agreements. They did not, however, have forces on the ground or much authority of any kind. UNEF was an ad hoc creation intended to facilitate the withdrawal of Israeli troops from Gaza and the Sinai and to mitigate the likelihood of a further outbreak of hostilities. It was disbanded when Egypt withdrew its consent to having UN troops stationed on its territory (Israel had never given such consent) in the lead up to the 1967 war. UNEF was conceived of as a force "altogether unique in history," the first time that soldiers were being sent to "make peace rather than to wage war."[17] In the years since, peacekeeping has become a regular, if sometimes controversial, instrument in the tool kit of international intervention.

From its inception, UNEF officials were cognizant of the force's novelty. In a pamphlet explaining the purpose of the force to its multinational soldiers, UNEF was described as "a military body but it has no military objective. It carries arms but its mission is peace, not war. . . . UNEF is a friendly and not a warlike force. In its operation there is no enemy. It is not a conquering force and it is not an army of occupation."[18] UN peacekeeping did not mark the first, nor the last, time that military forces were imagined as agents for peace. UNEF's creation did, though, represent a new way of thinking about the possibilities of mobilizing armies for peace and about international engagement in the cause of humanity.

The UNEF experiment in Gaza was crucial in shaping what came to be the familiar contours of first-generation peacekeeping. It illuminates how its principles, and its limits, emerged from the challenges of this ad hoc experience. I have explored this broad import elsewhere.[19] Here my focus is on UNEF's participation in the security dynamic in Gaza. UNEF's single greatest security concern was stability: stability of force relations, of borders, and of population. And each of these matters was directly connected in UN thinking to the organization's mission to "maintain or restore international peace and security."[20] Maintaining this peace and security required creating a full-fledged international community, with concomitant ideals, institutions, and personnel. Peacekeeping forces were one of these institutions and have to be understood as a component of what Ruti Teitel calls "humanity's law."[21] The variety of instruments that are part of the growing body of international humanitarian law—including UN resolutions and conventions, international criminal tribunals, and the International Criminal Court (ICC)—are meant both to protect vulnerable people and groups and, Teitel argues, to expand the "reach of the notion of humanity."[22]

The meaning of this expanding category of humanity is, of course, neither simple nor stable. As Miriam Ticktin and I explore elsewhere,[23] humanity has been variously conceptualized as a sentiment linked to the idea of the humane, as a biological object, even if a manipulable one, and as a threat.[24] In the context of UN peacekeeping in Gaza, humanity was identified as a space of relation. For UNEF's founders, the notion of an international community was a mechanism for instantiating the abstract ideal of universal humanity. And Palestinians were also committed to this idea. Over the years, beginning before 1948 and intensifying after, Palestinians have claimed a place in humanity in a number of venues, seeking the restoration of their political rights.[25] The idea of humanity invoked in these efforts is a relational one, emphasizing membership in the international community (itself a product of political claim making) and the obligations that members in that community have to one another. At a macro level, the idea of international community is expressed in global laws and institutions—the humanity's law that Teitel describes—but it also finds expression at the small scale, when the "international" personnel of these institutions come into contact with people defined as "locals." By 1956 Palestinians already had many years of engaging with the international community in largely failed efforts, first to win support for their position in Palestine and later to seek a resolution to their displacement. As a result of such failures, Palestinians have often felt poorly served by the international community. None of the commissions sent to Palestine over the years of the British Mandate brought Palestinians closer to their political goals. The efforts of the UN mediator Count Bernadotte to negotiate a settlement of the conflict and of the refugee problem—efforts that ended with his assassination in 1948 by Zionist militants—did not return people to their homes. The many UN resolutions that express support for Palestinian claims have never been implemented. Despite such repeated disappointments, which have only continued in the years after the UNEF experiment, Palestinians have continued to both engage the international community and place considerable hope in international law and the United Nations as mechanisms for pressing their claims.[26]

As a peacekeeping mission, UNEF had limited aims and was not designed to solve the Arab-Israeli conflict. Its planners hoped it could keep a fragile calm in Gaza and, as importantly, that it could help shift international practice around conflicts in general. On the ground in Gaza, UNEF brought the international community close. Even if its soldiers were not an audience for pressing Palestinian political claims, as "internationals" they did provide an opportunity to instantiate the international community as a concrete space of relationships. Not only in patrolling the border but also by employing Gazans in their camps and occasionally interacting with Gazans elsewhere, the presence of these soldiers made it possible for international community to be realized, and to disappoint, on the small scale.[27]

The experience of UNEF in Gaza illuminates not just the character of commitments to the idea of international community but also concrete expressions of this community on the ground. A range of concerns shaped relations between UNEF soldiers and the Gazan population: concerns about propriety (especially about soldiers approaching local women), about local politics, and about cooperation with Egyptian officials. Each of these concerns in turn affected how Gazans were incorporated into the space of the international community. UNEF's time in Gaza was characterized by a persistent tension with the local population, along with overall success in fulfilling its mission. UNEF's experience in Gaza therefore highlights broader tensions in humanity's law, which seeks to universalize the international community,[28] but also introduces new sorts of distinctions into that community (as, for instance, new divides between the saviors and the saved are produced).[29]

Principles from Practice: Internationals on the Ground in Gaza

UNEF forces went into Gaza with the intention of taking over local administration for an undetermined length of time. Israel had declared its withdrawal to be conditional on the United Nations keeping Egypt from returning to Gaza. Although the United Nations did not accept the proposition that Egypt no longer had authority in Gaza, it did hope to delay its return. Recognizing the necessity of governing Gaza for some period, internal UN discussions proposed establishing a committee composed of UNEF personnel with a representative from UNRWA to make "decisions regarding the administration of Gaza" even though "the General Assembly has never directly permitted the use of UNEF as [an] organ responsible for civilian administration."[30] As it entered Gaza, the force announced to the population: "Until further arrangements are made, the UNEF has assumed responsibility for civil affairs in the Gaza Strip."[31]

UNEF kept the peace quite successfully for ten years, but its administrative responsibilities lasted less than ten days. Egyptian officials were somewhat suspicious of UNEF from the beginning, concerned that its deployment might be part of a plan to "internationalize" Gaza.[32] The immediate cause of the Egyptian Administration's return was, though, concrete: the shooting death (apparently by a ricocheting bullet) of a Gazan by a UNEF soldier in the course of trying to control a demonstration on the fourth day of UNEF's presence in Gaza (see Figure 6). Ralph Bunche, UN under secretary-general, described the shooting incident as "unfortunate but apparently considered necessary by UNEF officers." Even as he expressed his "wish that an appeal to the crowd to disperse might have first been tried,"[33] Bunche insisted that "UNEF was acting properly in every respect since, in the absence of any effective local authority at that early stage of the takeover, UNEF had not only the right of self-protection but the duty to do whatever it could to maintain law and order in the interest of all the people of Gaza."[34] Once it became widely known that a Gazan had died, domestic political pressure on Nasser made an Egyptian return unavoidable.[35]

The initial account of the shooting, written by E. L. M. Burns (the first commander of UNEF) before he learned that a Gazan had been killed, emphasized that the crowd, which was "cheering Nasser and demanding return of Egyptians to [the] Gaza Strip," had become "rather threatening trying to break in [the] gate," leading the soldiers on scene to fire over the heads of the crowd.[36] Although both Bunche and Burns placed much of the blame for the event on the threatening crowd and praised the soldiers for having the "situation well in hand," other UN officials identified a problem in the soldiers' attitudes about the local population. As one commented: "The UNEF went into Gaza, briefed

FIGURE 6 *UNEF troops arrive in Gaza City, 1957. Source: UN Photos.*

by 'old Palestine hands,' not as friends but as jittery policemen expecting trouble." These unspecified Palestine hands seem most likely to have been British officials who, only a few years earlier, had abandoned the Palestine Mandate in the face of ongoing conflict.

This event, and its significant consequences, underscores the extent to which it was not just ideals but also individuals—with all their complicated attitudes about the mission, place, and population—who brought UNEF to life in Gaza. It further illuminates the significant questions about the role—and indeed the personas—of the soldiers who made up the force. Were they to fear the local population? To protect them? Were they police, soldiers, or something else? The ad hoc, improvisational, character of the force meant both that there were few preexisting principles to answer these questions. UNEF was an experiment that developed "mid-emergency . . . and had to be quickly established out of nothing."[37] Its principles and its subject positions emerged from the on-the-ground practice of its work.

UNEF was brought to conclusion not because of any UNEF soldiers' actions but as a result of decisions by the Egyptian government. As regional tensions heated up in advance of the 1967 war, the Egyptian government demanded that the force withdraw. On May 16, 1967, the Egyptian chief of staff sent a letter to UNEF: "I gave my instructions to all armed forces to be ready for action against Israel, the moment it might carry out any aggressive action against any Arab country. . . . For the sake of complete security of all UN troops which install [observation posts] along our borders, I request that you issue your orders to withdraw all there troops immediately."[38] UNEF forces began pulling back on May 19, though at the start of the war on June 5 there were still 2,500 UNEF personnel in Gaza. The evacuation was completed under Israeli occupation of the Strip.[39]

The UN secretary-general's July report on UNEF noted: "An operation such as UNEF is not an end in itself. . . . The true function of a peace-keeping effort is to create a climate of quiet which is more congenial to efforts to solve the underlying problems that lead to conflict."[40] It was the end—what many at the time called the "failure"—of UNEF that defined this "true" function. The authority of peacekeeping forces derived from the consent of the "host country" and "automatically and instantly vanishes once it is challenged by the host country." When consent was withdrawn, "the basis for UNEF's presence ceased to exist."[41] If the national organization of the force indicated one limit to UNEF's "internationalism"—understood as "a willingness to overlook national interest in favour of the welfare of humanity as a whole"[42]—this consent requirement highlighted another. International community, as it turned out, could be only very partially enacted on the ground in Gaza. The work of the force over its ten-year presence highlights these challenges.

Border Patrol and the Security Space

With UNEF's mission quickly defined as one of security not ad-ministration—what Ralph Bunche called a "buffer function"—its pri-mary work became patrolling the Armistice Demarcation Line (ADL) that marked the boundary of the Gaza Strip, along with the international border between Egypt and Israel, to prevent crossings or conflict (see Fig-ure 7).[43] The importance of the border as security space has already been evident in Egyptian policing practice, both in efforts to curtail movement across the line and in carefully managed crossings for military purposes. For Egyptian administrators the border was one security space among

FIGURE 7 *Redigging the Armistice Demarcation Line, 1959. Source: UN Photos.*

many, for UNEF it came to be *the* security space. UNEF personnel had encounters in the interior of Gaza, and their border-patrol work had clear consequences for that interior space, but UNEF's security jurisdiction was the border.

Maintaining the space of Gaza was central to the peacekeeping mission, but that space also posed unique problems. Here the first issue was not about internationalism but, rather, "internationality": the idea that "for any piece of land, and for any human being, there should be a definite answer to the question 'which nation is responsible?'"[44] There was no existing sovereign authority in Gaza, although Palestinians certainly claimed that right.[45] UNEF's presence could not solve Gaza's internationality problem. To do so would require political action beyond its mandate to resolve the issues of Palestinian displacement and the absence of a Palestinian state. But by patrolling and therefore protecting the border, UNEF was able to alleviate some of its consequences.

Thus, while Gaza's events helped define the character of UNEF, UNEF's presence helped define the space of Gaza. According to a report produced in 1959 by an employee of CARE (a humanitarian and development agency then working in Gaza): "With UNEF on the borders Gaza's real source of trouble is kept quiet. Before UNEF arrived private investors were afraid to take ventures in an area like Gaza that, in 24 hours, could even cease to exist as Arab territory with Arab inhabitants. If UNEF were to leave, however, there seems every likelihood that political conditions here would go right back to where they were in 1956."[46] Border control, the creation of a security space, also fulfilled a secondary humanitarian function.[47] In this context, establishing a security space was a means of protection in addition to a mechanism of control. The effect of UNEF's presence in Gaza was to produce a security space analogous to the "humanitarian space" of relief organizations.[48] Humanitarian actors describe a humanitarian space as one of both action (enabling the delivery of relief supplies) and survival (protecting people from the often violent conditions that made relief necessary). UNEF's work in the border zone had a similar effect. It did not end conflict or resolve the future status of Gaza, but it did produce stability in the interior for the population.

What did this border security work look like on the ground? It was, for the most part, fairly mundane. UNEF soldiers maintained observation towers along the ADL, conducted regular patrols, and were responsible for apprehending anyone who crossed the line (see Figure 8). One UNEF officer described the work as follows: "Their job of guarding the armistice line was boring. There were no major incidents to the best of my knowledge during the year I was there. Men would sit in observation posts training their binoculars on Israel. Occasionally a few sheep would violate the border."[49] However boring this work may have been, Captain J. A. Swettenham also commented, "Morale was generally high, accounted for by the facts that their strengths contained a high percentage of conscripts who might as well be in Egypt as at home, pay was

FIGURE 8 *Sentry from Swedish UNEF contingent, 1959. Source: UN Photos.*

higher than the national scales, tour of duty in many cases was for only six months, and their light tasks enable them to make full use of leave quotas and welfare trips to Jerusalem in Jordan."[50]

UNEF records show that some people did cross into the border zone and that most such crossings were both benign and banal: the most common sort were farmers working land or shepherds going after animals.[51] The statements that were gathered after any incident (whether or not someone was successfully captured) illuminate the everyday dynamics of the security regime. In one case, two Bedouin who were apprehended with sickle and hoe in hand indicated that they had gone to cut grass and insisted that they did not know that they were not supposed to cross the ADL. This last assertion was disputed by one of the UNEF soldiers who stated that he had seen one of these men "on many occasions in the area where he was apprehended. Many times have I chased him back away from the border."[52] In another incident, a man crossed the line to go after his donkeys, which had strayed into Israel. Under questioning, he acknowledged that he knew it was forbidden and dangerous to cross but did so "because I saw the animals only a few metres inside Israel."[53]

As routinized as patrols largely were, not everything that happened along the border was entirely so predictable or so insignificant. UNEF and the Egyptian Administration had a shared interest in stopping politically motivated border crossings. The response to such incidents underscores the fact that in its border work UNEF always shared responsibility with, and depended on the cooperation of, the Palestinian police and Egyptian security apparatus. In a case in which UNEF soldiers shot and killed one of a group of armed Palestinians caught crossing back from Israeli territory, management of the event was quickly taken over by Egyptian forces. UNEF turned the body over to Egyptian officials and asked them to "endeavor to identify and take action against the other members of the group, who had contravened the regulation against infiltration."[54] These officials quickly reported that the group was made up of "members of auxiliary police who had decided among themselves to make raid into ICT [Israeli Controlled Territory]. . . . They have been arrested and will be tried by military court."[55] This sort of event confirms that it was UNEF's presence, rather than its particular actions, that had the most significant impact on keeping the peace. Not a whole lot happened along the border, but when something of potential significance did happen, Egyptian security personnel took over management of the incident.[56]

Limits and Possibilities of Relations in Gaza

Just as UNEF's structure and mission was formed through an often unpredictable combination of decisions in UN headquarters and events on the grounds, so too were relationships between UNEF soldiers and the Gazan population shaped by the regulations that governed these interactions as well as the encounters (planned and unplanned) that people had on the streets, in military camps, and in other spaces in the Gaza Strip. If UNEF was an ad hoc experiment in peacekeeping, so too was the shape that the international community took when it was brought down to ground in Gaza. UNEF regulations strictly limited the kinds of contacts that its soldiers could have with the Gazan population in large part to avoid problems that might arise from such interactions.

Concern with propriety, here understood as both the preservation of a sense of national pride and a concern about proper gender relations, undergirded these regulations. According to the standing orders: "Members of the force will avoid close contact with the local inhabitants bearing in mind that any of the local population seen frequently in their company may suffer considerable embarrassment as a result."[57] To avoid such embarrassment, personnel were prohibited from going into Gazans' houses without prior coordination and were strictly forbidden to speak with women. Consequently, they "do not normally come into contact with the population except for official purposes."[58] Egyptian policing records make clear that UNEF soldiers did in fact sometimes have social relationships with Gazans and that those relations were cause for some concern.[59] UNEF's presence around the Strip also sometimes created worries among Gazans. Police reports on public opinion recount accusations that UNEF soldiers were involved in fatal traffic accidents and rumors that UNEF forces were permitting Israelis to enter the Strip at night.[60]

As peacekeeping has developed over the years, and as numerous problems in interactions between soldiers and local civilians have occurred, many observers have attributed such problems to a lack of understanding of local cultural forms, political conditions, and meaning systems. Tamara Duffey argues that although such knowledge is vital, "peacekeepers often lack cultural insight into the population they are attempting to develop positive community relations with."[61] Much of the anthropological literature on peacekeeping identifies cultural training as necessary but insufficient in the form it is provided. Rubinstein suggests that soldiers are often supplied with "cultural briefs" that offer some useful tidbits of cultural knowledge (e.g., for the Middle East: don't show the soles of your shoes; don't see women without their headscarves) but provide little real understanding of how people think and act, and therefore of how they may respond to peacekeepers' actions.[62]

A briefing paper prepared for UNEF soldiers, "Some Moslem Belief and Customs," described some basic features of Islam—mosques, prayers, dress, and holidays—as well as "Arab customs" such as hospitality. The note ended with the comment: "Palestinian Arabs have great pride. No matter how wretched or ragged a man may look don't single him out for ridicule and don't laugh at him."[63] Knowing something about the people one comes into contact with is surely a positive thing, but the UNEF experience in Gaza suggests that the work of cultural education that is meant to provide such knowledge can also have the effect of enforcing distance. That is, an effect of this training may have been not only that it failed to furnish soldiers with a sufficiently complex knowledge of local culture but also that in emphasizing cultural differences as the starting point for interactions it helped enforce distance in those interactions. Indeed, the ways that the culture concept can work to produce a sense of otherness even as it is deployed in projects of understanding is one of the oft-raised critiques by anthropologists about this core idea of the discipline.[64]

Social distance has been typical of most peacekeeping operations in which "military personnel are physically separated from the local populations."[65] Rubinstein contrasts this "control and separation" with how humanitarian workers generally operate. When in the course of research with Gazans, I have asked people about their memories of UNEF, the separateness of the force is evident. Most people recalled having almost no personal relationship with UNEF soldiers. Those who did were people who worked in the camps. However much planners wanted UNEF to be perceived as "a friendly and not a warlike force," there were significant constrains in how much its members could be "friends" with Gazans.[66] These regulations were intended to protect UNEF's overall mission, and therefore the ideal of international community that it represented, but they may have done so at the expense of limiting the relationships that could develop in Gaza. One should not, to be sure, overstate what kinds of relationships might have emerged without such regulations, nor imagine that they were the only barrier to such developments, but it is nonetheless significant that a disjuncture between the idea and practice of international community was built into UNEF's operational structure.

The ideals that UNEF was meant to represent did not emanate only from its planners and leaders. Many soldiers sought opportunities within the structured distance of their relationships to reach out to Gazans and express what they identified as humanitarian concern for the population. Charitable giving was the easiest form of such expression. A committee set up to gather such contributions explained: "Beyond their official duties, many of our colleagues, both military and civilian, have on several occasions expressed their desire to do something for those who need help. It is now time that this sentiment of solidarity we all feel in face of such human misery should take a concrete form and that we organise a means of helping the local population."[67] Although some soldiers seem to have objected to charity as a means of resolving the "adverse conditions," many UNEF personnel participated in annual holiday charitable projects. Charitable giving was an unofficial action on the part of UNEF soldiers, but there were occasions when members of the force engaged in ad hoc humanitarian operations in the course of their work. UNEF personnel helped test Gazan children for tuberculosis[68] and they assisted in efforts to fight a locust infestation in 1959, for which they received thanks from the governor-general.[69]

Another sort of good work that seems to have been quite common, judging from its repeated mention in the historical record, was UNEF's provision of water to locals. Because collecting water was women's work,[70] assisting with this activity meant that soldiers did have some interactions with Gazan women, despite the strict prohibition of regulations. A press account, complete with photograph, described this practice as an exchange, in which women traded information on border activity for water.[71] In his memoirs, a Swedish soldier described providing water as a "support task" for a nearby Bedouin camp. Because filling their jars with water made it hard for women to maintain usual standards of modesty among Bedouin women and keep their faces fully covered, Skold described how "the oldest women would come up to the truck while the others carried their jars to a place 5–10 meters away. The old one then filled jar after jar and took them back for the young ones to carry home to the tents."[72] This goodwill effort was thus not only an opportunity for interactions; it also produced at least some small changes in both local practices and the enactment of UNEF regulations. A 1964 report by Swedish researchers on conditions and attitudes among Gazans indicated that UNEF's charitable efforts were well received by the population: "UNRWA did immensely much more in their fields but received little gratitude. . . . They were judged according to what they did not do, whereas the UNEF built up a lot of good will by simple deeds because it was expected to do nothing of the kind and was judged according to what it did."[73]

The positive feelings that such actions apparently engendered were part of a spectrum of reactions to UNEF, some of which were considerably more negative. In 1963, for example, local intelligence personnel reported that people were grumbling about the force's presence and that graffiti had been discovered demanding its withdrawal.[74] Negative feelings were also produced by and sometimes expressed in difficult encounters between UNEF soldiers and Gazans. Reports in UNEF files describe patrols fired on as they drove along the border, roads obstructed by locals who then threw stones at soldiers, public drunkenness by UNEF soldiers, and car accidents that injured or killed Gazans.[75] A report on the experiences of the Colombian battalion in its first year reflected on conditions: "The first reaction of the local populace when the Colombian troops entered . . . was gratefulness and friendly feeling; but apparently at least, this feeling quickly changed, it is not known exactly why; this last position of the local populace has been manifested in some incidents which have consisted in word and work aggression; particularly the thefts committed in spite of the maximum security measures have been very troublesome."[76]

To understand more clearly the relationships that led to the coexistence of positive and negative evaluations of UNEF, it is helpful to look more closely at some of the sites and sorts of encounters between soldiers and Gazans, including confrontations on the streets and challenges in the workplace. It was in these sorts of interactions that the question of propriety arose most clearly. The most sustained opportunities for interactions between soldiers and Gazans were a result of the employment of locals in UNEF camps, serving as working cooks, watchmen, mechanics, batmen, and laborers.[77] When conflicts developed between UNEF personnel and locals, several different ideas framed how those conflicts were understood. At different times, the languages of both cultural specificity and universal humanity were deployed.

In some instances, the language of cultural respect seems to have been used strategically. In one such case (some facts of which were a subject of dispute between UNEF and Egyptian officials), Indian soldiers attempting to take into custody a Palestinian woman who was cutting grass in the border area were challenged (or attacked) by a large group of locals, after which the woman escaped. In a letter to the UNEF commander, the Egyptian military liaison stated: "It is not uncommon in this part of the world in a situation like that, that a relative or relatives spring to the help of a young girl taken away by soldiers who could not, through the difficulty of languages, explain their intentions correctly. According to local customs, which should be understood, this was chivalrous act on the part of the relatives who tried to help the girl in distress."[78] The commander's response did not challenge this claim that local propriety was at stake in this encounter but argued that the attack was inappropriate nonetheless. Propriety was a concept that helped structure the interactions between UNEF soldiers and Gazans, both through formal regulation and through more general concern. It was not, though, a concept with a single, or always a shared, meaning.

In other cases, it was less the culture of Gazans and more the biases of particular UNEF soldiers that seemed to structure the encounter. For example, in one case, a Norwegian soldier on guard at a water tower shot and wounded three Bedouin men who had, as they often did, approached the tower to collect water and, according to the soldier, "on this occasion kept pestering him for cigarettes."[79] However, an investigation of the events revealed negative attributes of this particular soldier. Even though he insisted that he shot at the ground to frighten the men away and that their wounding was accidental, the angle of the shot cast doubt on his story. Further questioning revealed that he had "certain views and prejudices against Arabs" that made him "temperamentally unsuited for continued service with UNEF in this region." Even though such attitudes could not be considered evidentiary in the case at hand, they seem clearly to have influenced a decision to send the soldier back to Norway to stand trial for negligence.[80] Certainly not all UNEF soldiers shared the attitude of this individual, but later experiences with peacekeeping operations confirm that racial and other prejudices cause frequent problems in these missions.[81]

In both of these cases, a lack of understanding about cultural difference seems to have shaped the incident and its interpretation. There were, it should also be noted, plenty of conflicts that seemed to have nothing to do with such matters. When a group of Gazans and Brazilian soldiers got into a physical confrontation that involved stone throwing, theft of goods, and destruction of property (with violence being done by both groups), the response by UNEF officials and Egyptian administrators focused on questions of criminality and proper procedure rather than any claim of cultural misunderstanding.[82]

Challenges that arose in the workplace, for example, were generally not talked about in the language of cultural difference; rather, they were viewed in terms of universal humanity and international community. Palestinians frequently made (and still make) humanity claims as part of their national political struggle; they argued that the international community had responsibility to support their claims both because of their membership in that community and because of that community's obligations to humanity.[83] In contrast to such national claims, the humanity claims to which labor issues gave rise were directed toward smaller-scale ends, focused on improving conditions rather than restoring national rights. The prevalence of this language across different settings speaks to how important it has been to Palestinians.

Given the high rates of unemployment in Gaza at this time—an Egyptian report from 1959 suggested that there was 87 percent unemployment—UNEF work was an important opportunity. Appreciation of the job did not mean, though, that Gazans were quiet in the face of perceived ill treatment. Local employees had a number of complaints about their work environment, many of which were connected to a concern about discriminatory treatment of "locals" in comparison to "internationals." Gazans argued that they were degraded by being checked on their way out of camp for stolen UNEF goods, especially since international staff members were not checked.[84] Describing the widespread complaints to the UNEF commander, the Egyptian military liaison officer noted that employees were referred to in a derogatory manner as "bloody locals" by at least one UNEF officer.[85] Here the complaint was precisely that in dividing people into the categories of "local" and "international," and in treating people differently based on those categories, standards of fairness and equality were undermined.

Other instances of problems in the labor conditions of locals gave rise to even more explicit use of the language of universal humanity. That UN officials regularly concurred with such complaints suggests that this language had broad resonance in principle, even if not always in practice. When night watchmen complained about the hours they were forced to work, they both compared their situation to other employees in Gaza and situated their complaint within the broader UN mission. Their petition stated that neither local police officers nor UNRWA watchmen had to work the hours they did and that both were treated with more compassion when they made mistakes at work. The watchmen pled with the UNEF commander to "be merciful" and change the rules, "taking into consideration that we are poor people, refugees who lost all their property and that the U/Nations [sic] was created to preserve peace all over the world and to do good and justice to all human beings."[86]

The UNEF legal adviser concurred that their working conditions were "contrary to fairness, equity and humanity and needs to be reconsidered in light . . . of the standards laid down in relation to conditions of employment and the right to rest and leisure in such documents as basic and fundamental in the work of the United Nations as the Universal Declaration of Human Rights."[87] Both the petition and the response utilize a language of universalism—expressed in terms of justice, equity, and humanity—and evince sensitivity to the institutional mechanisms required to enact these universal values. Relationships on the ground did not always live up to these universal standards, nor did they indicate an entirely comfortable relationship between Gazans and UNEF soldiers.

If the international community was in part a space of concrete relations, these complicated interactions confirm it had no unitary form. This relationship developed within structured limits. It was sometimes characterized by acrimony and mutual suspicion, highlighting the challenges of engagement. It was also sometimes characterized by appreciation and respect, confirming that this possibility was never wholly absent.

Whatever tensions existed among UNEF soldiers, Gazan locals, and Egyptian officials, the fact that UNEF's basic mission—to keep the peace—was accomplished successfully for ten years should not be forgotten. When UNEF disbanded, the disappointment of many UN members was acute. They mourned what they saw as the failure of this new instrument for peace. The UN secretary-general acknowledged this disappointment: "We must remember that United Nations peace keeping is a highly novel and sophisticated concept. . . . [W]e must face the fact that the world is not yet altogether ready for such sophisticated and reasonable concepts and methods."[88] The end of UNEF did not, of course, mean the end of UN peacekeeping. It did, though, require an evaluation of what kind of instrument peacekeeping was and what its place was in the broader field of humanity's law. The work of peacekeeping forces such as UNEF illuminates both the universalist ideals such interventions are intended to promote and the ways that ideas such as international community are experienced in encounters between peacekeeping personnel and local populations. In interventions like peacekeeping, lofty ideas about global possibility are worked out in small-scale and frequently messy interactions among people. The presence of UNEF in Gaza underscores the importance of the "international community" as both an actor in and an audience for the local security society.

Conclusion
The Policing Imperative

THE EXTENSIVE SECURITY APPARATUS developed to police the Gaza Strip during the Egyptian Administration was guided by intersecting concerns about national interest, social propriety, and everyday illegality. In pursuit of security in each of these areas, the police extended their reach across the public domain and into many aspects of private life. In this process, Palestinians were identified as, at once, security threats and vulnerable subjects who needed protection. And both threat and protection seemed to require expansive policing. That this police practice—with its heavy surveillance, emphasis on informing, and often severe punishments—exerted a repressive influence on life in Gaza is beyond dispute. This judgment is not, however, a sufficient stopping point for understanding its impact on Gazans. Even as policing in Gaza was not generally characterized by the liberal technique of "letting things happen,"[1] it was a space for getting things done, both by the police and by people. Even as I identify the capacity for action that remained within this expansive and repressive police apparatus, I remain cognizant of the tremendous constraints on possibility the system created as well as the real violence it sometimes did. Even so, the Gazan instance indicates the range of things that people do and the variety of ways they press their claims even within a highly repressive environment. It also shows the extent to which police are responsive to this reality and how police practices can provide a way for people to exert influence.

One of the most constraining forms of police activity—widespread surveillance—was also a particularly important mechanism for making the government aware of popular demands. With a focus on the documentation of "public opinion" (*al-ra'y al-'amm*), surveillance provided an avenue for petitioning the administration. For instance, the frequent complaints about high prices and the failure of merchants to adhere to price controls that appear in police reports on public opinion are often followed by a statement that the people "wish the authorities would find a solution,"[2] and that "the authorities need to impose supervision."[3] These demands did sometimes produce a response. After many reports of complaints about prices, the governor-general held a meeting with merchants and declared that they must obey price controls so that "all citizens, and especially those with limited incomes, can meet their basic needs."[4] A central feature of Gaza's security dynamic was that the mechanisms and categories through which control was exerted were also the avenues through which people could act.

Gaza's security society was centrally shaped by the specificities arising from the 1948 *nakba*. All Gazans were technically stateless—targets of humanitarian intervention and sources of the particular security concerns caused by displacement and dispossession—even as the category of "Palestinian citizen" continued to matter for how they were governed and policed. These facts made uncertainty both a fundamental, existential condition and a security technique that could be operationalized by police personnel. Demographic categories like "native" and "refugee"; political status categories like "citizen," "refugee," and "humanity"; and policing categories like "criminal," "spy," and "informer" were all unstable and at the same time crucial for security practice. Suspicion structured many relationships, but that suspicion did not foreclose either action or connection. Rather, suspicion, uncertainty, and instability were all key features in policing as governance and in policing as a means of action.

To the extent that people were able to get things done through the mechanisms of security society, it was not through proposing a counternarrative to the discourse of threat or an alternative Gazan subjectivity to that proffered by the security apparatus. Rather, they operated from within those positions to generate leverage for change or advantage. Simply being Palestinian made people both potential threats and objects of care. And being all those things sometimes created opportunities for impact and effect. The identification of the people as a security threat motivated and mandated a broad system of surveillance and deep involvement in all aspects of life. The extent of this perceived danger also meant that the people in action—whether through protest, public talk, or even general discontent—were not always and only repressed but could sometimes generate a recalculation of the threat landscape to result in a change of policy. In addition to deploying the idea of the people, the identification of security threats also divided the collectivity into constituent parts (both arrays of categories and assortments of individuals) that could police each other. And here too, Gazans sometimes used the language of threat, to national interest and moral order, as a means of exerting control over other Gazans. This happened both through forms of social policing and by requesting direct police intervention. This array of security practices deepened people's entrenchment in complex webs of relations and produced a degree of distance among them, in large part by increasing their suspicions of one another.

The breadth of surveillance, the layered work of reputation making, and the range of concerns that circulated in Gaza are captured in a series of reports in 1960 about one Ibrahim, a resident of the Maghazi refugee camp in the central Gaza Strip. The first report was generated by the receipt of information that two UN Emergency Force (UNEF) soldiers had been seen entering Ibrahim's house. When questioned, Ibrahim said that they had come for dinner. He worked as a "barman" at the UNEF headquarters in Gaza City. A further report by a police officer indicated that Ibrahim had thrown a party for a Canadian officer because he believed the officer respected the Arab workers and tried to help them. This report concluded by noting that Ibrahim "has good morals and a good reputation and is not now engaged in any activity to harm that reputation." The third report, though, traced his personal history and offered a somewhat less positive evaluation. In 1951 he went illegally to Egypt, where he worked with British forces in the Suez Canal zone. He returned to Gaza with a certificate from the British and began working as a cook for the UN Relief and Works Agency for Palestine Refugees in the Near East (UNRWA). During the 1956 Israeli occupation he worked as a cook for the Israeli governor of Deir al-Balah and informed on people who had weapons. He was seen going to the Israeli intelligence office frequently. After the Israeli withdrawal he left to Saudi Arabia for a year and then returned to work for UNEF. A year prior he had requested permission to own a gun, a request that was denied because of his behavior during the Israeli occupation and his poor reputation at that time.[5] Reputation, so important in how people were policed and what opportunities they had, was also changeable and even ephemeral.

Most people in Gaza were not entangled in quite as many problematic relationships as was Ibrahim, and his story is especially useful in showcasing the security landscape. What people thought of him, his reputation in the community, was relevant information for the police. That he had a social connection with internationals was what brought him to the attention of the police and was clearly of interest to them, and a possible cause for concern, as was the fact that he worked as a barman (in the report this English word is transliterated into Arabic). Worries about politics and propriety came together in this observation. That he had previously crossed the border illegally made criminality part of his profile. And his earlier work for Israeli occupation forces, especially acting as an informant, added treachery on top of that. What security personnel did with all this information is not included in the available documentary record, as with so many of the stories and encounters I have described. Since Ibrahim was not, at the time of reporting, engaged in any problematic activity, I expect that the information was simply made part of his file (as if that were a small thing!). Whereas before he invited UNEF soldiers into his home he may have existed for the police primarily as part of larger categories—"Palestinian," "refugee," "camp resident"—he was henceforth also an individual subject and probably perennial suspect.[6] His individuality then contributed additional meaning to the collective categories of which he was a member. Such was the work of wide and deep policing: it both identified suspect categories and persons (producing opportunities for police involvement) and contributed to a generalized condition of uncertainty and suspicion (ensuring the possibility of such involvement even in the absence of a particular opportunity).

The policing of Gaza under Egyptian rule, the policing of Egypt under Nasser and after, and the policing of much of the rest of the world indicate a security imperative to collect and retain, even if not always to parse, vast quantities of information. In Gaza and Egypt under Nasser this collection relied primarily on the low-tech deployment of large numbers of police personnel and the engagement of a broad sector of the population. Governments are increasingly relying on higher-tech methods of information gathering, but the imperative remains the same. The dynamics of policing and security work in Gaza show that increased surveillance is not simply a matter of security personnel imposing themselves on people and intruding into their lives, although it surely is that, but also a matter of people inviting the police into their lives and sometimes seeking an expanded security presence. When we seek to understand what is an increasingly global security society, we have to account for this feature of policing dynamics.

Security dynamics in Egyptian-ruled Gaza shed light on enduring questions about the mechanisms by which people come to participate in repressive police projects. As significant as coercion is in such participation, it is only part of the answer. Policing records describe an array of circumstances of participation. These include seeking personal advantage, making calculations that other threats were greater than police intrusion, and even belief in the policing project. People's participation in surveillance was not always clandestine, and sometimes it wasn't entirely under police control. In 1960 a teacher was brought in for questioning because the police had information that he was claiming to be a "Criminal Investigation Department [CID] representative" who could do anything he wanted to any of his colleagues at the school.[7] Ahmad answered this charge by saying that "this republican government is an Arab government built on the basis of the people governing themselves," and that he was only doing his national duty.

He was responding, he said, to a social problem in the school that posed a danger to "public security, Arab unity, and the Arab people." This problem was a conflict of political opinion among the teachers and principal in the school. He gave several instances of anti-Nasser behavior by others in the school, including that the principal had refused permission to a teacher's request that a student recite a recent speech by Nasser "giving the communists and collaborators in the Arab world a tough time." What precisely led Ahmad to take up the mission of policing the school, and to cloak himself in CID authority he had not been granted when he did so, cannot be known. But his motivations were clearly something more than simple coercion (especially since he was not asked to take on this role). He was trying to get something done, perhaps for himself, perhaps for his Gazan community, perhaps for his Arab nation, and deploying the tactics and authority of the police seemed to be the way to do it.

This instance, like so many others, also confirms the connection between moral concern and the policing of politics. Both were matters that troubled the government and its security forces as well as the public and its constituent parts. Both involved the exercise of power, as imposition and as persuasion. Both operated to constrain people's activities while at the same time sometimes creating new avenues for action. To understand how the police extended their reach across and into the diverse spaces of life in Gaza, it has been necessary to consider both. In this process, and in relation to both propriety and politics, fear was a key component. People feared police violence, and they also feared popular illegality and immorality. They worried about the effects on themselves and their families of a refusal to participate, and they worried about the effects on their community of failures to engage in social policing. People also saw the police as a source of protection: against political enemies, moral threats, and criminal activity. Each of these forms and sites of fear were at once produced and manipulated by security services and arose out of the conditions in which people lived.

Gaza's experience shows that techniques of security and surveillance also provide means for pursuing other politics. The control, invited and imposed, exercised by security systems does not have to be the end of the story. As we think about what conditions are necessary for civic and political action now—a question that has tremendous importance—it is worth remembering that the possibility of such action can exist even in highly policed and constrained circumstances. Large collective protests and individual acts of explicit resistance are among these possibilities.[8] And so too are smaller-scale efforts to shift the landscape. We can refuse the categories of suspicion that often make us willing, and sometimes even eager, to participate in these systems. We can try to find other means of building collectivity and pursuing politics.[9] The lives of Gazans under Egyptian rule and our lives today, in whatever country we live, are shaped in this nexus of possibility and constraint.

Policing After Egypt

The Egyptian Administration of Gaza ended with the Israeli occupation of the Strip (along with the West Bank, the Golan Heights, and the Sinai) in June 1967. The occupation introduced new security dynamics and new policing imperatives. Both the military forces (Palestine Liberation Army and fedayeen) supported by Egyptian authorities and independent Palestinian organizations took up active resistance against the occupation. And Israeli occupiers, despite their preference for a relatively "invisible occupation" whenever possible,[10] acted aggressively to stamp out this resistance.[11] In a counterinsurgency campaign under Ariel Sharon's command, Israeli forces killed large numbers of Gazans, bulldozed large portions of the refugee camps (to create wide roads that enabled easy military access), and ultimately established Jewish settlements throughout Gaza.[12] In addition to "thinning out" the refugee camps through bulldozing, Israeli authorities sought to encourage movement out of the camps by building new neighborhoods elsewhere in Gaza.[13]

The counterinsurgency campaign succeeded in undercutting organized resistance for many years, but not in creating consent to Israeli rule. Many Palestinians continued government work, making the practical choice to support their families in circumstances of what looked to be a long-term occupation. This included many police officers. And as in other colonial conflict situations, these Palestinian police were put in a difficult position. One retired police officer described to me the efforts of police to keep themselves apart from the security operations of the occupation. He recalled how the army tried to use the police in their efforts to capture members of the resistance. For instance:

> There was someone that they knew was working for the [Palestine Liberation Organization, or PLO]. They wanted to catch him. They had a map and they knew where his house was. They took me and another policeman in their jeep. We came to the street and they asked me to knock on the door. But

this is impossible—if I knocked, the owner of the house would come out and see me before his eyes. Then the army would come in. I would not survive twenty-four hours before being shot and killed. The owner of the house would say, 'This is the policeman who brought them.' . . . When I refused I was hit.

Abu Said went on to tell me that he was able to convince the authorities that they should not put Palestinian policemen at risk in this way. This accommodation lasted until the outbreak of the First Intifada in 1987, at which point "they started to humiliate us. They obliged us to wear uniforms day and night." The intifada changed many things.[14] It was not until the uprising that working in the police came to be widely seen as a form of collaboration. The Unified Leadership of the Uprising (UNLU) ordered policemen to resign.[15] Those who did were paid a salary by the PLO to compensate for their lost income.[16]

The creation of the Palestinian Authority (PA) as a result of the 1993 Oslo Accords and the subsequent withdrawal of Israel from direct administrative work in the occupied territories led to another shift in policing. Making policing more "indigenous" also meant bringing along some of the same expansion of security services found in other Arab countries, in this instance in pursuit of Israeli security as much as Palestinian regime stability. The terms of the agreement established six security branches, with a heavy emphasis on political rather than civil crime.[17] The agreement also created a jurisdictional separation between internal and external security: Palestinian police were responsible for controlling the population within the PA's areas of authority and Israeli forces continued to operate against perceived Palestinian threats.

After the outbreak of the Second Intifada (Al-Aqsa Intifada), these security arrangements were destabilized. Not only did the Palestinian policing of Palestinians on behalf of Israel become increasingly untenable in the face of Israeli military assaults on population centers, but the reoccupation of Palestinian cities brought an end to civilian policing. As the Second Intifada wound down, with no gains for Palestinians, security services became a focus (perhaps the central focus) of international donors.[18] In the West Bank numerous resources have been put into training and deploying a professionalized and effective security apparatus.[19] The goal of this interest, and the purpose of the apparatus, is to control Palestinian militancy and to increase the security of Israel and Israelis. As with much about the post-Oslo world, the Palestinian population has often been the target rather than the beneficiary of this security work.[20]

Gaza has had a different security trajectory. Israel pulled its settlers and soldiers out in 2005, henceforth conducting its occupation from the borders (including the sea).[21] The territory came under the control of Hamas in 2007.[22] Policing was an area in which Hamas sought to distinguish itself from what it deemed to be Fatah's failure to maintain security.[23] As Yezid Sayigh noted in 2010:

> The Hamas-run Ministry of Interior exercises effective control over its operational branches and civilian departments alike, and largely accords its civil police the primacy claimed, but not yet attained, by its West Bank counterpart service. Keenly aware of deep public discontent with the armed lawlessness of the pre-2007 era, the Hanieh government has consistently stressed security as its particular strong suit, and has been notably successful in imposing its overall control and basic law and order (and not merely through intimidation and coercion), as even its critics acknowledge.[24]

Reflecting on the broad security milieu under Hamas rule, Nathan Brown describes a situation that bears great similarity to the conditions described in this book: "It is an authoritarianism that polices and regulates opposition but allows it to operate within certain limits, enforces a set of constantly shifting red lines to govern political speech and action in public, and screens government employees for their political loyalties."[25] Brown explicitly compares the security dynamic, both policing practices and public responses, to Egypt under Mubarak.[26]

Governing and security dynamics in Egypt also remain relevant to the situation in Gaza. Gaza has been under an Israeli instigated blockade since 2007.[27] Since the southern part of Gaza borders Egypt, this blockade could have been successful only with Egyptian cooperation. And under Mubarak, the Egyptian government heavily controlled movement in and out of Gaza. After Hamas took control of Gaza, and therefore also of the Rafah border crossing into Egypt, the Egyptian government formally closed the border. In practice, the crossing was opened on an ad hoc basis, with the claim of humanitarian concern.[28] At the same time, despite its significant security concerns, the government took only limited action against the extensive network of tunnels that had been developed for the import of otherwise banned goods into Gaza. These tunnels were vital for the economy and survival of the Strip, and they were a significant source of income for Hamas.

When Mubarak was deposed in February 2011, many Palestinians hoped for a dramatically different Egyptian policy toward Gaza. This was not forthcoming. Whether under military rule (first in the form of the Supreme Council of the Armed Forces, and later under the rule of General Sisi) or under Muhammad Morsi (Muslim Brotherhood), promises to fully open the border have not been fulfilled. The fall of Mubarak did reinvigorate Gaza's place in the Egyptian discourse of security threats. And here there were differences between Muslim Brotherhood and military rule. Even as the Morsi government never implemented the freedom of movement that Palestinians hoped for, one of the charges made against it in Egypt was precisely that it was collaborating with the Hamas government in Gaza. Rumors circulated that Hamas was sending money and fighters to the Sinai to destabilize the Egyptian government and Islamize the area.

In the wake of the military takeover of its government in July 2013, Egypt intensified the project that had already begun under Morsi to destroy the tunnels that had served as a vital lifeline for the Strip.[29] According to a UN official, by the end of July of that year, 80 percent of the tunnels had been destroyed, leading to shortages of fuel and building materials.[30] At the same time, the military made statements that suggested a willingness to launch attacks on perceived security threats in Gaza.[31] When Israel attacked Gaza in July 2014, the government of newly elected President Sisi was ambivalent about, or even supportive of, the assault. The intense hostility to the Muslim Brotherhood that dominated Egyptian public discourse after the military coup carried over, seemingly in its entirety, to the evaluation of Hamas and interpretation of events in Gaza. During the Egyptian Administration of Gaza, Gazans were perceived as both threats and objects of protection. In 2014, they increasingly appeared to be viewed by the Egyptian government, and a portion of the Egyptian people, solely as threats. I cannot predict where things will go from here. One thing is certain: the story of Egypt and Gaza's entangled security relation continues.

Notes

Introduction

1. Israel State Archives (ISA), RG 115, box 2007, unnumbered file, police reports from March 22 and March 26, 1961.

2. Ibid., police reports from November 19 and December 17, 1961.

3. Ibid., police reports from April 30, May 9, and May 17, 1964.

4. Service and security are invariably intertwined. I explore the complex work of bureaucratic service in my first book: Ilana Feldman, *Governing Gaza: Bureaucracy, Authority, and the Work of Rule, 1917–67* (Durham, NC: Duke University Press, 2008). This study of policing should be seen as a companion to that project.

5. Rashid Khalidi, "The Palestinians and 1948: The Underlying Causes of Failure," in *The War for Palestine*, ed. Eugene L. Rogan and Avi Shlaim, 12–36 (Cambridge: Cambridge University Press, 2001), 12.

6. Fawaz Gerges, "Egypt and the 1948 War: Internal Conflict and Regional Ambition," in *The War for Palestine*, ed. Eugene L. Rogan and Avi Shlaim (Cambridge: Cambridge University Press, 2001), 150–175.

7. Avi Shlaim, "The Rise and Fall of the All-Palestine Government in Gaza," *Journal of Palestine Studies* 20, 1 (Fall 1990): 37–53.

8. Ilana Feldman, "Waiting for Palestine: Refracted Citizenship and Latent Sovereignty in Gaza," *Citizenship Studies* 12, 5 (2008): 447–463, 453.

9. Feldman, *Governing Gaza*.

10. Feldman, "Waiting for Palestine." For discussion of ways that ideas about citizenship were affected by humanitarian practice, see Ilana Feldman, "Difficult Distinctions: Refugee Law, Humanitarian Practice, and Political Identification in Gaza," *Cultural Anthropology* 22, 1 (2007): 129–169.

11. Policing in Gaza under Egyptian rule was also part of a broader landscape of postcolonial security states across the Arab world. See Volker Perthes, "*Si vis stabilitatem, para bellum*: State Building, National Security, and War Preparation in Syria," in *War, Institutions, and Social Change in the Middle East*, ed. Steven Heydemann, 149–173 (Berkeley: University of California Press, 2000); Elizabeth Picard, "State and Society in the Arab

World: Towards a New Role for the Security Services?" in *The Many Faces of National Security in the Arab World*, ed. Bahgat Korany, Paul Noble, and Rex Brynen, 258–274 (New York: St. Martin's Press, 1993); Dale Eickelman and M. G. Dennison, "Arabizing the Omani Intelligence Services: Clash of Cultures?" *International Journal of Intelligence and Counterintelligence* 7 (1994): 1–28; Lisa Wedeen, *Ambiguities of Domination: Politics, Rhetoric, and Symbols in Contemporary Syria* (Chicago: University of Chicago Press, 1999).

12. As Curtis Ryan describes it, "Police surveillance and arbitrary arrest were pervasive features of the repressive apparatus of the Nasserist state." Curtis Ryan, "Political Strategies and Regime Survival in Egypt," *Journal of Third World Studies* 18, 2 (2001): 34.

13. Peter Mansfield, *Nasser's Egypt* (Baltimore, MD: Penguin Books, 1965), 211. For a fictionalized account of the effects of the prison experience, see Sonallah Ibrahim, *That Smell* (New York: New Directions, 2013), along with his *Notes from Prison*. Ibrahim is an Egyptian novelist who spent time in prison for communist activity during this period.

14. Virginia Sherry, "Security Forces Practices in Egypt," *Criminal Justice Ethics* 12, 2 (1993): 2, 42–44.

15. One of the events that catalyzed millions to go out into the streets was the death by beating of a young man, Khaled Said, at the hands of policemen, apparently because he had a video recording of police involvement in a drug deal. At the same time, one of the things that made many Egyptians wary of the unfolding of events in the first years after Mubarak's ouster was the relative disappearance of public order and security (crime increased and rumors about crime increased even more) and the absence of the police from the streets. The July 2013 military coup not only returned a general to power but also brought an emboldened security apparatus back into full action.

16. Laleh Khalili, *Time in the Shadows: Confinement in Counterinsurgencies* (Stanford, CA: Stanford University Press, 2013).

17. Sir Charles Jeffries, *The Colonial Police* (London: Max Parrish, 1952), 153; Laleh Khalili, "The Location of Palestine in Global Counterinsurgencies," *International Journal of Middle East Studies* 42, 3 (2010): 413–433, 417.

18. PRO/National Archives, Colonial Office (CO) 850/268/1, "Malayan Personnel: Police—clarification of Position of Ex-Palestine Police Officers"; 850/267/10, "Malayan Personnel: Police—re-engagement terms."

19. Georgina Sinclair, *Colonial Policing and the Imperial Endgame, 1945–1980* (Manchester, UK: Manchester University Press, 2006), 115.

20. James Ferguson, "Seeing Like an Oil Company: Space, Security, and Global Capital in Neoliberal Africa," *American Anthropologist* 107, 3 (2005): 377–382.

21. David Anderson, "Policing the Settler State: Colonial Hegemony in Kenya, 1900–1952." Responding to reports about a lack of police discipline, the Arab paper *Filastin* (June 29, 1921) rejected them as part of a smear campaign launched by the Zionist press against the "national police."

22. Frantz Fanon, *The Wretched of the Earth* (New York: Grove Press, 1965); Adam Hochschild, *King Leopold's Ghost: A Story of Greed, Terror, and Heroism in Colonial Africa* (Boston: Houghton Mifflin, 1999).

23. Priya Satia, "The Defense of Inhumanity: Air Control in Iraq and the British Idea of Arabia," *American Historical Review* 111 (February 2006); Caroline Elkins, *Imperial Reckoning: The Untold Story of Britain's Gulag in Kenya* (New York: Henry Holt, 2005).

24. See Steven Pierce, "Punishment and the Political Body: Flogging and Colonialism in Northern Nigeria," in *Discipline and the Other Body: Correction, Corporeality, Colonialism*, ed. Steven Pierce and Anupama Rao, 186–214 (Durham, NC: Duke University Press, 2006).

25. CO 733/180/1/771015, April 8, 1930, letter from Dowbiggin to Chancellor.

26. R. J. B. Spicer, a key figure in the development of the Palestine police who was inspector general from 1931 to 1937, argued strongly in favor of regulating marriage between British police and Jewish women (these were the most frequent sorts of international marriages). He suggested that marriage be disallowed during an initial three-year probationary period (CO 733/195/87015, November 19, 1931, letter from officer administering the government to Cunliffe-Lister, secretary of state for the colonies). In spite of the concerns raised about the legality of such a rule by other officials, he was adamant about its importance (CO 733/212/97015, August 15, 1932; CO 733/229/17215, August 23, 1933). He believed that upon such a marriage "the man loses all standing and value as a Policeman" (CO 733/229/17215, May 10, 1933, extract of conversation between Spicer and Downie).

27. CO 935/4/2, Dowbiggin Report, 71. In a memoir about his service in the force Colin Imray comments, "One of RGB's [Spicer] profitable ideas was that British and Palestinians should patrol together and learn each other's way of life." Colin Imray, *Policeman in Palestine*, (Bideford, UK: Edward Gaskell, 1995), 33. In his history of the force Edward Horne also notes the importance of this change: "Now by merging the work of the British and the Palestinians, some very good results emerged. It bred a new police spirit in the British section, it stiffened the Palestinian personnel and made them much more resolute and finally it led to a greater understanding between all races in the force and the morale and efficiency of the men rose accordingly." Edward Horne, *A Job Well Done (Being a History of the Palestine Police Force 1920–1948)* (Essex, UK: Anchor Press, 1982), 168.

28. As fond as they might be of "the natives," and many of them were very fond, British police generally viewed the Palestinian Arab population as lawless and a bit uncivilized. Roger Courtney, for example, averred: "Surely there never were people so ready to murder one another as Arabs. Gentlemanly and dignified though they were in their ordinary moments, especially with strangers or guests, the fact remained that when they *did* let themselves go, they went crazy." Roger Courtney, *Palestine Policeman: An Account of Eighteen Dramatic Months in the Palestine Police Force During the Great Jew-Arab Troubles* (London: Herbert Jenkins, 1939), 100. Courtney argued that this absence of self-control resulted from a lack of proper discipline of children. He commented: "An Arab child was regarded

by his parents as sacrosanct. He was never spanked. He was allowed to do just as he liked. It is impossible to think of children more spoiled—not even the children of the Jews, with whom child worship certainly was bad enough. . . . Consequently, undisciplined from without and even more undisciplined within himself, the average Arab grew up into a pretty poor specimen of a man so far as control of his passions was concerned" (ibid.).

29. Imray, *Policeman in Palestine*, 40.

30. Palestine Police Force, *Annual Administrative Report*, 1938, 1.

31. Horne, *A Job Well Done*, 142.

32. Most of the fighting during the revolt took place in the northern part of Palestine, and people from Gaza often went north to participate. This geographic distance from the center of the revolt without doubt affected conditions of policing in Gaza, although it is clear that it did not exempt Gaza from tensions. As far as local manifestation of the revolt was concerned, it was mostly expressed through the bombing of railroad tracks and utility lines.

33. Gad Krozier, "From Dowbiggen to Tegart: Revolutionary Change in the Colonial Police in Palestine During the 1930s," *Journal of Imperial and Commonwealth History* 32, 2 (2004): 115–133, 129.

34. Louis Althusser, *Lenin and Philosophy* (New York: Monthly Review Press, 1971).

35. Ian Loader and Aogan Mulcahy, *Policing and the Condition of England* (Oxford: Oxford University Press, 2003), 40; Max Weber, "Politics as a Vocation," in *Essays in Sociology*, ed. H. H. Garth and C. W. Mills, 26–45 (New York: Macmillan, 1946).

36. Michel Foucault, *Discipline and Punish: The Birth of the Prison*, trans. Alan Sheridan (New York: Vintage Books, 1979).

37. David Arnold, "The Armed Police and Colonial Rule in South India, 1914–1947," *Modern Asian Studies* 11, 1 (1977): 101–25; Stuart M. Hall et al. *Policing the Crisis: Mugging, the State, and Law and Order* (New York: Holmes & Meier, 1978); Gary W. Potter and Victor E. Kappeler, eds., *Constructing Crime: Perspectives on Making News and Social Problems* (Prospect Heights, IL: Waveland Press, 1998).

38. David Lyon, ed., *Surveillance as Social Sorting: Privacy, Risk and Automated Discrimination* (New York: Routledge, 2002); David Lyon, *Surveillance Studies: An Overview* (New York: Polity, 2007).

39. Peter Nyers, "Abject Cosmopolitanism: The Politics of Protection in the Anti-Deportation Movement," *Third World Quarterly* 22, 6 (2010): 1069–1093.

40. William Garriott, ed., *Policing and Contemporary Governance: The Anthropology of Police in Practice* (New York: Palgrave Macmillan, 2013).

41. Ian Loader, "Policing, Recognition, and Belonging," *Annals of the American Academy of Political and Social Science* 605, 1 (2006): 201–221.

42. Ibid., 208.

43. Ibid., 214.

44. Ibid., 215.

45. Ibid., 214.

46. Loader (ibid.) indicates that deep policing gives people confidence about their place in community and a shared pursuit of security. In the case of Gaza—and in other places as well—the shaping effects of policing were not necessarily so stabilizing or comforting.

47. Michel Foucault, *Security, Territory, Population: Lectures at the College de France, 1977–1978*, ed. Michel Senellart (New York: Macmillan, 2009), 20.

48. Ibid., 45.

49. Ibid., 21.

50. Ibid., 11.

51. Hannah Arendt, *The Origins of Totalitarianism* (San Diego, CA: Harcourt Brace Jovanovich, 1968); Oleg Kharkhordin, "The Soviet Individual: Genealogy of a Dissimulating Animal," in *Global Modernities*, ed. Mike Featherstone, Scott Lash, and Roland Robertson, 209–226 (London: Sage, 1995).

52. Partha Chatterjee, *Politics of the Governed: Reflections of Popular Politics in Most of the World* (New York: Columbia University Press, 2006).

53. He states that he does not say much about the "dark side of political society" precisely because he "cannot claim to fully understand how criminality or violence are tied to the ways in which various deprived population groups must struggle to make their claims to governmental care" (Chatterjee, *Politics of the Governed*, 75).

54. This dynamic illustrates Michel Foucault's argument that government operates through simultaneously individualizing and totalizing operations. See Colin Gordon, "The Soul of the Citizen: Max Weber and Michel Foucault on Rationality and Government," in *Max Weber, Rationality and Modernity*, ed. Scott Lash and Sam Whimster, 293–316 (Boston: Allen & Unwin, 1987).

55. Arendt, *Origins of Totalitarianism*, 423–425.

56. I use the word *propriety* to gloss a range of Arabic terms that speak to proper and improper behavior—*adab, akhlaq, 'aib, haram*—all of which appear in the record of police work.

57. Asef Bayat, *Life as Politics: How Ordinary People Change the Middle East* (Stanford, CA: Stanford University Press, 2010).

58. See Feldman, *Governing Gaza*, chapter 5, for an extended discussion of the complexity of care under duress.

59. On "critical," see Veena Das, *Critical Events* (Cambridge: Oxford University Press, 1995). On "exemplary," see Lisa Wedeen, "Seeing Like a Citizen, Acting Like a State: Exemplary Events in Unified Yemen," *Comparative Studies in Society and History* 45, 4 (2003): 680–713.

60. Veena Das (*Critical Events*, 6) suggests that such events introduce "new modes of action." Sally Falk Moore argues that they can redirect social processes and "reflect instability and incipient change." "From Tribes and Traditions to Composites and Conjunctures," *Social Analysis* (2005): 254–272, 255.

Chapter 1

1. Dar Al-Watha'iq (DW), Qawa'im Al-Mushir, group 33, file 36/s/g/26-1, "Palestine Affairs Administration—Armistice."

2. Such training was a long-standing part of Palestinian police practice. Ottoman regulations for municipal police, for example, mandated that they "patrol the beat assigned to them and carry out their duties in the proper manner. . . . They may not speak to persons in the streets save in connection with their duties." The law further stated that municipal sergeants "may not sit in drinking shops, coffee shops, or casinos. They may however sit outside coffee shops to rest" (CO 733, file 57397, A. S. Mavrogordato, E. Mills, W. J. Johnson, and R. E. H. Crosbie, report on municipal and local policing, June 30, 1927, appendix C). These rules against socializing while on duty seem designed to enforce professional distance.

3. Efforts to manage this problem during the Mandate included trying not to station policemen in their homes districts until well into their careers, as well as projects to increase solidarity within the force, and therefore among Jewish, Arab, and British personnel (CO 733/180/1/771015, letter from Dowbiggin to Chancellor, April 8, 1930; CO 935/4/2, Dowbiggin Report, 71).

4. American Friends Service Committee Archives (AFSC), file 29, FS Sect Palestine, background material on Nuseirat, March 15, 1949.

5. Ibid.; AFSC, file 41, FS Sect Palestine, February 18, 1949; AFSC, file 30, FS Sect Palestine, February 22, 1949. AFSC reports also describe the involvement of Palestinian police in keeping order during rations distribution: "Tall, mustached Abdul Kareem, of the Palestinian Police stands guard. He wears the dark uniform of the local gendarmes, and their wide, high black lambs-wool hat, and carries a stick. . . . Despite the policeman's best efforts, people creep into the enclosure. He clears it out vigorously one minute. Ten minutes later twenty people, tall sheiks, colorful Bedouin women in their heavy coins, shy refugee women with their veils held in their teeth, often with a nursing infant under it, old men and frisky little boys, fill the place" ("background material on Nuseirat").

6. Abu Iyad and Eric Rouleau, *My Home, My Land: A Narrative of the Palestinian Resistance*, trans. Linda Butler Koseoglu (New York: Times Books, 1981), 13.

7. For discussion of the tensions between native Gazans and refugees, see Ilana Feldman, "Difficult Distinctions: Refugee Law, Humanitarian Practice, and Political Identification in Gaza," *Cultural Anthropology* 22, 1 (2007): 129–169; Ilana Feldman, "Home as a Refrain: Remembering and Living Displacement in Gaza," *History and Memory* 18, 2 (2006): 10–47.

8. Colonial policing was often underpinned by anxiety about native inscrutability and irrationality. This is what Partha Chatterjee, looking at British colonialism in India, has called "the rule of colonial difference." *The Nation and Its Fragments: Colonial and Postcolonial Histories* (Princeton, NJ: Princeton University Press, 1993). Arjun Appadurai identifies fear, and often hatred, of minorities as being at the heart of what he calls "preda-

tory identities." *Fear of Small Numbers: An Essay on the Geography of Anger* (Durham, NC: Duke University Press, 2006), 51.

9. Michelle Alexander, *The New Jim Crow: Mass Incarceration in the Age of Colorblindness* (New York: New Press, 2012).

10. Didier Fassin, *Enforcing Order: An Ethnography of Urban Policing* (Malden, MA: Polity, 2013).

11. Juliana Ochs, *Security and Suspicion: An Ethnography of Everyday Life in Israel* (Philadelphia: University of Pennsylvania Press, 2011), 83. Ochs also notes the gap between the effectiveness of this practice of suspicion in identifying actual militants and its effect in producing and reproducing racial categories: "Publicly circulated imaginaries of suspicion did not necessarily correspond to the appearance of Palestinian militants, and people's everyday vigilance rarely deterred Palestinian bombers" (Ochs, *Security and Suspicion*, 84). In the United States the conviction that suspicion is a security technique is summed up in the phrase "if you see something, say something," which has proliferated, especially in public transit spaces, after 9/11.

12. Stuart Hall et al., *Policing the Crisis: Mugging, the State, and Law and Order* (New York: Holmes and Meier, 1978).

13. Teresa Caldeira, *City of Walls: Crime, Segregation, and Citizenship in São Paulo* (Berkeley: University of California Press, 2000).

14. Neither the divide between governor and governed nor differences within the population were understood in racial terms. This is not to say that racial—or more commonly color—difference does not matter, either in Palestine or in the Middle East more generally. It does, but it was not a key category of suspicion.

15. Surveying the European landscape, Hannah Arendt famously identified statelessness as a key boundary of political possibility. In her view, what people were most deprived of in the loss of a polity were not the specific rights of citizens, but their ability to be human. She described the capacity to make "opinions significant and actions effective" (Hannah Arendt, *The Origins of Totalitarianism* [San Diego, CA: Harcourt Brace Jovanovich, 1968], 296) as the essential requirement of the "human condition" (Hannah Arendt, *The Human Condition* [Chicago: University of Chicago Press, 1958]). According to Arendt, relations of policing were central in structuring and constraining this possibility for some people. Those expelled from humanity, and from politics, were outside the domain of law and were left at the mercy of the police. It was, in fact, only by committing a crime and violating the law that stateless persons could acquire legal protection, hence crossing into the space generally reserved for citizens. As Arendt says of the stateless, "Only as an offender against the law can he gain protection from it." (*Origins of Totalitarianism*, 286).

16. Arendt, *Origins of Totalitarianism*, 269. According to the UN High Commissioner for Refugees (UNHCR) *Global Trends 2013* report, the year 2013 saw the greatest number of displaced people since World War II: 51.2 million at year's end (http://www.unhcr.org/trends2013/).

17. ISA, RG 115, box 2114, file 2, report on travel to Lebanon, August 9, 1966; ISA, RG 115, box 2005, file 5, request for permit to open newspaper, June 24, 1965; ISA, RG 115, box 2005, file 19, investigation of UNRWA social services club, November 19, 1957; ISA, RG 115, box 2007, file 19, investigation of request to open a Young Men's Muslim Association.

18. ISA, RG 115, box 1983, file 14, statement to police, February 24, 1965; ISA, RG 115, box 1983, file 3, investigation report, September 19, 1966.

19. In this, Gaza's experience suggests the longevity of concerns and practices that are sometimes identified as new. Arjun Appadurai (*Fear of Small Numbers*, 103), for instance, argues that the intertwining of social uncertainty and state security concerns is a feature of new, particularly post-9/11, world orders.

20. Distinct from the suggestion of some observers of the post-9/11 security climate in the United States that "a culture of suspicion is the anti-thesis of order and security because it undermines the ontological security of social interactions," in Egyptian-ruled Gaza security and insecurity were co-constituted. Janet Chan, "The New Lateral Surveillance and a Culture of Suspicion," in *Surveillance and Governance: Crime Control and Beyond*, ed. Mathieu Deflem, 223–240 (Bingley, UK: Emerald/JAI, 2008), 234. This condition made relationships perpetually unstable, but one cannot say that suspicion only undermined security.

21. For discussion of the weapons scandal and its importance for the 1952 Free Officers revolution in Egypt, see Anouar Abdel-Malek, *Egypt: Military Society, the Army Regime, the Left, and Social Change Under Nasser* (New York: Random House, 1968), 45.

22. Interview, Gaza City, February 14, 1999.

23. Hussein Abu Naml, *Qita' Ghazzah, 1948–1967: Tatawwarrat Iqtisadiyya wa-Siyasiyya wa-Ijtimaiyya wa-Askariyya* (Beirut: PLO Research Center, 1979), 181.

24. Interview, Rafah, May 2, 1999. The real turning point, another person told me, was the Free Officers revolution and Nasser's rise to power in Egypt (interview, Gaza City, February 14, 1999).

25. Report from the director of Palestine Intelligence, July 20, 1954, reproduced in Ehud Ya'ari, *Mitsrayim veha-Feda'in, 1953–1956* (Givat Haviva, Israel: Center for Arabic and Afro-Asian Studies, 1975), 35.

26. Yezid Sayigh, *Armed Struggle and the Search for State: The Palestinian National Movement, 1949–1993* (Oxford: Oxford University Press, 1997), 61.

27. Ibid., 62.

28. Husayn Abu Naml, "Harb al-Fedayeen fi Qita' Ghazzah," *Shu'un Filastiniyya* 62 (January 1979): 177–199.

29. United Nations Archives, S-0530-0206, assorted intelligence files, "Notes on Police Situation in Gaza at 29 May 1957."

30. I got this information from an Israeli propaganda pamphlet, published after the 1967 occupation of Gaza and presented as an argument against Egyptian rule in Gaza, which includes a chart of the CID's organizational structure. The text indicates that the

chart came from captured Egyptian documents (the same sort of documents that are my principal sources here). This particular document is not in the files I have, so I cannot verify its authenticity, but, even as it was deployed for propaganda purposes, I have no reason to doubt it. The English translation provided is highly editorial, but the original Arabic is included in the book, and it is to that text that I refer. David Zohar, *Gamal over Gaza: Egyptian Neocolonialism in Gaza—A Record of Twenty Years of Oppression* (Jerusalem: Ministry for Foreign Affairs [Israel], Information Division, 1968).

31. On the activities of the "underground" Muslim Brotherhood in the first years of the administration, see Ibrahim Skeik, *Ghazzah 'Abr al-Tarikh: Qita' Ghazzah Taht Al-Idara Al-Masriyya, 1948–1956* (n.p., 1982).

32. See Ziad Abu Amr, *Usul Al-Haraka al-Siyasiyya fi Qita' Ghazzah, 1948–1967* (Akka: Dar al-Aswar, 1987). Rema Hammami notes that "the movement was thus the best resourced party in Gaza at the time, and the largest, with about 1,500 members." "Between Heaven and Earth: Transformations in Religiosity and Labor Among Southern Palestinian Peasant and Refugee Women, 1920–1993" (PhD diss., Temple University, 1994), 124.

33. James Jankowski, *Nasser's Egypt, Arab Nationalism, and the United Arab Republic* (Boulder, CO: Lynne Rienner Publishers, 2002), 152; Kirk Beattie, *Egypt During the Nasser Years: Ideology, Politics, Civil Society* (Boulder, CO: Westview Press, 1994), 131.

34. Mu'in Basisu, *Descent into the Water: Palestinian Notes from Arab Exile* (Wilmette, IL: Medina Press, 1980), 54.

35. Ibrahim Ahmed, a former refugee camp officer, told me that the agreement governing cooperation between Egypt and UNRWA in the camps went so far as to specify that "UNRWA employees could not go to the police stations. So I used to go to the police or to the government when they needed something" (interview, Gaza City, March 24, 1999).

36. Feldman, "Difficult Distinctions"; Ilana Feldman, "The Quaker Way: Ethical Labor and Humanitarian Relief," *American Ethnologist* 34, 4 (2007): 689–705.

37. When I asked about these matters, few native Gazans would actually admit to hostility toward refugees. Most responded to questions about these relations by saying things like, "There was sympathy and love. I, for example, would take a refugee to live in my house. There was sympathy, we welcomed them from the beginning" (interview, Gaza City, March 23, 1999). I did hear enough comments from Gazans to make clear that refugees were not simply imagining the tensions.

38. Interview, Rafah, October 29, 1999.

39. Feldman, "Difficult Distinctions." Abu Nizar, a refugee who later became a fedayee (guerrilla fighter), offered his interpretation of native Gazan fear: "The refugees were so many and the natives, the original people of Gaza, were few. The natives feared the refugees and restrained themselves. That is, when someone made a mistake and insulted a refugee by saying 'you are a refugee and you left your village,' he was afraid to fight with that refugee lest the refugees who were many beat him" (interview, Shati camp, February 22, 1999).

40. Abu Nizar, interview, Shati camp, February 22, 1999.

41. Laura Bier details the importance of gender, and especially of "the woman question" in Egypt during the Nasser era. Laura Bier, *Revolutionary Womanhood: Feminisms, Modernity, and the State in Nasser's Egypt* (Stanford, CA: Stanford University Press, 2011). In Gaza the new spaces of refugee camps—and the enormous transformation of the physical landscape—brought new anxieties about social relations (gendered and otherwise). Egyptian officials commented regularly about their concerns about the effect of camp life on refugee society. Ilana Feldman, *Governing Gaza: Bureaucracy, Authority, and the Work of Rule (1917–67)* (Durham, NC: Duke University Press, 2008), 149.

42. ISA, RG 115, box 1983, file 1, letter from student to headmaster, December 24, 1957.

43. ISA, RG 115, box 1983, file 1, report from police officer to CID inspector, December 24, 1957; letter from CID director to the head of Gaza's education department, December 31, 1957.

44. ISA, RG 115, box 1983, file 1, report from CID officer to director of internal security, February 9, 1958; letter from students to director of public security, March 24, 1958.

45. Reports from interrogations—most often about petty crimes or minor political expression (such as graffiti or pamphlets)—are among the most common documents in the police files to which I have access.

46. See ISA, RG 115, box 2114, file 2, police interrogation of Ismail Atwa, July 17, 1966.

47. ISA RG 115, box 2114, file 5, multiple transcripts of questioning about dog bites.

48. Fingerprint technology was developed in colonial India and was part of a process of both identifying individual suspects and marking suspect populations. Chandak Sengoopta, *Imprint of the Raj: How Fingerprinting Was Born in Colonial India* (London: Macmillan, 2003); Jacqueline Azzopardi Cauchi and Paul Knepper, "Empire, the Police, and the Introduction of Fingerprint Technology in Malta," *Criminology and Criminal Justice* 9, 1 (2009): 73–92.

49. ISA, RG 115, box 2114, file 17.

50. All names of interview subjects are pseudonyms.

51. Michel Foucault, *Discipline and Punish: The Birth of the Prison*, trans. Alan Sheridan (New York: Vintage Books, 1979).

52. ISA, RG 115, box 2024, file 14, report of Refugee Affairs Department. The report also argued that this whole area of responsibility should be removed from the department's portfolio, as it had not been part of it in the past, and it came with no budget allotment.

53. ISA, RG 115, box 2007, file 9, report of committee meeting, September 3, 1959.

54. ISA, RG 115, box 2007, file 9, report of committee meeting, October 13, 1959.

55. I reference these memoirs repeatedly in this book, as they are an unusual and significant source for understanding security practice as experienced by a dissident.

56. Basisu, *Descent into the Water*, 68.

57. Ibid., 47–48.

58. Interview, Shati camp, February 22, 1999.

59. Interview conducted by Doaa' El Nakhala, Gaza City, December 31, 2012.

60. Ian Loader, "Policing, Recognition, and Belonging," *Annals of the American Academy of Political and Social Science* 605, 1 (2006): 201–221, 214.

Chapter 2

Sections of this chapter are revisions of material that first appeared in Ilana Feldman, "Observing the Everyday: Policing and the Conditions of Possibility in Gaza (1948–67)," *Interventions: International Journal of Postcolonial Studies* 9, 3 (2007): 414–433.

1. ISA, RG 115, box 2024, file 4, report from police officer, January 26, 1967.

2. Ilana Feldman, "Observing the Everyday: Policing and the Conditions of Possibility in Gaza (1948–67)," *Interventions: International Journal of Postcolonial Studies* 9, 3 (2007): 414–433.

3. Nancy Campbell uses the phrase "technologies of suspicion" to describe the deployment of widespread surveillance in the United States. "Technologies of Suspicion: Coercion and Compassion in Post-disciplinary Surveillance Regimes," *Surveillance and Society* 2, 1 (2004): 78–92.

4. In my thinking about the life of the category of "the people" in Egypt's policing of Gaza, I have been influenced by Khaled Fahmy's analysis of the ways that General Sisi—like Nasser and Sadat before him—works with monolithic conceptual categories of army, state, and people in his claims and approach to security. Fahmy suggests that the Muslim Brotherhood uses similar strategies but, instead of *sha'ab* (people), they speak of *umma* (Muslim community), and instead of army, they speak of mosque. "Egypt's Perplexing Fascination with The Military" (lecture, George Washington University, Washington DC, October 9, 2013). Dynamics in Gaza under Egyptian rule were not identical, and notably the state did not have the same role, stability, or existence as it did in Egypt. For extended arguments about this style of governing without stability, which I call "tactical government," see Ilana Feldman, *Governing Gaza: Bureaucracy, Authority, and the Work of Rule (1917–67)* (Durham, NC: Duke University Press, 2008). To the extent that "the people" was mobilized as a category of threat and protection, it certainly referenced the life of this category in Egypt itself but was not placed in precisely the same triadic relation.

5. David Lyon, *Surveillance Society: Monitoring Everyday Life* (Philadelphia: Open University Press, 2001).

6. Sean P. Hier and Josh Greenberg, eds., *Surveillance: Power, Problems, and Politics* (Vancouver: University of British Columbia Press, 2009); Torin Monahan, ed., *Surveillance and Security: Technological Politics and Power in Everyday Life* (New York: Routledge, 2006); Andrew Lakoff and Stephen J. Collier, eds., *Biosecurity Interventions: Global Health and Security in Question* (New York: Columbia University Press, 2008).

7. Hannah Arendt, *The Origins of Totalitarianism* (San Diego, CA: Harcourt Brace Jovanovich, 1968), 296.

8. ISA, RG 115, box 2005, file 3, letter to CID director, September 24, 1960.

9. Such was the case in several reports about night patrols (surveillance of activity) submitted by police officers. Patrols of the main streets in Gaza—Omar Mukhtar, Thalathini—to observe the "cars and passersby" and watch for "car thieves and suspect persons" turned up no evidence of wrongdoing. The reports did all note that "the weather was rainy," a relative rarity in Gaza that could certainly have inhibited both criminal activity and observational capacity (ISA, RG 115, box 2096, file 21, reports from police officers, 1967).

10. The horizontal quality of surveillance suggests a more threatening version of Benedict Anderson's "horizontal comradeship." *Imagined Communities* (London: Verso, 1991), 7.

11. Arendt, *Origins of Totalitarianism*, 422. See also Oleg Kharkhordin, "The Soviet Individual: Genealogy of a Dissimulating Animal," in *Global Modernities*, ed. Mike Featherstone, Scott Lash, and Roland Robertson, 209–226 (London: Sage, 1995). And, regionally closer, see Lisa Wedeen, *Ambiguities of Domination: Politics, Rhetoric, and Symbols in Contemporary Syria* (Chicago: University of Chicago Press, 1999); Virginia Sherry, "Disappearances: Syrian Impunity in Lebanon," *Middle East Report* 27, 203 (1997): 31–33.

12. Michael T. Thornhill, "Britain, the United States and the Rise of an Egyptian Leader: The Politics and Diplomacy of Nasser's Consolidation of Power, 1952–4," *English Historical Review* 119, 483 (2004): 892–921. On concern about factionalism by police in Gaza, see ISA RG 115, box 2005, file 4, police investigation, December 7, 1964.

13. For examples of this sort of mundane police report, see ISA, RG 115, box 2005, file 3, report from police officer to CID director, December 12, 1960, and box 2096, file 21, reports from police officers, 1967.

14. There were plenty of police reports that were about "something"—either criminal or political activity. My particular interest here is in the effects of the reports of nothing.

15. ISA, RG 115, box 2096, file 22, report from police officer to Deir al-Balah CID inspector, January 4, 1960.

16. Ibid., report from police officer to Deir al-Balah CID inspector, January 5, 1960.

17. Ibid., report from police officer to Deir al-Balah CID inspector, January 7, 1960.

18. Interview, Gaza City, February 16, 1999.

19. ISA RG 115, box 1983, file 1 and file 5.

20. ISA, RG 115, box 2096, file 21, report from police officer to CID director, January 19, 1967.

21. ISA, RG 115, box 2096, file 21, reports of February 15 and 28, 1967.

22. Ibid., statement of Hussein Sharif.

23. Hannah Arendt, *The Human Condition* (1958; Chicago: University of Chicago Press, 1998), 40.

24. Propriety, Pierre Mayol says, "represses what is 'not proper,' 'what one does not do.' . . . [I]t takes care of decreeing the 'rules' of social custom, inasmuch as the social is the space of the other, and the medium for the position of self as a public being." "Propriety," in *The Practice of Everyday Life*, vol. 2, *Living and Cooking*, ed. Luce Giard, 15–34 (Minneapolis: University of Minnesota Press, 1998), 17.

25. As Mayol says, "If propriety imposes its own coercion, it is in the hopes of a 'symbolic' benefit to acquire or maintain" (ibid., 19).

26. ISA, RG 115, box 2096, file 21, reports of January 1 and 21, 1967.

27. Less highlighted in these particular incidents but also of importance in the policing of propriety (and explored more in Chapter 5) is the possible intersection of this security threat with the threats to the national interest that occupied so much police attention.

28. I should note that the records I have are not of regular informers on the payroll—although such informers certainly had to exist—but of more opportunistic instances of informing by people who might not do so regularly.

29. Hillel Cohen describes the multiplicity of reasons that Palestinian citizens of the new State of Israel worked as informers and collaborators. *Good Arabs: The Israeli Security Agencies and the Israeli Arabs, 1948–1967* (Berkeley: University of California Press, 2010).

30. ISA, RG 115, box 2005, file 3, statement of student Musa Eid, April 15, 1960.

31. Ibid., statement of Ahmed Abu Sharbin, teacher of Musa who found the publications, April 16, 1960.

32. Ibid., documents from April 21 and 26, 1960.

33. Here I should reiterate that in the Israel State Archives (ISA) I was not allowed to see files that were explicitly about security matters. I can only speculate on what is contained in those files, but I would imagine that it is there that names of persons involved in serious political activity are found and details of their activities recorded. In the files that I did research in, most (though not all) political informing was of anonymous activity.

34. ISA, RG 115, box 2005, file 4, statement to CID, May 5, 1964.

35. Ibid.

36. While Khalil and Hassan very well might not have known who the authors of the pamphlets were, had they desired to build an informing relationship with the CID, they might have ventured a guess.

37. Shira Robinson discusses practices of informing by people who were not necessarily paid informants among Palestinian citizens of Israel during this same time period. *Citizen Strangers: Palestinians and the Birth of Israel's Liberal Settler State* (Stanford, CA: Stanford University Press, 2013).

38. DW, Qawa'im Al-Mushir, group 8, file number 1-27/s g/14, letters between director of military intelligence and war minister, April and May 1949.

39. Ibid., letter from Mahmud Shurab to director of the Information Department of the CID in Gaza, n.d.

40. ISA, RG 115, box 2007, file 7, report from CID inspector to CID director, November 19, 1957. Relations between Egypt and Saudi Arabia were very poor at this time, making any Saudi-sponsored organization an object of suspicion.

41. Ibid., letter from acting director of Palestine affairs to governor-general, September 26, 1957.

42. ISA, RG 115, box 1983, file 12, report from CID inspector to the head of the department, March 17, 1966.

43. It is probably no coincidence that most of this falsifying was around nonpolitical activity. It is one thing to try to harm someone by implicating them in criminal activity, quite another to link them with outlawed and heavily repressed political organizations. Furthermore, in terms of an interest in doing damage to reputations, being accused of criminal activity might be considerably more harmful within the community than being thought to be political.

44. ISA, RG 115, box 1983, file 12 also includes several reports of arrests made on the basis of information provided by informers.

45. Paul Cooper, "Ethical Approaches for Police Officers When Working with Informants in the Development of Criminal Intelligence in the United Kingdom," *Journal of Social Policy* 26, 1 (1997): 1–20.

46. Michael L. Rich, "Coerced Informants and Thirteenth Amendment Limitations on the Police-Informant Relationship," *Santa Clara Law Review* 50, 3 (2010), 681; Hillel Cohen in *Good Arabs* traces the informing process for Palestinians on the other side of the armistice line during this same time period.

47. ISA RG 115, box 1983, file 12.

48. Ami Ayalon, *Reading Palestine: Printing and Literacy, 1900–1948* (Austin: University of Texas Press, 2004); Dale F. Eickelman and Jon W. Anderson, *New Media in the Muslim World: The Emerging Public Sphere* (Bloomington: Indiana University Press, 2003); Jürgen Habermas, *The Structural Transformation of the Public Sphere: An Inquiry into a Category of Bourgeois Society* (Cambridge: MIT Press, 1989); Armando Salvatore and Mark LeVine, *Religion, Social Practice, and Contested Hegemonies: Reconstructing the Public Sphere in Muslim Majority Societies* (New York: Palgrave Macmillan, 2005).

49. The council, established in 1957, did give Gazans greater voice in government, although the governor-general retained final authority. The National Union, the only party allowed in Gaza, was established in 1959. It was created, as the governor-general put it, "with the goal of actualizing the message of Arab nationalism and building a democratic socialist society and to engender cooperation among all Palestinians to liberate the rest of their homeland" (DW, Qawa'im Al-Mushir, group 41, file 90105, letter from governor-general to director of the Defense Minister's Office, December 17, 1960). This was Gaza's version of the National Union established in Egypt during the same period and, like that Union, should be seen largely as a mechanism for involving Gazans in the Nasserist project.

50. The police reports I discuss here were not public files but rather part of the internal work of police and could be seen only by the appropriate authorities. The fact that the majority of police were Gazan, though, means that some Gazans did see them. For regulations of movement of files (police and others), see ISA, RG 115, box 2114, file 1, and box 2023, file 19.

51. Arendt connected action to the "human condition of plurality" (*Human Condition*, 7). As she saw it, action is fundamentally about relations among people, is "the only activity that goes on directly between men without the intermediary of things or matter," and is furthermore "*the* condition . . . of all political life" (ibid., 7). Following from this position, for her the "frailty of human affairs" derives in part from this dependence on others: "To be isolated is to be deprived of the capacity to act. . . . [A]ction and speech are surrounded by and in constant contact with the web of acts and words of other men" (ibid., 188).

52. Among the police files of the administration are reports about *nadawat* held by such organizations as the Arab UNRWA Employees Association, the Women's Advancement Society, the General Union of Arab Workers, the Association of Palestinian Employees in the Gaza Strip (see ISA, RG 115, box 2007, files 13 and 15–17), and of government-sponsored *nadawat* in various towns and camps (see ISA, RG 115, box 2024, files 6, 7, 10, and 20; box 2007, file 15; box 2056, file 26).

53. ISA, RG 115, box 2007, file 13, report from police officer to CID inspector, October 6, 1963.

54. ISA, RG 115, box 2023, file 6, report from police officer to CID inspector, January 5, 1960.

55. ISA, RG 115, box 2096, file 15, report from police officer to CID inspector, February 23, 1963.

56. Haidar Abdul Shafi, a physician who founded the Gaza branch of the Palestinian Red Crescent Society, was a major figure in Palestinian politics. He was one of the Palestinian representatives in the 1991 Madrid Conference and in the negotiations that followed (until the Oslo process took over). In no small part because of his widely recognized integrity, he was consistently one of the most respected figures on the Palestinian political scene. He died in 2007.

57. Police reports on public opinion frequently opened with that phrase, saying that such-and-such topic was "on people's tongues."

58. Reports on public opinion are all over the archival record. See especially ISA, RG 115, box 2024, files 3, 4, 6, 7, 10, and 20.

59. Box 2024, file 10, report from policeman to police inspector, January 3, 1966.

60. Ibid., policeman's report to police inspector, January 25, 1966.

61. ISA, RG 115, box 2096, file 14, October 14, 1965. The suggestion was that without small change available, merchants would be able to sell goods at higher prices.

62. ISA, RG 115, box 2096, file 14, letter from governor-general to director of internal affairs and public security, October 21, 1965.

63. ISA, RG 115, box 2096, file 14, letter from CID director to director of internal affairs and public security, November 15, 1965.

64. ISA, RG 115, box 2024 file 10, policeman's report to police inspector, January 25, 1966.

65. Arendt, *Human Condition*, 201.

Chapter 3

1. Interview, Shati camp, February 22, 1999.

2. Interview, Gaza City, April 11, 1999.

3. Interview, Gaza City, February 23, 1999.

4. ISA, RG 115, box 1983, file 16, report from CID inspector to CID director, June 5, 1966.

5. ISA, RG 115, box 1983, file 16, report from CID inspector to CID director.

6. ISA, RG 115, box 2007, unnumbered file: 1960, series of reports on individuals.

7. ISA, RG 115, box 2114, file 11, report from police officer to CID inspector, November 6, 1961.

8. ISA, RG 115, box 2096, file 11, report from police officer to CID inspector, September 12, 1964.

9. ISA, RG 115, box 2114, file 23, report from CID director to Rafah administrative governor, November 11, 1958, and letter from Rafah administrative governor to CID director, December 1, 1958.

10. In Gaza's twenty-first-century conditions, cross-border smuggling once again became big business. The Israeli-Egyptian blockade on Gaza produced a vibrant "tunnel economy" where a huge range of commodities were brought into Gaza through tunnels dug under the border with Egypt. In Egyptian-administered Gaza smuggling was not principally a result of a lack of goods in the Strip. In fact, Egypt made the area a free-trade zone in the latter part of its administration, ensuring that a much wider array of commodities were available, for much lower prices, in Gaza than elsewhere in the region. Sara Roy, *The Gaza Strip: The Political Economy of De-development* (Washington DC: Institute for Palestine Studies, 1995), 90.

11. The extent to which government officials were engaged in such smuggling themselves is an open question. There was surely some civil service participation in this activity—there is evidence of it in the CID files—but how widespread it was is not clear. An Israeli Foreign Office publication produced shortly after the 1967 occupation of Gaza and the West Bank accused Egyptian administrators of running large scale smuggling operations. Given that this publication was clearly a piece of propaganda designed to besmirch the Egyptian Administration, and thus make the Israeli occupation appear more benign, it is impossible to determine the veracity of that claim. Likely, it is a much exaggerated version of the truth. David Zohar, *Gamal over Gaza: Egyptian Neocolonialism in Gaza—A Record of Twenty Years of Oppression* (Jerusalem: Ministry for Foreign Affairs, Information Division, 1968).

12. See, for example, ISA RG 115, box 2096, file 11, letter of August 8, 1965; ISA RG 115, box 1983, file 12, letter of August 16, 1966; ISA RG 115, box 2023, file 22.

13. When the Gaza representative failed to attend a meeting in September 1963, the War Ministry sent a sharply worded letter to the governor-general, underlying the importance of a Gazan presence at the meeting because of its "special place in facing Israel and the neighboring countries." The governor-general responded by appointing the director of the CID himself as the representative to the meetings. (ISA, RG 115, box 2007, file 9, letter from War Ministry to governor-general, September 14, 1963; and reply, September 21, 1963).

14. ISA, RG 115, box 2007, file 9, report of September 3, 1959, meeting.

15. ISA, RG 115, box 2007, file 9, report of June 23, 1962, meeting.

16. Brenda Chalfin, *Neoliberal Frontiers: An Ethnography of Sovereignty in West Africa* (Chicago: University of Chicago Press, 2010); Brenda Chalfin, "Sovereigns and Citizens in Close Encounter: Airport Anthropology and Customs Regimes in Neoliberal Ghana," *American Ethnologist* 35, 4 (2008): 519–538.

17. DW, Qawa'im Al-Mushir, group 41, file 90805, letter from governor-general of Gaza to minister of finance, March 5, 1959.

18. ISA, RG 115, box 2096, file 8, reports and transcripts of interrogations, August 1964.

19. ISA, RG 115 box 2114, file 5. In one report about a dog bite the victim indicated that he had gone to the doctor, who told him he had to report the bit to the police.

20. ISA, RG 115, box 2114, file 8, April 1966 police report on loss of turkey and transcripts of five witness statements. Another file records the detailed investigation that ensued when a dog bit several people, including a child (ISA RG 115, box 2114, file 5).

21. The wallet contained 17 Egyptian pounds, his ID, military training diploma, university ID card, and a bus card from Cairo Co. (box 2114, file 8, letter from investigating detective, Rimal police station, to the Gaza CID, February 4, 1966). Detailed crime reports such as these are available only from the last few years of the administration. Presumably these files were regularly culled—compiled into anonymous statistics and the original details discarded. The Israeli occupation of 1967, when these files were seized, froze the "normal" filing process in its conditions in June 1967.

22. ISA, box 2114, file 8, inspection report by policeman, n.d.

23. Ibid., report on and transcript of Ahmed's statement, February 4, 1966.

24. Ibid., transcript of Salem's questioning, February 6, 1966; and see confirming statement of policeman.

25. Ibid., police report of interview with Ahmed, February 6, 1966.

26. Ibid., police report, n.d.

27. John Comaroff, and Jean Comaroff, "Policing Culture, Cultural Policing: Law and Social Order in Postcolonial South Africa," *Law and Social Inquiry* 29, 3 (2004): 513–545.

28. Lila Abu-Lughod, "Seductions of the 'Honor Crime,'" *differences* 22, 1 (2011): 17–63.

29. Lila Abu-Lughod, "Do Muslim Women Really Need Saving? Anthropological Reflections on Cultural Relativism and Its Others," *American Anthropologist* 104, 3 (2002): 783–790; Chandra Talpade Mohanty, "Under Western Eyes: Feminist Scholarship and Colonial Discourses," *Feminist Review*, 30 (1988): 61–88; Gayatri Spivak, "Can the Subaltern Speak?" in *Marxism and the Interpretation of Culture*, ed. Cary Nelson and Larry Grossberg, 271–313 (Urbana: University of Illinois Press, 1988).

30. A report on one reconciliation noted that it was attended by "a number of personalities of the Strip" (ISA, RG 115, box 2024, file 6, monthly report by Deir al-Balah governor, August 25, 1966).

31. ISA, RG 115, box 2024, file 3, report on conditions in the Gaza area for the period December 21, 1962–January 20, 1963, January 23, 1963.

32. This management of customary law was very often a production of this law. See Francis G. Snyder, "Colonialism and Legal Form: The Creation of Customary Law in Senegal," *Journal of Legal Pluralism* 19 (1981): 49; Martin Chanock, "Making Customary Law: Men, Women, and Courts in Colonial Northern Rhodesia," in *African Women and the Law: Historical Perspectives*, ed. Margaret Jean Hay and Marcia Wright, 53–67 (Boston: Boston University African Studies Center, 1982); Martin Chanock, "A Peculiar Sharpness: An Essay on Property in the History of Customary Law in Colonial Africa," *Journal of African History* 32, 1 (1991): 65–88.

33. Veena Das, "Communities as Political Actors: The Question of Cultural Rights," in *Critical Events: An Anthropological Perspective on Contemporary India*, ed. Veena Das (Oxford: Oxford University Press, 1995); Michael Eilenberg, "Flouting the Law: Vigilante Justice and Regional Autonomy on the Indonesian Border," *Austrian Journal of South-East Asian Studies* 4, 2 (2011): 237–253; Steffen Jensen and Lars Buur, "Everyday Policing and the Occult: Notions of Witchcraft, Crime and 'the People,'" *African Studies* 63, 2 (2004): 193–211.

34. Comaroff and Comaroff, "Policing Culture," 515.

35. Partha Chatterjee, "Religious Minorities and the Secular State: Reflections on an Indian Impasse," *Public Culture* 8, 1 (1995): 11–39; Gyanendra Pandey, "The Secular State and the Limits of Dialogue," in *The Crisis of Secularism in India*, ed. Anuradha Dingwaney Needham and Rajeswari Sunder Rijan, 157–176 (Durham, NC: Duke University Press, 2007).

36. Lars Buur and Steffen Jensen, "Introduction: Vigilantism and the Policing of Everyday Life in South Africa," *African Studies* 63, 2 (2004): 139–152; Nicholas Dirks, "The Policing of Tradition: Colonialism and Anthropology in Southern India," *Comparative Studies in Society and History* 39, 1 (1997): 182–212; Lata Mani, "Contentious Traditions: The Debate on Sati in Colonial India," in *Recasting Women: Essays in Indian Colonial History*, ed. Kumkum Sangari and Sudesh Vaid, 88–126 (New Brunswick, NJ: Rutgers University Press, 1990).

37. Stuart Hall et al, *Policing the Crisis: Mugging, the State and Law and Order* (New York: Holmes & Meier, 1978). Paul Amar highlights the importance of sexuality and gen-

der in security panics in Egypt. *The Security Archipelago: Human-Security States, Sexuality Politics, and the End of Neoliberalism* (Durham, NC: Duke University Press, 2013).

38. Lila Abu-Lughod notes that some crimes that have been described in the press as honor crimes in fact seem to have other causes at their root. "Seductions of the 'Honor Crime,'" 27.

39. ISA, RG 115, box 2024, file 5, report from officer of Khan Yunis CID to director of CID, May 1, 1965.

40. Ibid., report from director of CID to director of internal security, May 4, 1965.

41. Ibid., report from Khan Yunis administrative governor to director of CID, May 18, 1965.

42. Ibid., police report, June 14, 1965.

43. Ibid., report from police officer to CID inspector, June 24, 1965.

44. Ibid., report from policeman to CID inspector, June 15, 1965.

45. Ibid., report from administrative governor of Khan Yunis to director of interior and public security, June 15, 1965.

46. Ibid., report from policeman to CID inspector, June 24, 1965.

47. Interview, Gaza City, April 25, 1999.

48. ISA, RG 115, box 2096, file 11, letter to director of the interior and CID director, November 28, 1965.

49. Ibid., letter from police officer to CID inspector, December 12, 1965.

50. During the administration, the prices of many basic commodities were controlled by the government—as they were (and some items still are) in Egypt.

51. ISA, RG 115, box 2096, reports from October 18, 1965, and November 11, 1965.

52. ISA, RG 115, box 2024, file 3, report from police officer to CID inspector, March 25, 1963.

53. ISA, RG 115, box 2024, file 3, report on conditions in village areas from police officers to a CID inspector, June 22, 1963.

54. ISA, RG 115, box 2056, file 14.

Chapter 4

1. *Sawt Al-'Uruba*, January 22 and 29, February 23, March 2, 1950; November 28, 1951.

2. Seyla Benhabib, "Twilight of Sovereignty or the Emergence of Cosmopolitan Norms? Rethinking Citizenship in Volatile Times," *Citizenship Studies* 11, 1 (2007): 19–36; Saskia Sassen, "Foundational Subjects for Political Membership: Today's Changed Relation to the National State," in *Territory, Authority, Rights: From Medieval to Global Assemblages* (Princeton, NJ: Princeton University Press, 2006); Gershon Shafir, "The Evolving Tradition of Citizenship," in *The Citizenship Debates*, ed. Gershon Shafir (Minneapolis: University of Minnesota Press, 1998).

3. Ilana Feldman, "Waiting for Palestine: Refracted Citizenship and Latent Sovereignty in Gaza," *Citizenship Studies* 12, 5 (2008): 447–463. As I noted there: "The extent

to which citizenship requires the nation-state to be a meaningful concept has been a subject of considerable debate. Arguing against positions such as Ong's about transnational citizenship, Bryan Turner avers that this concept only has meaning within a nation-state framework 'because it is based on contributions and a reciprocal relationship between duty and rights, unlike human rights for which there are as yet no explicit duties' (Bryan Turner, "Classical Sociology and Cosmopolitanism: A Critical Defense of the Social," *British Journal of Sociology* 57, 1 [2006]: 146). To loose the concept from its moorings in the nation-state is, he argues, to 'distort the meaning of the term, indeed to render it meaningless" (ibid.). But what if there is an idea of a nation-state, but not its actuality? Gaza under Egyptian Administration provides an instance neither of deterritorialized, transnational citizenship nor of citizenship juridically codified by a nation-state. This case suggests that it is not only an existing nation-state that can define such rights and duties and that there can be citizenship without fully realized sovereignty."

4. Karl Marx, "On the Jewish Question," in *The Marx-Engels Reader*, ed. Robert C. Tucker, 26–46 (New York: W.W. Norton, 1978).

5. Benedict Anderson, *Imagined Communities: Reflections on the Origin and Spread of Nationalism* (London: Verso, 1991), 35–36.

6. To respond to the security threat posed by an irresponsible press—a threat that had been made evident to the government in the 1929 riots in Palestine—the Press Ordinance—which amended the previous Ottoman regulations—was enacted in 1933 (*Palestine Gazette*, no. 340, January 19, 1933). This ordinance confirmed government as the sole arbiter of the rights of the press, including granting permits for newspapers to publish. It provided for the closure of newspapers that published "seditious" materials and the seizure of their property. Further, the press law called for the constant surveillance of press activities as a means of minimizing such illegal publication. This latter activity was to be accomplished through the Press Bureau, a government office that was also responsible for providing information *to* the press. This office, charged with both censorship and dissemination of information, was established after responsibility for press supervision was removed from the Criminal Intelligence Division of the police in 1928 (CO 733, file 87168, control of press, report on the control of the press in Palestine, by R. A. Furness, June 16, 1931).

7. *Sawt Al-'Uruba*, February 11, 1950.

8. CID records also include reports about discussions of Gaza in the Egyptian press, a matter of concern in part because these materials also circulated in Gaza. ISA, RG 115, box 2005, file 13, letter from CID director to director of internal security, February 5, 1958.

9. ISA, RG 115, box 2005, file 13, letter from censor to publisher of *Al-'Awda*, December 7, 1957. The Gaza censor also monitored the Egyptian press, complaining sometimes that articles about Gaza were published without appropriate censorship (ISA, RG 115, box 2005, file 9, passim, and file 13, letter from CID director (censor) to director of interior and public security). On other occasions, the censor demanded to know the sources for articles published in local papers, as well as the names of reporters who worked on the

story (ISA, RG 115, box 2005, file 2, letter from CID director to editor of *Al-Tahrir* newspaper, June 2, 1965). There is no indication in the file about how the editor responded to this demand or what the consequences of noncompliance would be.

10. Mu'in Basisu, *Descent into the Water: Palestinian Notes from Arab Exile* (Wilmette, IL: Medina Press, 1980), 39.

11. Ibid., 24.

12. Charles Hirschkind, *The Ethical Soundscape: Cassette Sermons and Islamic Counterpublics* (New York: Columbia University Press, 2006).

13. ISA, RG 115, box 2007, unnumbered file, letter from director of interior and public security to CID director, June 20, 1960.

14. Ibid., *Al-Tahrir*, June 20, 1960.

15. ISA, RG 115, box 2005, file 3, statements from April 7, 1960.

16. ISA, RG 115, box 2005, file 15, assorted surveillance and informing reports about newspapers found lying around, 1958.

17. ISA, RG 115, box 2096, file 21, telegram, February 5, 1967.

18. ISA, RG 115, box 2096, file 21, interrogation report, February 7, 1967.

19. John Waterbury, *The Egypt of Nasser and Sadat: The Political Economy of Two Regimes* (Princeton, NJ: Princeton University Press, 1983), 314.

20. Gamal Abdel Nasser, *President Gamal Abdel Nasser on Palestine* (speech given in 1962) (Cairo, United Arab Republic: Information Department, n.d.).

21. UN Archives, S-0530-0144, file 46, "Announcing Constitutional System of Gaza Sector," March 9, 1962 (UN translation).

22. ISA, RG 115, box 2007, unnumbered file, problems in Chest Illnesses Hospital in Bureij.

23. ISA, RG 115, box 2007, file 16b, report from CID officer to CID inspector about Khan Yunis mayoralty, May 2, 1964.

24. ISA, RG 115, box 2007, file 16b, report from CID officer at Khan Yunis to CID director about general conditions in Khan Yunis, May 3, 1964.

25. Ibid., memo from CID director on the mayoralty of Khan Yunis, May 2, 1964.

26. Ibid., report from CID officer to CID director about Khan Yunis mayor, May 3, 1964.

27. Ibid., letter from CID inspector to CID director, n.d.

28. ISA, RG 115, box 2007, file 8. Other files report on demonstrations against King Hussein and in support of Nasser. Even in these cases where the content of the demonstration was not oppositional, the police were concerned about independent action (ISA, RG 115, box 2024, file 10, interrogations and reports about a November 27, 1966, demonstration).

29. UNRWA, *UNRWA: A Brief History, 1950–1982* (Vienna: UNRWA, 1982), 251.

30. Benny Morris, *Israel's Border Wars, 1949–1956: Arab Infiltration, Israeli Retaliation, and the Countdown to the Suez War* (Oxford, UK: Clarendon Press, 1993), 326. Apparently,

the number of Egyptian dead surprised the Israelis, who had hoped that they might flee and thus minimize the number of casualties. Livia Rokach, *Israel's Sacred Terrorism: A Study Based on Moshe Sharett's Personal Diary and Other Documents* (Belmont, MA: Association of Arab-American University Graduates, 1980), 44. Faced with what they feared would be viewed internationally as proof that "we initiate aggression and reveal ourselves as being bloodthirsty and aspiring to perpetrate mass massacres," Moshe Sharett, the Israeli prime minister, commanded Israeli embassies to claim that the attack had been a response to an unprovoked Egyptian infiltration (Sharett's diary, March 1, 1955, cited in ibid., 45).

31. Morris, *Israel's Border Wars*, 327.

32. Rokach, *Israel's Sacred Terrorism*, 45.

33. Husayn Abu Naml, "Harb al-Fedayeen fi Qita' Ghazzah" *Shu'un Filistiniyya* 62 (January 1979): 170–199, 182.

34. *Al-Ahram*, November 22, 1951.

35. Abu Naml, "Harb al-Fedayeen," 170.

36. Basisu, *Descent into the Water*, 32.

37. Ibid., 31.

38. Abu Naml, "Harb al-Fedayeen," 174.

39. Ibid.

40. Basisu, *Descent into the Water*, 33–34.

41. Ibid., 33. Basisu's recollections are confirmed by other accounts of the demonstrations. See Abu Naml "Harb al-Fedayeen."

42. Basisu, *Descent into the Water*, 34.

43. Abu Naml, "Harb al-Fedayeen," 172.

44. Basisu, *Descent into the Water*, 38.

45. UNRWA inactive files, box 2, E-810-5, Sinai Project—Construction Agreement. UN General Assembly Resolution 194 states: "Resolves that the refugees wishing to return to their homes and live at peace with their neighbours should be permitted to do so at the earliest practicable date, and that compensation should be paid for the property of those choosing not to return and for loss of or damage to property which, under principles of international law or in equity, should be made good by the Governments or authorities responsible" (UN, A/RES/194 [III], December 11, 1948).

46. UNRWA inactive files, box 2, E/810—Part 1, Egypt—Sinai Project General, Summary Record of Discussion Held in Colonel Gohar's Office in Cairo at 10:30 a.m. on August 18, 1955.

47. UNRWA, *Annual Report Covering the Period 1 July 1955 to 30 June 1956*, 25.

48. Feldman, "Waiting for Palestine."

49. UNRWA inactive files, box 2, E/810—Part 1, Egypt—Sinai Project General, to Henry R. Labouisse—Director, UNRWA, from Alexander E. Squadrilli—UNRWA Representative to Egypt, November 2, 1955.

50. These paragraphs were originally published in Ilana Feldman, "Home as a Refrain: Remembering and Living Displacement in Gaza," *History and Memory* 18, 2 (2006): 10–47.

51. Interview, Gaza City, February 14, 1999.

52. Interview, Shati camp, February 22, 1999.

53. UN, S-0530-0206, "The Egyptian Fedayeen Organization," n.d.

54. UN, S-0530-0206, "Intelligence Report—fedayeen," February 22, 1960.

55. This history is detailed by Yezid Sayigh in "Escalation or Containment? Egypt and the Palestine Liberation Army, 1964–67," *International Journal of Middle East Studies* 30, 1 (1998): 97–116.

56. Deborah Cowen, "Fighting for 'Freedom': The End of Conscription in the United States and the Neoliberal Project of Citizenship," *Citizenship Studies* 10, 2 (2006): 167–183.

57. Yezid Sayigh, "Escalation or Containment?" In 1966 UNEF officials indicated that "the importance of PLA presence . . . remains mostly political as their military capability is limited" (UN S-0530-0035, file 411, notes for commander's conference, February 7, 1966).

58. ISA, RG 115, box 1983, file 15; box 2096, file 21.

59. ISA, RG 115, box 2024, file 10, report on general conditions and public opinion. January 25, 1966.

60. UN Archives, S-0530-0151, file C-32, Military Service Law 4/65 of March 7, 1965, explanatory note.

Chapter 5

Material in this chapter was adapted from Ilana Feldman, "Ad Hoc Humanity: UN Peacekeeping and the Limits of International Community in Gaza," *American Anthropologist* 112, 3 (2010): 416–429.

1. Arthur Veysey, "Egypt's Lost Towns Awaken as War Stops: Gaza's Citizens Come out to Buy Food," *Chicago Tribune*, November 6, 1956, 9.

2. "Israeli Cabinet Approves Steps to Restore Gaza Life to Normal," *Washington Post*, November 25, 1956, A1.

3. "Israel Will Start Gaza Mail Service," *New York Times*, December 3, 1956, 3.

4. William Frye, *A United Nations Peace Force* (New York: Oceana Publications, 1957), 4.

5. UN Archives, S-0313-0004, file 8, About UNEF: A Pocket Guide for Members of the United Nations Emergency Force, n.d.

6. Peter Redfield, "Doctors, Borders, and Life in Crisis," *Cultural Anthropology* 20, 3 (2005): 328–361.

7. Paul Rabinow, "Midst Anthropology's Problems," *Cultural Anthropology* 17, 2 (2002): 135–149.

8. UN Archives, S-0330-0002, file 6, UNEF: Report of the secretary-general, July 12, 1967.

9. This kind of arrangement has continued to be typical of peacekeeping forces. Eyal Ben-Ari and Efrat Elron, "Blue Helmets and White Armor: Multi-Nationalism and Multi-Culturalism Among UN Peacekeeping Forces," *City and Society* 13, 2 (2001): 271–302; Tamara Duffey, "Cultural Issues in Contemporary Peacekeeping," *International Peacekeeping* 7, 1 (2000): 142–168.

10. UN Archives, S-0165-0001, file 5, UN press release, March 18, 1958, and S-530-0004, file OR 110, staff paper on UNEF, June 23, 1960. UNEF was initially composed of troops from ten countries: Canada, Brazil, Colombia, Indonesia, India, Denmark, Norway, Finland, Sweden, and Canada. Later there were just seven, because Finland, Indonesia, and Colombia withdrew their contingents.

11. UN Archives, S-0530-0142, file LEG 700, legal status of the force, n.d.

12. UN Archives, S-0330-0002, file 6, UNEF: Report of the secretary-general.

13. Jarat Chopra, "The UN's King of East Timor," *Survival* 42, 3 (2000): 27–39; Tanja Hohe, "The Clash of Paradigms: International Administration and Local Political Legitimacy in East Timor," *Contemporary Southeast Asia* 24, 3 (2002): 569–589; Sherene Razack, *Dark Threats and White Knights: The Somalia Affair, Peacekeeping, and the New Imperialism* (Toronto: University of Toronto Press, 2004).

14. UN Archives, S-0370-0029, file 17, memo, March 27, 1957.

15. According to a 1964 report, 16 of 3,656 staff in Gaza were international (UN Archives, S-0330-0002, file 14, a pilot report from Gaza, February 1964, by Ingrid and Johan Galtung).

16. Norrie MacQueen argues that the establishment of UNEF was continuous with earlier efforts in Palestine, although she does acknowledge the significance of the fact that "for the first time, a substantial force rather than an observer group was deployed." MacQueen, *Peacekeeping and the International System* (New York: Routledge, 2006), 67.

17. UN Archives, S-0313-0004, file 8, About UNEF, n.d.

18. UN Archives, About UNEF.

19. Ilana Feldman, "Ad Hoc Humanity: Peacekeeping and the Limits of International Community in Gaza," *American Anthropologist* 112, 3 (2010): 416–429.

20. The United Nations, founded in 1945, was established with the purpose of "maintain[ing] international peace and security," and its charter authorized the Security Council to deploy armed forces to accomplish this mission. UN peacekeeping was not an enforcement action, as outlined in chapter 7 of the charter, nor a negotiated settlement of a conflict as envisioned in its chapter 6. Rather, it has been described as "an unwritten chapter six-and-a-half" that emerged out of "political improvisation and legal flexibility." Miltiadis Sarigiannidis, "Legal Discourses on Peacemaking/Peacekeeping/Peacebuilding: International Law as a New Topos for Human Security," *International Journal* 62, 3 (2007): 527. In the years since UNEF's mission, peacekeeping as a form of

UN intervention has both become more codified (as principles emerged from its practice) and been modified in response to changing global conditions and criticisms of some of its procedures.

21. Ruti Teitel, "Humanity's Law: Rule of Law for the New Global Politics," *Cornell International Law Journal* 35 (2002): 355–387.

22. Ruti Teitel, "For Humanity," *Journal of Human Rights* 3, 2 (2004): 225–237, 227.

23. Ilana Feldman and Miriam Ticktin, *In the Name of Humanity: The Government of Threat and Care* (Durham, NC: Duke University Press, 2010).

24. Thomas Laqueur, "Mourning, Pity, and the Work of Narrative in the Making of 'Humanity,'" in *Humanitarianism and Suffering: The Mobilization of Empathy*, ed. Richard. D. Brown and Richard A. Wilson, 31–57 (Cambridge: Cambridge University Press, 2009); Adriana Petryna, *Life Exposed: Biological Citizens After Chernobyl* (Princeton, NJ: Princeton University Press, 2002); Carl Schmitt, *The Concept of the Political* (Chicago: University of Chicago Press, 1996).

25. Lori Allen, "Martyr Bodies in the Media: Human Rights, Aesthetics, and the Politics of Immediation in the Palestinian Intifada," *American Ethnologist* 36, 1 (2009): 161–180; Ilana Feldman, "Refusing Invisibility: Documentation and Memorialization in Palestinian Refugee Claims," *Journal of Refugee Studies* 21, 4 (2008): 498–516.

26. John Quigley, *The Case for Palestine: An International Law Perspective* (Durham, NC: Duke University Press, 2005).

27. Peter Andreas similarly explores the multiple roles that UN peacekeeping soldiers took on in Sarajevo: *Blue Helmets and Black Markets: The Business of Survival in the Siege of Sarajevo* (Ithaca, NY: Cornell University Press, 2008).

28. Teitel, "For Humanity."

29. Didier Fassin, "Humanitarianism as a Politics of Life," *Public Culture* 19, 3 (2007): 499–520.

30. UN Archives, S-0164-0003, file 6, memo from secretary general to executive assistant, March 7, 1957.

31. UN Archives, S-0164-0003, file 6, press release, March 7, 1957,

32. In a cable to the secretary-general, Ralph Bunche noted, "There seems to be little doubt that Egyptians had developed strong suspicions concerning U.N. motives and objectives in Gaza. 'Internationalization of Gaza' much bandied about here and is a common straw man target" (UN Archives, S-0370-0032, file 4, March 13, 1957). Worries about internationalization also became a subject of concern in the policing of Gazans and any attachment to that idea was seen as a threat.

33. UN Archives, S-0370-0032, file 4, Bunche to secretary-general, March 11, 1957.

34. UN Archives, S-0164-0003, file 6, UN press release, March 13, 1957.

35. As one UN official commented in a note on the events: "If [Nasser] did not take a dramatic and immediate decision, his position in the country would have been difficult" (UN Archives, S-0165-0002, file 3, March 15, 1957).

36. UN Archives, UN S-0370-0032, file 4, code cable from Burns to secretary-general, March 10, 1957.

37. Ibid.

38. Nils Skold, *United Nations Peacekeeping After the Suez War—UNEF I: The Swedish Involvement*, trans. Stig Nihlen (New York: St. Martin's Press, 1996), 159.

39. Ibid., 161–163.

40. UN Archives, S-0330-0002, file 6, UNEF: report of the secretary-general, July 12, 1967.

41. UN Archives, S-0330-0002, file 6, notes on withdrawal of United Nations Emergency Force (UNEF), June 3, 1967.

42. Liisa Malkki, "Things to Come: Internationalism and Global Solidarities in the Late 1990s," *Public Culture* 10, 2 (1998): 431–442, 434.

43. UN Archives, S-0316-0009, file 4, briefing, May 20, 1967.

44. Malkki, "Things to Come," 434.

45. Ilana Feldman, "Waiting for Palestine: Refracted Citizenship and Latent Sovereignty in Gaza," *Citizenship Studies* 12, 5 (2008): 447–463.

46. CARE Records, box 839, discursive reports, Egypt 1955–83, n.d., Gaza Strip.

47. As peacekeeping has developed over the years, it has been linked increasingly closely to humanitarian practices that seek to keep people alive. In fact, peacekeeping is now often described as a form of humanitarian intervention. Andrew Cottey, "Beyond Humanitarian Intervention: The New Politics of Peacekeeping and Intervention," *Contemporary Politics* 14, 4 (2008): 429–446, although it remains quite different from actions focused on the delivery of food, medical treatment, and other material assistance.

48. Michel Agier and Françoise Bouchet-Sangier, "Humanitarian Spaces: Spaces of Exception," in *In the Shadow of "Just Wars": Violence, Politics, and Humanitarian Action*, ed. Fabrice Weissman, 297–313 (Ithaca, NY: Cornell Press, 2004); Robert Rubinstein, *Peacekeeping Under Fire: Culture and Intervention* (Boulder, CO: Paradigm Publishers, 2008).

49. J. A. Swettenham, "Some Impressions of the UNEF: 1957 to 1958," Directory or History, National Defence Headquarters, Ottawa Canada (1959), http://www.cmp-cpm.forces.gc.ca/dhh-dhp/his/rep-rap/doc/ahqr-rqga/ahq078.pdf, 11.

50. Ibid.

51. UNEF files also record incidents of Israeli young women crossing into Gaza—some coming in with UNEF soldiers and some apparently seeking a way out of Israel. One girl who crossed said that she was "fed up with living from [*sic*] kibbutz . . . and wished to see Cairo," whereas the other had "quarreled with her parents and complained her father beat her" (UN Archives, S-0319-0003, file 17, August 16, 1966). In another case, drunk Canadian soldiers brought three Israeli young women ("known prostitutes," according to one account) across the border, where they were discovered after spending

the night in UNEF barracks. The women were taken into Egyptian custody and eventually were sentenced to five years in prison for infiltrating the ADL. The soldiers seem to have been returned to Canada; the file on this matter does not specify whether they were punished for their transgression (S-0319-0001, file 2).

52. UN Archives, S-0530-0142, file UNMO 1300, investigation report, June 3, 1959.

53. UN Archives, S-0530-0142, file UNMO 1300, investigation report, September 15, 1959.

54. UN Archives, S-0319-0001, file 28, press release, February 12, 1959.

55. UN Archives, S-0319-0001, file 28, incident reports, February 12–13, 1959.

56. A Swedish former UNEF member noted that forces were not permitted to investigate thefts of UNEF goods but, rather, had to request that local police investigate (Skold, *United Nations*, 130).

57. UN Archives, S-0530-0070, file PE 224 1, UNEF daily camp routine order, April 2, 1963.

58. UN Archives, S-0530-200, file 37-1, April 2, 1958, relations with the local administration and population and with the Egyptian authorities.

59. I describe some of these reports in other chapters. See ISA, RG 115, box, 2114, file 23; ISA, RG 115, box 2023, file 6.

60. ISA, RG 115, box 2033, file 3, January 30, 1962, report from police officer to Criminal Investigation Department (CID) inspector. Other reports describe UNEF involvement in drug smuggling (ISA, RG 115, box 1983, file 8, reports from May 1958).

61. Tamara Duffey, "Cultural Issues," 151. Lack of cultural knowledge and sensitivity has also been cited as a problem in peacekeeping missions elsewhere. On Lebanon, see Marianne Heiberg and Johan Jorgen Holst, "Comparing UNIFIL and the MNF," *Survival* 28, 5 (1986): 399–422; on Somalia, see Duffey "Cultural Issues"; Rubinstein, *Peacekeeping Under Fire*. On East Timor, see Hohe, "Clash of Paradigms."

62. Robert Rubinstein, "Intervention and Culture: An Anthropological Approach to Peace Operations," *Security Dialogue* 36, 4 (2005): 527–544, 532.

63. UN Archives, S-0165-0004, file 1, some Moslem customs and beliefs, April 17, 1957.

64. Lila Abu-Lughod, "Writing Against Culture," in *Recapturing Anthropology: Working in the Present*, ed. Richard Fox, 137–162 (Santa Fe, NM: SAR Press, 1991).

65. Robert Rubinstein, "Cross-Cultural Considerations in Complex Peace Operations," *Negotiation Journal* 19, 1 (2003): 29–49, 40.

66. UN Archives, S-0313-0004, file 8, About UNEF.

67. UN Archives, S-0530-0210, File Charity General, n.d., memo from "The Committee" to military and civilian personnel of UNEF.

68. UN Relief and Works Agency, "Annual Report of the Director of the United Nations Relief and Works Agency for Palestine Refugees in the Near East: Covering the period 1 July 1957 to 30 June 1958," UN Doc. A/3931.

69. DW, Qawa'im Al-Mushir, group 41, file 90205, July 13, 1959.

70. Ilana Feldman, *Governing Gaza: Bureaucracy, Authority, and the Work of Rule, 1917–1967* (Durham, NC: Duke University Press, 2008).

71. UN Archives S-0330-0002, file 14, "Canada's Desert Force," *Weekend*, no. 13, 1964.

72. Skold, *United Nations*, 138.

73. UN Archives, S-0330-0002, file 14, Galtung Report. It should be noted that UN leaders objected to what they considered a generally critical tone in the report.

74. ISA, RG 115, box 2024, file 3, reports from January 1 and February 23, 1963. Such attitudes were of concern to Egyptian security in part because they went against Egyptian policy of support for UNEF's presence.

75. See UN Archives, S-0319-0001, file 25; S-0319-0001, file 13; S-0314-0001, file 26; S-0530-0151, file C-33.

76. UN Archives, S-0530-0005, file OR 311, n.d. (1957), A concise history of activities of the Colombian battalion in the United Nations Emergency Force and some comments about them.

77. Both Gazans and Egyptians from the Sinai were employed by UNEF.

78. UN Archives, S-0319-0001, file 32, letter from Hilmy to Burns, May 7, 1959.

79. UN Archives, S-0319-0002, file 11, Gyani to Bunche, August 14, 1962.

80. He was convicted of these charges, but his sentence was suspended (UN Archives, S-0319-0002, file 11, letter from Norway's UN representative to Ralph Bunche, April 11, 1963).

81. Keith Allred, "Peacekeepers and Prostitutes: How Deployed Forces Fuel the Demand for Trafficked Women and New Hope for Stopping It," *Armed Forces and Society* 33, 1 (2006): 5–23; Razack, *Dark Threats*.

82. UN Archives, S-0319-0001, file 14, n.d., summary of the facts of the case.

83. When I conducted research in Gaza in the late 1990s, I often heard such sentiments. As one person told me: "I am a human being and I want to live as a human being. . . . You are nothing without your country and this is the conviction of the Palestinians. I need to live with dignity. A human being is not made only to eat and drink" (interview, Gaza City, November 12, 1999).

84. UN Archives, S-0530-0130, file 2, notes of meeting with certain members of locally recruited staff, July 1959.

85. UN Archives, S-0530-0130, file 2, letter from Hilmy to Burns, July 11, 1959.

86. UN Archives, S-0530-0085, file PE 530, petition from UNEF watchmen to UNEF commander, January 25, 1963.

87. UN Archives, S-0530-0085, file PE 530, from UNEF legal and political advisor to UNEF commander, February 14, 1963.

88. UN Archives, S-0316-0009, file 14, closing remarks by secretary-general at dinner of United Nations Association of Canada, June 2, 1967.

Conclusion

1. Michel Foucault, *Security, Territory, Population: Lectures at the College de France, 1977–1978*, ed. Michel Senellart (New York: Macmillan, 2009), 45.

2. ISA, RG 115, box 2024, file 20, report on political situation in Gaza, April 11, 1966.

3. ISA, RG 115, box 2024, file 10, police report on general situation in Shati refugee camp, January 15, 1966.

4. ISA, RG 115, box 2024, file 10, report from CID inspector to CID director, October 1966.

5. ISA RG 115, box 2023, file 6, reports on January 6, 9, and 12, 1960.

6. Such file making was part of what Michel Foucault describes as "the constitution of the individual as a describable, analyzable object." *Discipline and Punish: The Birth of the Prison*, trans. Alan Sheridan (New York: Vintage Books, 1979), 190.

7. ISA, RG 115, box 2023, file 6, police interrogation, March 8, 1960.

8. The US National Security Agency surveillance practice that came to light in 2013 after Edward Snowden leaked an enormous cache of documents is an important diagnostic of our time, but so too is Snowden's choice to make that information public. In an earlier period, anti–Vietnam War activists who burglarized an FBI office in 1971 to get evidence of the bureau's often-illegal surveillance of activists. Mark Mazzetti, "Burglars Who Took on F.B.I. Abandon Shadows," *New York Times*, January 7, 2014, http://www.nytimes.com/2014/01/07/us/burglars-who-took-on-fbi-abandon-shadows.html?_r=0.

9. A conviction that this is possible surely contributed to the uprisings in the Arab world that began in Tunisia in December 2010. The paths that these uprisings have taken in the following years serves as a reminder of both the resiliency of security systems and the difficulties in seeking alternatives.

10. Neve Gordon, *Israel's Occupation* (Berkeley: University of California Press, 2008), 49.

11. Ann Mosely Lesch, "Gaza: History and Politics," in *Israel, Egypt, and the Palestinians: From Camp David to Intifada*, ed. Ann Mosely Lesch and Mark Tessler, 223–237 (Bloomington: Indiana University Press, 1989).

12. Eyal Weizman, *Hollow Land: Israel's Architecture of Occupation* (New York: Verso, 2007), 70.

13. Lesch, "Gaza," 230.

14. The First Intifada (uprising) against Israeli occupation began in Gaza in 1987. It started with demonstrations after an Israeli driver killed a Palestinian child in Gaza. It grew into a societywide refusal to cooperate with the occupation. It ended in 1993 with the signing of the Oslo Accords between Palestinian leaders and Israel. The Second Intifada—also known as the Al-Aqsa Intifada—began in 2000 after Ariel Sharon made a deliberately provocative visit to the Haram Al-Sharif. It petered out a few years later.

15. Beverly Milton-Edwards, "Policing Palestinian Society," *Policing and Society: An International Journal of Research and Policy* 7, 1 (1997): 19–44, 24.

16. Rhoda Kanaaneh, *Surrounded: Palestinian Soldiers in the Israeli Military* (Stanford, CA: Stanford University Press, 2009), 24.

17. Nigel Parsons, "Israeli Biopolitics, Palestinian Policing: Order and Resistance in the Occupied Palestinian Territories," in *Policing and Prisons in the Middle East: Formations of Coercion*, ed. Laleh Khalili and Jillian Schwedler, 57–76 (New York: Columbia University Press, 2010), 60.

18. Lori Allen, *The Rise and Fall of Human Rights: Cynicism and Politics in Occupied Palestine* (Stanford, CA: Stanford University Press, 2013).

19. Yezid Sayigh, "Policing the People, Building the State: Authoritarian Transformation in the West Bank and Gaza," *Carnegie Papers*, February 2011, http://carnegie-mec .org/2011/02/28/policing-people-building-state-authoritarian-transformation-in-west -bank-and-gaza/awvd.

20. Tariq Dana, "The Beginning of the End of Palestinian Security Coordination with Israel?" *Jadaliyya*, July 4, 2014, http://www.jadaliyya.com/pages/index/18379/the -beginning-of-the-end-of-palestinian-security-c.

21. Lisa Hajjar, "Is Gaza Still Occupied and Why Does It Matter?" *Jadaliyya*, July 14, 2014, http://www.jadaliyya.com/pages/index/8807/is-gaza-still-occupied-and-why-does -it-matter.

22. Hamas first won parliamentary elections in 2006. Israel and its allies essentially refused to acknowledge the legitimacy of this electoral victory and worked to impede its capacity to govern. In 2007 fighting between Fatah and Hamas led to Hamas taking sole control of Gaza, with the Fatah-led PA in control in the West Bank.

23. In the summer of 2014, reconciliation between Fatah and Hamas led to the creation of a new unity government for both the West Bank and Gaza. In July 2014 Israel launched an assault on the Palestinian population in the name of going after Hamas, first in the West Bank and then in Gaza. As of this writing, the full consequences of this attack for the Palestinian government and the population of Gaza remain uncertain.

24. Yezid Sayigh, "Hamas Rule in Gaza: Three Years On" (Middle East Policy Brief No. 41, March 2010, Crown Center for Middle East Studies, Brandeis University, Waltham, MA), 3.

25. Nathan Brown, "Gaza Five Years On: Hamas Settles In," paper, June 11, 2012, Carnegie Endowment for International Peace, http://carnegieendowment.org/files/ hamas_settles_in.pdf.

26. Sayigh also suggests a comparison with "the nondemocratic model of civil-military relations under communist party rule in the former Soviet Union or Warsaw Pact countries," arguing that the civilian control over the police forces Hamas has accomplished "is not to say the Gaza security sector is democratically governed or entirely focused on impartial, public service." "Policing the People," 16.

27. After Hamas won parliamentary elections in 2006, Israel, the United States, and the European Union imposed severe sanctions on the Palestinian Authority. After Hamas

took over Gaza in 2007 restrictions were eased in the West Bank and a full blockade imposed on Gaza.

28. F. Mareah Peoples, "Egypt at the Rafah Border and the Prospects for Gaza," Peace Research Institute Oslo, 2012, http://file.prio.no/Publication_files/Prio/Mareah-Peoples -Egypt-at-the-Rafah-Border-PRIO-Paper-2012.pdf, 8.

29. Nidal al-Mughrabi, "Egypt Floods Gaza Tunnels to Cut Palestinian Lifeline," Reuters, February 13, 2013, http://www.reuters.com/article/2013/02/13/us-palestinians -egypt-tunnels-idUSBRE91CoRF20130213.

30. "U.N. Says Egypt Crackdown Closes 80 Percent of Gaza Tunnels," Reuters, July 23, 2013, http://www.reuters.com/article/2013/07/23/us-palestinians-egypt-tunnels -un-idUSBRE96M10J20130723.

31. In October 2013 there were media reports on this willingness, but other reports noted that it may have been more about rhetoric than actual planning. See Yasser Okbi, "Report: Egypt's Army Planning to Attack Targets in Gaza," *Jerusalem Post*, March 10, 2013, http://www.jpost.com/Middle-East/Report-Egypts-army-is-planning-to-attack -targets-in-Gaza-327769; Asmaa al-Ghoul, "Egypt-Gaza Border Quiet Despite Political Rhetoric," *Al-Monitor*, October 9, 2013, http://www.al-monitor.com/pulse/originals/2013/ 10/egypt-gaza-hamas-border.html.

Bibliography

Archives and Libraries
American Friends Service Committee Archives (AFSC), Philadelphia, PA
Dar Al-Watha'iq (DW), Egyptian National Archives, Cairo
Israel State Archives (ISA), Jerusalem
National Archives (formerly Public Record Office), London
New York Public Library, New York, NY
United Nations Archives, New York, NY
United Nations Relief and Works Agency for Palestine Refugees in the Near East
(UNRWA) Archives, Amman

Books and Articles
Abdel-Malek, Anouar. *Egypt: Military Society, the Army Regime, the Left, and Social Change Under Nasser.* New York: Random House, 1968.

Abdel Nasser, Gamal. *President Gamal Abdel Nasser on Palestine.* Cairo, United Arab Republic: Information Department, n.d.

Abu Amr, Ziad. *Usul Al-Haraka al-Siyasiyya fi Qita' Ghazzah, 1948–1967.* Akka: Dar al-Aswar, 1987.

Abu Iyad, with Eric Rouleau. *My Home, My Land: A Narrative of the Palestinian Resistance.* Translated by Linda Butler Koseoglu. New York: Times Books, 1981.

Abu-Lughod, Lila. "Do Muslim Women Really Need Saving? Anthropological Reflections on Cultural Relativism and Its Others." *American Anthropologist* 104, 3 (2002): 783–790.

———. "Seductions of the 'Honor Crime.'" *differences: A Journal of Feminist Cultural Studies* 22, 1 (2011): 17–63.

———. "Writing Against Culture." In *Recapturing Anthropology: Working in the Present,* edited by Richard Fox, 137–162. Santa Fe, NM: SAR Press, 1991.

Abu Naml, Husayn. "Harb al-Fedayeen fi Qita' Ghazzah." *Shu'un Filastiniyya* 62 (January 1979): 177–199.

———. *Qita' Ghazzah, 1948–1967: Tatawwarat Iqtisadiyya wa-Siyasiyya wa-Ijtimaiyya wa-Askariyya.* Beirut: PLO Research Center, 1979.

Agier, Michel, and Françoise Bouchet-Sangier. "Humanitarian Spaces: Spaces of Exception." In *In the Shadow of "Just Wars": Violence, Politics, and Humanitarian Action,* edited by Fabrice Weissman, 297–313. Ithaca, NY: Cornell University Press, 2004.

Alexander, Michelle. *The New Jim Crow: Mass Incarceration in the Age of Colorblindness.* New York: New Press, 2012.

Allen, Lori. "Martyr Bodies in the Media: Human Rights, Aesthetics, and the Politics of Immediation in the Palestinian Intifada." *American Ethnologist* 36, 1 (2009): 161–180.

———. *The Rise and Fall of Human Rights: Cynicism and Politics in Occupied Palestine.* Stanford, CA: Stanford University Press, 2013.

Allred, Keith. "Peacekeepers and Prostitutes: How Deployed Forces Fuel the Demand for Trafficked Women and New Hope for Stopping It." *Armed Forces and Society* 33, 1 (2006): 5–23.

Althusser, Louis. *Lenin and Philosophy and Other Essays.* Translated by Ben Brewster. New York: Monthly Review Press, 1971.

Amar, Paul. *The Security Archipelago: Human-Security States, Sexuality Politics, and the End of Neoliberalism.* Durham, NC: Duke University Press, 2013.

Anderson, Benedict. *Imagined Communities.* New York: Verso, 1991.

Anderson, David. "Policing the Settler State: Colonial Hegemony in Kenya, 1900–1952." In *Contesting Colonial Hegemony: State and Society in Africa and India,* edited by Shula Marks and Dagmar Engels, 248–264. London: British Academic Press, 1994.

Andreas, Peter. *Blue Helmets and Black Markets: The Business of Survival in the Siege of Sarajevo.* Ithaca, NY: Cornell University Press, 2008.

Appadurai, Arjun. *Fear of Small Numbers: An Essay on the Geography of Anger.* Durham, NC: Duke University Press, 2006.

Arendt, Hannah. *The Human Condition.* Chicago: University of Chicago Press, 1958.

———. *The Origins of Totalitarianism.* San Diego, CA: Harcourt Brace Jovanovich, 1968.

Arnold, David. "The Armed Police and Colonial Rule in South India, 1914–1947." *Modern Asian Studies* 11, 1 (1977): 101–125.

Ayalon, Ami. *Reading Palestine: Printing and Literacy, 1900–1948.* Austin: University of Texas Press, 2004.

Basisu, Mu'in. *Descent into the Water: Palestinian Notes from Arab Exile.* Wilmette, IL: Medina Press, 1980.

Bayat, Asef. *Life as Politics: How Ordinary People Change the Middle East.* Stanford, CA: Stanford University Press, 2010.

Beattie, Kirk. *Egypt During the Nasser Years: Ideology, Politics, Civil Society.* Boulder, CO: Westview Press, 1994.

Ben-Ari, Eyal, and Efrat Elron. "Blue Helmets and White Armor: Multi-Nationalism and Multi-Culturalism Among UN Peacekeeping Forces." *City and Society* 13, 2 (2001): 271–302.

Benhabib, Seyla. "Twilight of Sovereignty or the Emergence of Cosmopolitan Norms? Rethinking Citizenship in Volatile Times." *Citizenship Studies* 11, 1 (2007): 19–36.

Bier, Laura. *Revolutionary Womanhood: Feminisms, Modernity, and the State in Nasser's Egypt.* Stanford, CA: Stanford University Press, 2011.

Brown, Nathan. "Gaza Five Years On: Hamas Settles In." Paper, Carnegie Endowment for International Peace, Washington DC. http://carnegieendowment.org/files/hamas_settles_in.pdf.

Buur, Lars, and Steffen Jensen. "Introduction: Vigilantism and the Policing of Everyday Life in South Africa." *African Studies* 63, 2 (2004): 139–152.

Caldeira, Teresa. *City of Walls: Crime, Segregation, and Citizenship in São Paulo.* Berkeley: University of California Press, 2000.

Campbell, Nancy. "Technologies of Suspicion: Coercion and Compassion in Post-Disciplinary Surveillance Regimes." *Surveillance and Society* 2, 1 (2004): 78–92.

Cauchi, Jacqueline Azzopardi, and Paul Knepper. "Empire, the Police, and the Introduction of Fingerprint Technology in Malta." *Criminology and Criminal Justice* 9, 1 (2009): 73–92.

Chalfin, Brenda. *Neoliberal Frontiers: An Ethnography of Sovereignty in West Africa.* Chicago: University of Chicago Press, 2010.

———. "Sovereigns and Citizens in Close Encounter: Airport Anthropology and Customs Regimes in Neoliberal Ghana." *American Ethnologist* 35, 4 (2008): 519–538.

Chan, Janet. "The New Lateral Surveillance and a Culture of Suspicion." In *Surveillance and Governance: Crime Control and Beyond*, edited by Mathieu Deflem, 223–240. Bingley, UK: Emerald/JAI, 2008.

Chanock, Martin. "Making Customary Law: Men, Women, and Courts in Colonial Northern Rhodesia." In *African Women and the Law: Historical Perspectives*, edited by Margaret Jean Hay and Marcia Wright, 53–67. Boston: Boston University Press, 1982.

———. "A Peculiar Sharpness: An Essay on Property in the History of Customary Law in Colonial Africa." *Journal of African History* 32, 1 (1991): 65–88.

Chatterjee, Partha. *The Nation and Its Fragments.* Princeton, NJ: Princeton University Press, 1993.

———. *Politics of the Governed: Reflections of Popular Politics in Most of the World.* New York: Columbia University Press, 2006.

———. "Religious Minorities and the Secular State: Reflections on an Indian Impasse." *Public Culture* 8, 1 (1995): 11–39.

Chopra, Jarat. "The UN's King of East Timor." *Survival* 42, 3 (2000): 27–39.

Cohen, Hillel. *Good Arabs: The Israeli Security Agencies and the Israeli Arabs, 1948–1967.* Berkeley: University of California Press, 2010.

Comaroff, John, and Jean Comaroff. "Policing Culture, Cultural Policing: Law and Social Order in Postcolonial South Africa." *Law and Social Inquiry* 29, 3 (2004): 513–545.

Cooper, Paul. "Ethical Approaches for Police Officers When Working with Informants in the Development of Criminal Intelligence in the United Kingdom." *Journal of Social Policy* 26, 1 (1997): 1–20.

Cottey, Andrew. "Beyond Humanitarian Intervention: The New Politics of Peacekeeping and Intervention." *Contemporary Politics* 14, 4 (2008): 429–446.

Courtney, Roger. *Palestine Policeman: An Account of Eighteen Dramatic Months in the Palestine Police Force During the Great Jew-Arab Troubles.* London: Herbert Jenkins, 1939.

Cowen, Deborah. "Fighting for 'Freedom': The End of Conscription in the United States and the Neoliberal Project of Citizenship." *Citizenship Studies* 10, 2 (2006): 167–183.

Das, Veena. *Critical Events.* Cambridge, UK: Oxford University Press, 1995.

Dirks, Nicholas. "The Policing of Tradition: Colonialism and Anthropology in Southern India." *Comparative Studies in Society and History* 39, 1 (1997): 182–212.

Duffey, Tamara. "Cultural Issues in Contemporary Peacekeeping." *International Peacekeeping* 7, 1 (2000): 142–168.

Eickelman, Dale F., and Jon W. Anderson. *New Media in the Muslim World: The Emerging Public Sphere.* Bloomington: Indiana University Press, 2003.

Eickelman, Dale, and M. G. Dennison. "Arabizing the Omani Intelligence Services: Clash of Cultures?" *International Journal of Intelligence and Counterintelligence* 7 (1994): 1–28.

Eilenberg, Michael. "Flouting the Law: Vigilante Justice and Regional Autonomy on the Indonesian Border." *ASEAS—Austrian Journal of South-East Asian Studies* 4, 2 (2011): 237–253.

Elkins, Caroline. *Imperial Reckoning: The Untold Story of Britain's Gulag in Kenya.* New York: Henry Holt, 2005.

Fanon, Frantz. *The Wretched of the Earth.* New York: Grove Press, 1965.

Fassin, Didier. "Humanitarianism as a Politics of Life." *Public Culture* 19, 3 (2007): 499–520.

———. *Enforcing Order: An Ethnography of Urban Policing.* Malden, MA: Polity, 2013.

Feldman, Ilana. "Ad Hoc Humanity: Peacekeeping and the Limits of International Community in Gaza." *American Anthropologist* 112, 3 (2010): 416–429.

———. "Difficult Distinctions: Refugee Law, Humanitarian Practice, and Political Identification in Gaza." *Cultural Anthropology* 22, 1 (2007): 129–169.

———. *Governing Gaza: Bureaucracy, Authority, and the Work of Rule, 1917–1967.* Durham, NC: Duke University Press, 2008.

———. "Home as a Refrain: Remembering and Living Displacement in Gaza." *History and Memory* 18, 2 (2006): 10–47.

———. "Mercy Trains and Ration Rolls: Between Government and Humanitarianism in Gaza." In *Interpreting Welfare and Relief in the Middle East*, edited by Inger Marie Okkenhaug and Nefissa Naguib, 175–194. Leiden, The Netherlands: Brill Press, 2008.

———. "Observing the Everyday: Policing and the Conditions of Possibility in Gaza (1948–1967)." *Interventions: International Journal of Postcolonial Studies* 9, 3 (2007): 414–433.

———. "Refusing Invisibility: Documentation and Memorialization in Palestinian Refugee Claims." *Journal of Refugee Studies* 21, 4 (2008): 498–516.

———. "Waiting for Palestine: Refracted Citizenship and Latent Sovereignty in Gaza." *Citizenship Studies* 12, 5 (2008): 447–463.

Feldman, Ilana, and Miriam Ticktin. *In the Name of Humanity: The Government of Threat and Care*. Durham, NC: Duke University Press, 2010.

Ferguson, James. "Seeing Like an Oil Company: Space, Security, and Global Capital in Neoliberal Africa." *American Anthropologist* 107, 3 (2005): 377–382.

Fetherston, A. B., and Carolyn Nordstrom. "Overcoming *Habitus* in Conflict Management: UN Peacekeeping and War Zone Ethnography." *Peace and Change* 20, 1 (1995): 94–119.

Foucault, Michel. *Discipline and Punish: The Birth of the Prison*. Translated by Alan Sheridan. New York: Vintage Books, 1979.

———. *Security, Territory, Population: Lectures at the College de France, 1977–1978*. Edited by Michel Senellart. New York: Macmillan, 2009.

Frye, William. *A United Nations Peace Force*. New York: Oceana Publications, 1957.

Garriott, William, ed. *Policing and Contemporary Governance: The Anthropology of Police in Practice*. New York: Palgrave MacMillan, 2013.

Gerges, Fawaz. "Egypt and the 1948 War: Internal Conflict and Regional Ambition." In *The War for Palestine*, edited by Eugene L. Rogan and Avi Shlaim, 150–175. Cambridge: Cambridge University Press, 2001.

Gordon, Colin. "The Soul of the Citizen: Max Weber and Michel Foucault on Rationality and Government." In *Max Weber, Rationality and Modernity*, edited by Scott Lash and Sam Whimster, 293–316. Boston: Allen & Unwin, 1987.

Gordon, Neve. *Israel's Occupation*. Berkeley: University of California Press, 2008.

Habermas, Jürgen. *The Structural Transformation of the Public Sphere: An Inquiry into a Category of Bourgeois Society*. Cambridge: MIT Press, 1989.

Hall, Stuart M., Chas Critcher, Tony Jefferson, John Clarke, and Brian Roberts. *Policing the Crisis: Mugging, the State, and Law and Order*. New York: Holmes & Meier, 1978.

Hammami, Rema. "Between Heaven and Earth: Transformations in Religiosity and Labor Among Southern Palestinian Peasant and Refugee Women, 1920–1993." PhD diss., Temple University, 1994.

Heiberg, Marianne, and Johan Jorgen Holst. "Comparing UNIFIL and the MNF." *Survival* 28, 5 (1986): 399–422.

Hier, Sean P., and Josh Greenberg, eds. *Surveillance: Power, Problems, and Politics*. Vancouver: University of British Columbia Press, 2009.

Hirschkind, Charles. *The Ethical Soundscape: Cassette Sermons and Islamic Counterpublics*. New York: Columbia University Press, 2006.

Hochschild, Adam. *King Leopold's Ghost: A Story of Greed, Terror, and Heroism in Colonial Africa*. Boston: Houghton Mifflin, 1999.

Hohe, Tanja, "The Clash of Paradigms: International Administration and Local Political Legitimacy in East Timor." *Contemporary Southeast Asia* 24, 3 (2002): 569–589.

Horne, Edward. *A Job Well Done (Being a History of the Palestine Police Force 1920–1948)*. Essex, UK: Anchor Press, 1982.

Ibrahim, Sonallah. *That Smell and Notes from Prison*. Translated by Robyn Creswell. New York: New Directions, 2013.

Imray, Colin. *Policeman in Palestine*. Bideford, UK: Edward Gaskell, 1995.

Jankowski, James. *Nasser's Egypt, Arab Nationalism, and the United Arab Republic*. Boulder, CO: Lynne Rienner Publishers, 2002.

Jeffries, Sir Charles. *The Colonial Police*. London: Max Parrish, 1952.

Jensen, Steffen, and Lars Buur. "Everyday Policing and the Occult: Notions of Witchcraft, Crime and 'the People.'" *African Studies* 63, 2 (2004): 193–211.

Kanaaneh, Rhoda. *Surrounded: Palestinian Soldiers in the Israeli Military*. Stanford, CA: Stanford University Press, 2009.

Khalidi, Rashid. "The Palestinians and 1948: The Underlying Causes of Failure." In *The War for Palestine*, edited by Eugene L. Rogan and Avi Shlaim, 12–36. Cambridge: Cambridge University Press, 2001.

Khalili, Laleh. "The Location of Palestine in Global Counterinsurgencies." *International Journal of Middle East Studies* 42, 3 (2010): 413–433.

———. *Time in the Shadows: Confinement in Counterinsurgencies*. Stanford, CA: Stanford University Press, 2013.

Kharkhordin, Oleg. "The Soviet Individual: Genealogy of a Dissimulating Animal." In *Global Modernities*, edited by Mike Featherstone, Scott Lash, and Roland Robertson, 209–226. London: Sage, 1995.

Kianni, Maria. "The Changing Dimensions of UN Peacekeeping." *Strategic Studies* 24, 1 (2004).

Krozier, Gad. "From Dowbiggen to Tegart: Revolutionary Change in the Colonial Police in Palestine During the 1930s." *Journal of Imperial and Commonwealth History* 32, 2 (2004): 115–133.

Lakoff, Andrew, and Stephen J. Collier, eds. *Biosecurity Interventions: Global Health and Security in Question*. New York: Columbia University Press, 2008.

Laqueur, Thomas. "Mourning, Pity, and the Work of Narrative in the Making of 'Humanity.'" In *Humanitarianism and Suffering: The Mobilization of Empathy*, edited by Richard D. Brown and Richard A. Wilson, 31–57. Cambridge: Cambridge University Press, 2009.

Lesch, Ann Mosely. "Gaza: History and Politics." In *Israel, Egypt, and the Palestinians: From Camp David to Intifada*, edited by Ann Mosely Lesch and Mark Tessler, 223–237. Bloomington: Indiana University Press, 1989.

Loader, Ian. "Policing, Recognition, and Belonging." *Annals of the American Academy of Political and Social Science* 605, 1 (2006): 201–221.

Loader, Ian, and Aogan Mulcahy. *Policing and the Condition of England.* Oxford: Oxford University Press, 2003.

Lyon, David. *Surveillance Society: Monitoring Everyday Life.* Philadelphia: Open University Press, 2001.

———, ed. *Surveillance as Social Sorting: Privacy, Risk and Automated Discrimination.* New York: Routledge, 2002.

———. *Surveillance Studies: An Overview.* New York: Polity, 2007.

MacQueen, Norrie. *Peacekeeping and the International System.* New York: Routledge, 2006.

Malkki, Liisa. "Citizens of Humanity: Internationalism and the Imagined Community of Nations." *Diaspora: A Journal of Transnational Studies* 3, 1 (1994): 41–68.

———. "Things to Come: Internationalism and Global Solidarities in the Late 1990s." *Public Culture* 10, 2 (1998): 431–442.

Mani, Lata. "Contentious Traditions: The Debate on Sati in Colonial India." In *Recasting Women: Essays in Indian Colonial History,* edited by Kumkum Sangari and Sudesh Vaid, 88–126. New Brunswick, NJ: Rutgers University Press, 1990.

Mansfield, Peter. *Nasser's Egypt.* Baltimore, MD: Penguin Books, 1965.

Marx, Karl. "On the Jewish Question." In *The Marx-Engels Reader,* edited by Robert C. Tucker, 26–46. New York: W. W. Norton, 1978.

Mayol, Pierre. "Propriety." In *The Practice of Everyday Life.* vol. 2, *Living and Cooking,* edited by Luce Giard and Pierre Mayol, 15–34. Minneapolis: University of Minnesota Press, 1998.

Milton-Edwards, Beverly. "Policing Palestinian Society." *Policing and Society: An International Journal of Research and Policy* 7, 1 (1997): 19–44.

Mohanty, Chandra Talpade. "Under Western Eyes: Feminist Scholarship and Colonial Discourses." *Feminist Review* 30 (1988): 61–88.

Monahan, Torin, ed. *Surveillance and Security: Technological Politics and Power in Everyday Life.* New York: Routledge, 2006.

Moore, Sally Falk. "From Tribes and Traditions to Composites and Conjunctures." *Social Analysis* (2005): 254–272.

Morris, Benny. *Israel's Border Wars, 1949–1956: Arab Infiltration, Israeli Retaliation, and the Countdown to the Suez War.* Oxford, UK: Clarendon Press, 1993.

Nyers, Peter. "Abject Cosmopolitanism: The Politics of Protection in the Anti-Deportation Movement." *Third World Quarterly* 22, 6 (2010): 1069–1093.

Ochs, Juliana. *Security and Suspicion: An Ethnography of Everyday Life in Israel.* Philadelphia: University of Pennsylvania Press, 2011.

Pandey, Gyanendra. "The Secular State and the Limits of Dialogue." In *The Crisis of Secularism in India,* edited by Anuradha Dingwaney Needham and Rajeswari Sunder Rajan, 157–176. Durham, NC: Duke University Press, 2007.

Parsons, Nigel. "Israeli Biopolitics, Palestinian Policing: Order and Resistance in the Occupied Palestinian Territories." In *Policing and Prisons in the Middle East: Formations of Coercion*, edited by Laleh Khalili and Jillian Schwedler, 57–76. New York: Columbia University Press, 2010.

Peoples, F. Mareah. "Egypt at the Rafah Border and the Prospects for Gaza." Peace Research Institute Oslo (PRIO), 2012, http://file.prio.no/Publication_files/Prio/Mareah-Peoples-Egypt-at-the-Rafah-Border-PRIO-Paper-2012.pdf.

Perthes, Volker. "*Si vis stabilitatem, para bellum*: State Building, National Security, and War Preparation in Syria." In *War, Institutions, and Social Change in the Middle East*, edited by Steven Heydemann, 149–173. Berkeley: University of California Press, 2000.

Petryna, Adriana. *Life Exposed: Biological Citizens After Chernobyl*. Princeton, NJ: Princeton University Press, 2002.

Picard, Elizabeth. "State and Society in the Arab World: Towards a New Role for the Security Services?" In *The Many Faces of National Security in the Arab World*, edited by Bahgat Korany, Paul Noble, and Rex Brynen, 258–274. New York: St. Martin's Press, 1993.

Pierce, Steven. "Punishment and the Political Body: Flogging and Colonialism in Northern Nigeria." In *Discipline and the Other Body: Correction, Corporeality, Colonialism*, edited by Steven Pierce and Anupama Rao, 186–214. Durham, NC: Duke University Press, 2006.

Potter, Gary W., and Victor E. Kappeler, eds. *Constructing Crime: Perspectives on Making News and Social Problems*. Prospect Heights, IL: Waveland Press, 1998.

Quigley, John. *The Case for Palestine: An International Law Perspective*. Durham, NC: Duke University Press, 2005.

Rabinow, Paul. "Midst Anthropology's Problems." *Cultural Anthropology* 17, 2 (2002): 135–149.

Ramsbotham, Oliver, Tom Woodhouse, and Hugh Miall. *Contemporary Conflict Resolution*. Boston: Polity, 2005.

Razack, Sherene. *Dark Threats and White Knights: The Somalia Affair, Peacekeeping, and the New Imperialism*. Toronto: University of Toronto Press, 2004.

Redfield, Peter. "Doctors, Borders, and Life in Crisis." *Cultural Anthropology* 20, 3 (2005): 328–361.

Rich, Michael L. "Coerced Informants and Thirteenth Amendment Limitations on the Police-Informant Relationship." *Santa Clara Law Review* 50, 3 (2010): 681–745.

Robinson, Shira. *Citizen Strangers: Palestinians and the Birth of Israel's Liberal Settler State*. Stanford, CA: Stanford University Press, 2013.

Rokach, Livia. *Israel's Sacred Terrorism: A Study Based on Moshe Sharett's Personal Diary and Other Documents*. Belmont, MA: Association of Arab-American University Graduates, 1980.

Roy, Sara. *The Gaza Strip: The Political Economy of De-Development*. Washington DC: Institute for Palestine Studies, 1995.

Rubinstein, Robert. "Cross-Cultural Considerations in Complex Peace Operations." *Negotiation Journal* 19, 1 (2003): 29–49.

———. "Intervention and Culture: An Anthropological Approach to Peace Operations." *Security Dialogue* 36, 4 (2005): 527–544.

———. *Peacekeeping Under Fire: Culture and Intervention*. Boulder, CO: Paradigm Publishers, 2008.

Ryan, Curtis. "Political Strategies and Regime Survival in Egypt." *Journal of Third World Studies* 18, 2 (2001): 25–46.

Salvatore, Armando, and Mark LeVine. *Religion, Social Practice, and Contested Hegemonies: Reconstructing the Public Sphere in Muslim Majority Societies*. New York: Palgrave Macmillan, 2005.

Sarigiannidis, Miltiadis. "Legal Discourses on Peacemaking/Peacekeeping/Peacebuilding: International Law as a New Topos for Human Security." *International Journal* 62, 3 (2007): 519–537.

Sassen, Saskia. *Territory, Authority, Rights: From Medieval to Global Assemblages*. Princeton, NJ: Princeton University Press, 2006.

Satia, Priya. "The Defense of Inhumanity: Air Control in Iraq and the British Idea of Arabia." *American Historical Review* 111 (2006): 16–51.

Sayigh, Yezid. *Armed Struggle and the Search for State: The Palestinian National Movement, 1949–1993*. Oxford: Oxford University Press, 1997.

———. "Escalation or Containment? Egypt and the Palestine Liberation Army, 1964–67." *International Journal of Middle East Studies* 30, 1 (1998): 97–116.

———. "Hamas Rule in Gaza: Three Years On." Middle East Brief No. 41, March 2010, Crown Center for Middle East Studies, Brandeis University, Waltham, MA.

———. "Policing the People, Building the State: Authoritarian Transformation in the West Bank and Gaza." Paper, February 2011, Carnegie Endowment for International Peace, Washington DC. http://carnegie-mec.org/2011/02/28/policing-people-build ing-state-authoritarian-transformation-in-west-bank-and-gaza/awvd.

Schmitt, Carl. *The Concept of the Political*. Chicago: University of Chicago Press, 1996.

Sengoopta, Chandak. *Imprint of the Raj: How Fingerprinting Was Born in Colonial India*. London: Macmillan, 2003.

Shafir, Gershon. "The Evolving Tradition of Citizenship." In *The Citizenship Debates*, edited by Gershon Shafir, 1–27. Minneapolis: University of Minnesota Press, 1998.

Sherry, Virginia. "Disappearances: Syrian Impunity in Lebanon." *Middle East Report* 27, 203 (1997): 31–33.

———. "Security Forces Practices in Egypt." *Criminal Justice Ethics* 12, 2 (1993).

Shlaim, Avi. "The Rise and Fall of the All-Palestine Government in Gaza." *Journal of Palestine Studies* 20, 1 (Fall 1990): 37–53.

Sinclair, Georgina. *Colonial Policing and the Imperial Endgame, 1945–1980*. Manchester, UK: Manchester University Press, 2006.

Skeik, Ibrahim. *Ghazzah 'Abr al-Tarikh: Qita' Ghazzah Taht Al-Idara Al-Masriyya, 1948–1956*. N.p.: 1982.

Skold, Nils. *United Nations Peacekeeping After the Suez War—UNEF I: The Swedish Involvement.* Translated by Stig Nihlen. New York: St. Martin's Press, 1996.

Snyder, Francis G. "Colonialism and Legal Form: The Creation of Customary Law in Senegal." *Journal of Legal Pluralism* 19 (1981): 49–90.

Spivak, Gayatri. "Can the Subaltern Speak?" In *Marxism and the Interpretation of Culture*, edited by Cary Nelson and Larry Grossberg, 271–313. Urbana: University of Illinois Press, 1988.

Swettenham, J. A. "Some Impressions of the UNEF: 1957 to 1958." Directorate of History, National Defence Headquarters, Ottawa, Canada, 1959.

Teitel, Ruti. "For Humanity." *Journal of Human Rights* 3, 2 (2004): 225–237.

———. "Humanity's Law: Rule of Law for the New Global Politics." *Cornell International Law Journal* 35 (2002): 355–387.

Thornhill, Michael T. "Britain, the United States and the Rise of an Egyptian Leader: The Politics and Diplomacy of Nasser's Consolidation of Power, 1952–4." *English Historical Review* 119, 483 (2004): 892–921.

Turner, Bryan. "Classical Sociology and Cosmopolitanism: A Critical Defense of the Social." *British Journal of Sociology* 57, 1 (2006): 133–151.

UN High Commissioner for Refugees. *Global Trends Report 2013.* http://www.unhcr.org/trends2013/.

UN Relief and Works Agency. *UNRWA: A Brief History, 1950–1982.* Vienna: UN Relief and Works Agency, 1982.

Waterbury, John. *The Egypt of Nasser and Sadat: The Political Economy of Two Regimes.* Princeton, NJ: Princeton University Press, 1983.

Weber, Max. "Politics as a Vocation." In *Essays in Sociology*, edited by H. H. Garth and C. W. Mills, 26–45. New York: Macmillan, 1946.

Wedeen, Lisa. *Ambiguities of Domination: Politics, Rhetoric, and Symbols in Contemporary Syria.* Chicago: University of Chicago Press, 1999.

———. "Seeing Like a Citizen, Acting Like a State: Exemplary Events in Unified Yemen." *Comparative Studies in Society and History* 45, 4 (2003): 680–713.

Weizman, Eyal. *Hollow Land: Israel's Architecture of Occupation.* New York: Verso, 2007.

Ya'ari, Ehud. *Mitsrayim veha-Feda'in, 1953–1956.* Givat Haviva, Israel: Center for Arabic and Afro-Asian Studies, 1975.

Zohar, David. *Gamal over Gaza: Egyptian Neocolonialism in Gaza—A Record of Twenty Years of Oppression.* Jerusalem: Ministry for Foreign Affairs (Israel), Information Division, 1968.

Index

Page numbers followed by "f" indicate material in figures.

Tamir Sorek, *Palestinian Commemoration in Israel: Calendars, Monuments, and Martyrs*
2015

Adi Kuntsman and Rebecca L. Stein, *Digital Militarism: Israel's Occupation in the Social Media Age*
2015

Laurie A. Brand, *Official Stories: Politics and National Narratives in Egypt and Algeria*
2014

Kabir Tambar, *The Reckonings of Pluralism: Citizenship and the Demands of History in Turkey*
2014

Diana Allan, *Refugees of the Revolution: Experiences of Palestinian Exile*
2013

Shira Robinson, *Citizen Strangers: Palestinians and the Birth of Israel's Liberal Settler State*
2013

Joel Beinin and Frédéric Vairel, editors, *Social Movements, Mobilization, and Contestation in the Middle East and North Africa*
2013 (Second Edition), 2011

Ariella Azoulay and Adi Ophir, *The One-State Condition: Occupation and Democracy in Israel/Palestine*
2012

Steven Heydemann and Reinoud Leenders, editors, *Middle East Authoritarianisms: Governance, Contestation, and Regime Resilience in Syria and Iran*
2012

Jonathan Marshall, *The Lebanese Connection: Corruption, Civil War, and the International Drug Traffic*
2012

Joshua Stacher, *Adaptable Autocrats: Regime Power in Egypt and Syria*
2012

Bassam Haddad, *Business Networks in Syria: The Political Economy of Authoritarian Resilience*
2011

Noah Coburn, *Bazaar Politics: Power and Pottery in an Afghan Market Town*
2011

Laura Bier, *Revolutionary Womanhood: Feminisms, Modernity, and the State in Nasser's Egypt*
2011

Samer Soliman, *The Autumn of Dictatorship: Fiscal Crisis and Political Change in Egypt under Mubarak*
2011

Rochelle A. Davis, *Palestinian Village Histories: Geographies of the Displaced*
2010

Haggai Ram, *Iranophobia: The Logic of an Israeli Obsession*
2009

John Chalcraft, *The Invisible Cage: Syrian Migrant Workers in Lebanon*
2008

Rhoda Kanaaneh, *Surrounded: Palestinian Soldiers in the Israeli Military*
2008

Asef Bayat, *Making Islam Democratic: Social Movements and the Post-Islamist Turn*
2007

Robert Vitalis, *America's Kingdom: Mythmaking on the Saudi Oil Frontier*
2006

Jessica Winegar, *Creative Reckonings: The Politics of Art and Culture in Contemporary Egypt*
2006

Joel Beinin and Rebecca L. Stein, editors, *The Struggle for Sovereignty: Palestine and Israel, 1993–2005*
2006